THE REALM OF REFORM

Presbyterianism and Calvinism
in a changing Scotland

Reflections edited by

R. D. Kernohan

THE HANDSEL PRESS

Edinburgh

British Library Cataloguing in Publication Data
A catalogue record for this publication is available from the British Library

ISBN 1 871828 48 1

Typeset in 10.7 pt. Garamond
at The Stables, Carberry

Printed by Polestar AUP Aberdeen Ltd

Cover design by John McWilliam

*Published with the assistance of the Hope Trust,
and the Drummond Trust, 3 Pitt Terrace, Stirling*

Our vows, our prayers we now present
Before Thy throne of grace:
God of our fathers, be the God
Of their succeeding race

CONTENTS

INTRODUCTION: QUESTIONS OF IDENTITY

The Realm of Reform is no tightly-controlled unitary state of mind

R.D. KERNOHAN

"How wonderful it must be to belong to the only country with a Reformed majority!": comment to the editor of this book from a young Calvinist minister in Hungary, then under Communism.

This book appears at what is both a solemn and an exciting time in the history of Scotland and the life of its people. There are great hopes, many uncertainties, some anxieties. In Scotland at least the new century may plausibly seem the beginning of a new era.

It has become fashionable to assert a Scottish identity or to claim that it has been rediscovered, even if some of us never thought it was lost. From Catalonia to California there will be at least passing mentions, sometimes more than passing interest, at the creation of a devolved Scottish Parliament and the realignment of the functions and direction of the already largely devolved Scottish Executive.

No-one in Scotland can be insensitive to the importance of the change. For many among the majority of Scots who voted for it, the new dispensation is a necessary redress of grievance and expression of identity, inspired in some degree by a sense of ill-usage. This makes it something more than an important innovation in a British constitution which has never been rigid or static. For some Scots it is a practical step towards what they see as a logical goal, the resumption of the sovereign identity of Scotland among the other nations of a uniting Europe, most of them far younger in their sense of national identity. Even those Scots who opposed parliamentary devolution, a significant minority who have no choice now but to seek the best from the new system, did so because they saw great dangers in the greatness of the change. They too were conscious of a Scottish identity, but fearful of losing it in the form with which they were comfortable and of disturbance to relationships which they cherish.

But it is easier to assert or defend an identity than to define it or explore all the ways in which it finds expression.

There are also specially acute difficulties when the identity of a nation is closely linked to religious traditions and when the ways in which it expresses itself have been influenced not just by the forms and sociology of religion but by its inner core of faith and passion.

For this is apparently not a great age of faith (at least in Western Europe and North America) and is certainly not one in which diligent observance of the outward forms of religion retains much status among social conventions.

But the consequences of this may involve both misunderstandings and miscalculations. This book seeks to correct misunderstandings and warn against miscalculations. It also seeks perspectives in which the future as well as the past of Scotland can be related to the influence, achievements, and present uncertainties of the Reformed Christianity which has historically been the most powerful religious influence on Scottish life and character.

Recognition of the importance of religious influences, traditions, and beliefs has been called "the missing dimension" of much modern political thinking and planning. This is most obviously true in relation to the former Soviet system, both in its direct attack on religion in the U.S.S.R. and the subtler pressures of East Central Europe. Communism not only underestimated the tenacity of religious belief but inadvertently created a situation in which the Churches - in Poland most obviously but also in East Germany and elsewhere - attracted interest and prestige as the only independent institutions through which national identity and wider aspirations could find expression.

However secular liberalism has made similar miscalculations, not least in its failure to appreciate the extent to which religious traditions mark out the frontiers of cultural and sometimes political divisions, even when religious belief and practice may not appear especially ardent. This is most obviously true in the tragic conflicts of what was Yugoslavia. It is also a factor in such different situations as those of the Baltic States, the Polish-Ukrainian borderlands, and parts of the Russian Federation. Even within the United Kingdom the hopes, fears, and complexities in Northern Ireland have been compounded by inability, especially in England, to understand the feelings and fears behind the "Troubles".

Yet in recognising that there are often common factors in the way religious traditions are deeply involved in very different cultural and political situations, we have to beware of general theories. Each nation is different. Even nations which are closely akin and associated in culture, language, political history, and religious outlook - as Scotland and England are within a wider British nationality - have been shaped in different ways.

One of the ironies of history is that these cultural differences linked to religious experience were taken for granted by both Scots and English in the two centuries between 1745 and 1945 when their political union seemed most secure. As has always been recognised, they were built into the Union by the maintenance of the distinctive Scots law, along with the Presbyterian order of the Scottish Church. There is of course, no such thing as the Presbyterian religion. Presbyterianism, in its Scottish and other varieties, merely provides a structure and system of law for a Reformed part of the universal or catholic Church whose only Head is Jesus Christ and whose supreme law-book is the Bible. But the structure does reflect the insights of John Calvin and others, of the Reformation era and since, into the nature of the Church and its authority; and it has been immensely important for Scottish life and character. What has not always been so clearly recognised is that, in the conditions of the time, acceptance of home rule for the Church, as well as the courts, necessarily involved devolution for universities, schools, and social services.

At a time when most Scots were committed, in some degree, to Presbyterianism and many had a taste for theology, with much enjoyment as well as endurance of long sermons, the distinctive religious identity of Scotland (which Episcopalians and Roman Catholics also expressed, though in very different ways) may even have encouraged a satisfying sense of nationality and provided a milder surrogate for nationalism. The distinctive religious identity of the only European country with a clear "Reformed majority" - as Scotland still seemed in our own time to the admiring Hungarian I quoted - was probably a factor, along with involvement in the British Empire, in insulating Scotland from the kind of nationalism which convulsed nineteenth and early twentieth century Europe and took such firm root in Ireland.

It was probably inevitable that as the role of Government increased and society became more secular, a process accelerated by the Disruption of the National Church in 1843, the political union would require reform and eventually face a challenge. The challenge might even have built up sooner if Britain's world role - so misleadingly described by a great Victorian historian as "the expansion

of England" - had not created an intensely strong sense of common
purpose and, in two world wars, common danger.

Indeed if this book were primarily a historical inquiry into the
way the Scottish Reformed religious tradition, mainly expressed in
Presbyterianism, reflected the outlook of the Scottish people, it would
have to reflect very different moods. Some of the moods would reflect
different times, but others would be apparent at the same time. For
example, it would record not only the identification of the Church
of Scotland, through the reports of its Church and Nation Committee
and the majority view of the General Assembly, with aspirations for
more self-government but its identification with the United Kingdom
and, while it endured, of all that was positive and constructive in the
British Empire, in which the Scots had such a large, influential, and
enthusiastic minority shareholding.

It would record the way the Scots Kirk so passionately shared
and so often expressed the predominant British national mood in
both world wars and their aftermath. Yet it would also have to note
that in many respects, long before the politics of European Union,
the distant heirs of Calvin and Knox still affirmed a European
dimension in their thinking, were influenced by it in their theology,
and expressed it in a wide range of personal contacts, sometimes with
German universities, sometimes with the Protestants of Central
Europe. See for example the way in which this European dimension
suddenly and vividly appears in Ian Mackenzie's very personal essay
about a changing Scotland.

But at this turn of the century the emphasis in Scottish thinking
is inevitably on what Scotland will be and should be, not what it has
been. The past matters, but not least because ignorance and
misinterpretation makes it harder to understand the nature of Scotland
today and only too easy to make false assumptions about the future.

It is also inevitable that celebration of Scotland's internal self-
government will emphasise fashionable moods, needs, and themes.
Moderators will be as tempted as cardinals to intersperse a little semi-
political populism into less popular preaching about sin and grace.
Organised Christianity will play down its awkward, exclusive claims.
As several contributions to this book recognise and even emphasise,
the new Scotland will be proclaimed not only as ecumenical but as
inter-faith and multi-cultural. Platitudes will resound about the role
of people of all faiths and none.

This is probably a natural reflection of the kind of Scotland that
moves into the new century, and no-one should over-react. Things

could be much worse - as they assuredly would be if a consensus of contemporary spiritual and secular wisdom had to be concocted to bless a new Parliament for England, or a new Constitution for the United States.

But there is still a place for a reasoned reaction in favour of much that is undervalued, neglected, even disparaged in the Reformed Christian place in Scottish character and history, and the implications of that role for the present and future Scotland.

To claim that place is not "reactionary" in any political or cultural sense. Indeed it will soon be apparent to readers of this book that most of its contributors sit distressingly leftward, politically or theologically or both, of the benignly liberal conservatism and unrepentant unionism of its editor. That is probably an appropriate balance in a tradition which owes so much not only to one necessary and dramatic act of ecclesiastical re-formation but to the idea that being Reformed necessarily involves a constant readiness, as conditions change, to reform the structures and thinking of the Church.

To an extent it is also inevitable that such a book as this at such a time as this should be a reflection of different insights within the Reformed Church as well as a reflection on them. Those who read the Acts of the Apostles, or Paul's letters, will neither be surprised nor daunted by such differences among Christians.

They are an inevitable reflection of the present condition of the Reformed tradition, and have their parallels in other sectors of the universal Church - not only in Anglicanism, with its inheritance of chronic dissension and miracles of comprehension, but in the once monolithic and still authoritarian Church of Rome. Indeed it may be true that one of the great ecumenical failures of the universal Church in the twentieth century was to concentrate so much on its slow and not very successful progress towards "organic union" at a time when deep differences about the meaning of Christian faith, biblical authority, and the nature of the Church were opening up within the different Christian traditions rather than between them.

But there is also an ecumenical paradox. While the new fault lines have opened up between liberal and conservative in every part of the Church, there has also been a surprising tenacity of denominational and confessional identity. This has been true not only in Western Europe and North America, where the mainstream Churches have struggled in an adverse cultural climate, but in Eastern Europe since the decline and fall of the Soviet Empire.

It is against that background that Scottish Christians will try to respond, with both a sense of duty and sense of occasion, to the the redefinition of Scotland's role within the United Kingdom and the continuing debate, probably stimulated by constitutional change, about Scottish identity and sovereignty. This book emerges from a feeling that the Reformed response cannot be wholly expressed through the formality of reports to be adopted by General Assemblies or eloquent sermons for great and State occasions. We also need to heed warnings (for example in Johnston McKay's essay) about exaggerating the influence of the modern Kirk as a national institution and in "the development of civic society". There is a also a role for those prepared to encourage, warn, reflect, and provoke - as Donald Macleod does in the one Reformed and Presbyterian contribution to this book from outside the Church of Scotland.

Although these reflections (and provocations) are bound to reflect differences of approach and opinion there are probably two important themes on which most Reformed Scottish Christians will agree.

The first, which Presbyterians will share with many other people of religious belief or outlook, will be to hope that the new departure in Scottish life will be inspired and guided by what Rudyard Kipling called an humble and a contrite heart.

There are various politicians and publicists in Scotland who might usefully take the *Recessional* advice from the Indian-born Englishman who at imperialism's zenith became its conscience as well as its publicist. He was hardly an evangelical Christian but he had a profound and necessary sense of dutiful dependence on God and was, as the editors of the handbook to the Kirk's 1928 hymn-book put it, "a singer of the faith that has made Britain great".

After the celebration of all great festivals, religious as well as national, there is always a need for a recessional, reappraising mood: what the life-style and idiom of an older Scotland called a return to auld claes and parritch. Scotland's move to internal self-government and the decentralisation of the United Kingdom are not occasions for "frantic boast and foolish word", or the loosening of "wild tongues that have not Thee in awe". No-one, wherever they hope the new arrangements to lead, should be "drunk with sight of power". The new departure is too serious a business for that, with too many difficulties ahead.

At this point it might seen neat to add Kipling's cautionary refrain: "Lest we forget". But the stylistic neatness wouldn't be quite right. For the second great theme for Reformed concern, and one where Presbyterians' reflections may, perhaps must, differ from those of the rest of Scotland is not about the danger of forgetting but the need to remember. Or rather to rediscover and recall our history and the way that it was shaped by the Great Reformation of Luther, Calvin, and Knox and the continuing experience and influence of Reformed Christianity.

All nations reinterpret their history and reassess their identity. These are continuous processes, even when not so obvious as in times of constitutional change and very evident nationalist impulses. This is a healthy process, for there is no finality to nationality. If one generation of historians tends to emphasise "nationalist" factors - though the word is an anachronism - in the crises of the National Covenant of 1638 or the Disruption of the Kirk in 1843 no permanent harm is done, provided our historians remain capable of understanding the religious impulses as well as the political factors involved. A later generation of revisionists will restore the balance.

But there are two dangers. One is that the assertion of Scottish nationality will undervalue and misunderstand the vigour of Scottish political, economic, intellectual, literary, scientific, and theological achievement in the 250 years years after the Act of Union and the extent to which Scottish identity must reflect the affinities as well as the differences among the nations of the United Kingdom.

The more serious danger, however, is that the quest for a Scottish identity has become most evident at a time when commitment to religious ways of life and the structures of religious institutions is least evident and rather unfashionable.

These fashions are by no means distinctively Scottish. They reflect a mood of the Western world. It is evident for example in the way that enthusiasts for European Union now emphasise a secular and not a Christian basis for its political philosophy and the extent to which the American constitutional commitment to religious freedom is interpreted in ways at odds with assumptions of the Founding Fathers and generations of their successors. And if the English people ever feel the urge to assert and define their identity there will be politically-correct attempts, in the name of multi-faith multi-culturalism, to devalue the role of English Christianity in it.

The problem in Scotland is that the mood for political change inevitably creates a crisis of identity and that at this critical moment in Scottish history the single most important element in the country's religious identity will not only be under-emphasised but misunderstood, disparaged, and caricatured.

To say that is not to be ultra-sensitive or thin-skinned. Some caricature can be beneficial as well as enjoyable. Succeeding generations of fellow-Presbyters have reason to be grateful to Robert Burns for *Holy Willie's Prayer*, though it is scarcely a fair assessment of the theological differences in a Kirk adjusting to the Age of Enlightenment.

There is caricature too in what our own times have voted the greatest work of literature by a precentor of the Kirk: James Hogg's *Confessions and Memoirs of a Justified Sinner*. Sir Walter Scott's caricature of the Covenanters in *Old Mortality*, which so irritated such contemporaries as Thomas McCrie, the biographer of Knox, is also acceptable as a work of art rather than definitive history; and Scott himself, Kirk elder and Episcopalian, switching even in his last days between the Prayer Book and the metrical Psalms, reveals the complexity of Scottish religious history and the danger of substituting slogans for subtleties. Such a good Presbyterian elder as John Buchan wasn't above a little good-humoured caricature. And even where the caricature seems spiteful and more akin to Continental anticlericalism, as in Lewis Grassic Gibbon, it can still reflect the way that the Scots Kirk, in weaknesses as well as strengths, was at the heart of Scottish life.

It is rather different in the age when the most widely presented literary image of modern Scotland is the one in *Trainspotting*, where the Kirk (as in so much of modern Scotland) intrudes only at funerals, either preaching a consolatory but superficial universalism or, less kindly and convincingly, in the form of "some ruling-class c***, a junior minister or something" with an alleged Oxbridge accent.

Fortunately there is no need to decide whether Irvine Welsh's eventual role in Scottish cultural history will match that of Scott, or even Grassic Gibbon. But perhaps there is a need for a wider appreciation of the role that Reformed Christian religion has played, even still plays, in Scottish life. Indeed that role is so widely misunderstood and travestied that the need for reappreciation ought not just to be a concern of those who in any sense adhere to the Presbyterian tradition, and even of other Scottish Christians, but for all those concerned about the integrity of history and the meaningful use of language.

We have always been accustomed to a little misunderstanding from across the Border, for example in that old joke (whose obsolescence is a comment on Scottish cultural changes) about the Scots keeping the sabbath and everything else they can get their hands on. It wasn't even surprising, for example, that when in 1984 Scotland celebrated their first international Rugby Grand Slam for nearly sixty years, the slightly less than gracious congratulations of *The Times* Rugby correspondent suggested that "Scotland won by showing us their Calvinistic face." He meant, I think, that they linked their skills to self-discipline and good order, not least on the day of the decisive match against Calvin's fellow-countrymen.

But far worse looseness of language and thought has crept into our own Scottish arguments, and not only from Irvine Welsh or his characters. Take for example a contribution to the rucks and mauls of Scottish Rugby politics in the professional age from David Johnston - a member of the triumphant "Calvinist XV" of 1984, for whom I had vast admiration as a player and some sympathy as a critic of the Scottish Rugby Union.

Criticising Jim Telfer, the grey eminence of Scottish Rugby tactics, Johnston, a lawyer whose professional words should be carefully chosen, told *The Scotsman*: "His Presbyterian gloom is all-pervading." The same style was imitated later by John Beattie in *The Herald* sports pages, but this time Scott Hastings - though actually from what beadles call "good Kirk folk" - was said to to have given the Scottish team colour and enthusiasm in place of "Presbyterian austerity and fear" (January 5, 1999).

This kind of journalese is inspired not only by Murrayfield but by Saint Andrew's House. If we are to believe a diarist in *Scotland on Sunday*, even New Labour's Secretary of State, the successful promoter of the Holyrood Parliament, embodies our Calvinist inheritance. When a chief constable got into a mixture of professional difficulty and personal embarrassment, so we were told, "Donald Dewar's Calvinism was utterly outraged". (December 27, 1998.)

Anyone rich enough to afford a complete cuttings service could muster even more ludicrous examples of ill-judged invocations of a misunderstood theological inheritance. For decades Scotland's licensing laws were denounced as Calvinistic, even while the most dangerous national drink could sometimes be colloquially known as a drop of the Auld Kirk. Glasgow councillors, among whom practising Presbyterians are hardly the largest ethnic-religious group, are credited with Calvinism when they try to curb revelry in the small hours. Even the Scottish Youth Hostels Association have found their rules, despite regular review and reform, denounced for "their Calvinistic ethos of the 1930s", hardly the golden age of the Reformation.

That was again in *The Herald*, but surpassed a few weeks later by one of the same paper's columnists complaining that "living in Glasgow is like being at a funeral every day .... The antidote to Presbyterian angst is hot weather." She then told us she went to Jamaica and found the dolphins there "altogether smoother than their Calvinist brothers." Look it up if you think such nonsense unpublishable: November 6, 1998.

These verbal usages and abusages are merely the outward and trivial symbols of a much more serious confusion and ignorance, and of a situation which it is more important to understand than to denounce or lament, excruciating though such bad journalism can be. That understanding will surely be helped by William Storrar's essay, even though it suggests that it may be easier for many leaders of modern Scotland to appreciate the virtues of a "civic Calvinism" than to restore a Reformed, reforming Christianity (in and beyond Presbyterianism) as the way, the truth, and the life for a changing Scotland.

For it is intrinsically difficult for a secular, liberal society which marginalises religion and regards its practices as matters of private inclination to understand the power of faith, whether in individuals or as ideology. The difficulty has been aggravated as sexual revolution turned out to be more influential than socialist revolution and the two dominant Western political influences, free-market conservatism and democratic socialism, were both deeply imbued with social and moral attitudes which were libertarian rather than liberal.

Christians can no longer assume that those estranged from the Church or indifferent to it will still generally share Christian ideas about family life or, in a much wider sense, the nature of the good life. They have also to recognise that those who themselves profess no religious allegiance and feel little religious interest, especially if they are a generation or two away from even conventional religious practice, require extraordinary powers of insight and imagination to enter into the thinking and understand the motivation of believers. All credit to those non-religious historians, writers, and sociologists who manage to do so.

It must be even more difficult for the outsider to understand the complexities and contradictions of faith than its simplicities. That may explain why our media are generally kinder to a Mother Teresa, even to such an effective plain-speaking evangelical as Billy Graham, than to Anglican archbishops or Presbyterian General Assemblies. But the greatest complexities and most acute contradictions are probably not in the faith of individual Christians, not even in the individual or collective leadership of the Church, but in the way religious beliefs and institutions shape the evolution of nations, societies, and cultures.

Perhaps it is there that much of modern Scotland most profoundly misunderstands its inheritance. It does so in two ways. The first is that it tends, without actually taking too much account of the evidence, to accept notions that Calvinism and Presbyterianism blighted Scottish cultural life. The second is that it takes far too narrow a view of what culture is and only grudgingly accepts that the Reformed Christian way of life and thought directly stimulated and encouraged a Scottish contribution to Western culture quite disproportionate to the size of the country or its economic condition before the nineteenth century.

There is a case against Calvinism in some of its forms. But even that case presents difficulties when it is forced upon Scottish history, and not least cultural history.

In music, for example, the Reformed tradition, though it created wonderful psalmody, did not fulfil the promise of Geneva. The different Protestant tradition from which Bach emerged in all his genius and marvellously applied piety has no Scottish parallel. But then it has no English parallel either. Calvinism cannot be blamed for the English failure to develop native musical genius from Purcell's time to that of Elgar, who didn't emerge from the Anglican tradition. And why did musical genius develop in some Roman Catholic countries but not at all in others? There is no Spanish Mozart.

Even in music the idea of Calvinist "blight" is hard to sustain. In practical terms there is no doubt that the musical life of the Churches, including most of those in the Calvinist tradition, has been a major factor in the stimulation and diversification of musical interests throughout the English-speaking world. Those of us in the mainstream of the Reformed tradition may also reasonably argue that we have been true to the Genevan concern that the people of the Church should be able to bear the main part in the music of worship; and that nothing has better demonstrated the capacity of the Reformed tradition to carry on reforming than the adaptation of changing musical styles into its worship and the integration of its own great hymns, from a Bonar or a Matheson, with the best of the Wesleyan, Lutheran, Anglican, and even Roman Catholic traditions. If that vigour is less obvious today than a generation ago - and that is arguable - the causes lie partly in the confusion of modern musical taste and partly in the inclination of congregations to cling to what served them so well in the past.

The idea that Calvinism or Presbyterianism blighted the visual arts and architecture in Scotland is probably as deeply entrenched but still harder to sustain. That the Reformation was accompanied by some popular vandalism is indisputable, though our most serious loss of architectural heritage came from long years of neglect and parsimony - the same straitened circumstances which created relatively few examples of fine post-Reformation architecture like Burntisland Church or Greyfriars in Edinburgh. It was not until the ages of the Enlightenment and the Evangelical revival that architects were adequately encouraged to use the opportunity provided by the Reformed need to hear the Word audibly preached and to feel gathered round the Table at the Lord's Supper.

There is room for argument about why Calvinist-dominated Scotland was a rather drab country artistically at a time when Calvinist-dominated Holland enjoyed its golden age. Limited resources, the loss of the court to London, and civil wars all played a part. One thing, however, is indisputable. Reformed religion and artistic achievement flourished together in the society of high purpose, economic progress, political stability, social mobility, and intellectual achievement which emerged in eighteenth and nineteenth-century Scotland. They were not at odds but in harmony; and they went along with the advancement of science, literature, and learning.

By this time Scotland, still celebrated for its Calvinism and identified throughout the world with Presbyterianism, had claimed a major place in the visual arts and laid the foundations for a great artistic tradition in national life. The tradition has been maintained in two centuries of changing tastes. Unfortunately some of the genres and styles in which nineteenth-century Scottish painting especially excelled became unfashionable, and not least those in which "historical" art often reflected an intensely Presbyterian view of Scottish history, as in some of Sir David Wilkie's greatest work.

Wilkie's fame endures; but how many of those who recognise his name as a very great Scotsman appreciate that (as argued by the leading art historian Duncan Macmillan) four of his pictures of preaching, the Lord's Supper, prayer, and Bible-reading "together constitute an equivalent to Poussin's *Seven Sacraments* translated into Protestant terms" (*Scottish Art 1460-1990* p. 189). Even among those who know Wilkie's international stature, how many would recognise the names or religious themes of George Harvey or Thomas

Duncan? More art-lovers today are probably familiar with the landscape work of Raeburn's pupil, the Reverend John Thomson of Duddingston, than with a number of artists who were not ministers but whose themes were more explicitly Presbyterian.

Yet even Thomson, very much a Moderate, went in for variations on his friend Scott's theme of "Old Mortality". And if the Edinburgh Presbytery of one generation is mocked for condemning the ministerial playwright John Home, that of a later generation takes credit for Thomson, combining parish ministry with artistic celebrity.

But the real case for Calvinism, and the Reformed tradition which evolved naturally from it as the Church re-formed to meet new conditions, does not lie in a defence against the farther-fetched of the charges against it. It lies in the spiritual priorities, moral concerns, and intellectual conditioning which it provided for a small and (until the end of the eighteenth century) relatively poor nation.

There is no need for us to to idealise a vanished Scotland of porridge, peasants, and piety and pretend life was ever one long *Cottar's Saturday Night*, even if we find some of Robert Burns's personal complexity in that poem and admire what Wilkie made of it in his picture. But some of of the most crucial facts are clear enough. The Reformed tradition and the living faith in Christ which it handed on to be discovered and experienced in every generation provided a mixture of true piety, high purpose, social concern, and (by the standards of the time) widespread educational opportunity and access to university or technical training. It helped to build these values into the New World of the United States and the British colonies. From the early nineteenth century it combined this "expansion of Scotland" with a wider missionary enthusiasm - see some of the examples mentioned by Lorna Paterson and Catherine Hepburn's thoughts on the "gift of a missionary childhood" - which has widened Scottish horizons and been a significant influence in many successor States of the former British Empire.

Reformed Scotland also expressed, more than most societies of the time, the idea of the "democratic intellect": not because Presbyterianism is pure democracy, for it isn't, but because it expressed the Christian concept of equality in the sight of God, opened a way for democratic elements in its structures, and redefined the place of the ministry of Word and Sacrament in the wider community of faith. The traditional view is that Presbyterianism (according to one's point of view) encouraged the lower orders to defy their betters, who thought they knew best, or provided the

confidence to challenge oppressors. Such a view has some warrant in
the up-country "Scotch-Irish" enthusiasm for the American
Revolution, the Scots Radical flirtation with Jacobinism after the
French Revolution, and the mood of a section of Ulster Presbyterians
before the tumults of 1798. In Scotland itself it found especially
vigorous expression in Presbyterian groups who opposed the
estabished order in Church and well as State.

But of course our social and political traditions are much more
complex, as the anti-revolutionary political conservatism of Thomas
Chalmers spectacularly demonstrates. Even in the great Victorian
divide in Scots Presbyterianism, which so damaged the concept of a
National Church, both sides brought something of lasting value to
politics.

The new alliance of Free Kirk and "Voluntaries" became a force
for ordered reform rather than radical protest. With English
Nonconformity, it ensured that Britain had a long and happy
transition from an *ancien régime* to a modern parliamentary
democracy with the Crown, so precious a part of our constitution,
as symbol of unity and authority.

But something also needs to be said for the more conservative
and often Conservative tradition of the Establishment, seen at its
best in such leaders as Norman Macleod and Archibald Charteris.
Not least, they should be credited with fighting the campaign for
disestablishment on a principle which can still be argued in the
twenty-first century: "the national recognition of religion". It
provided a large part of the basis for the eventual Presbyterian reunion
of 1929 which gave the Church of Scotland its present character. It
remains defensible in an age when Christian thinking inevitably
becomes more widely ecumenical and politics has to take account
not only of those lapsed from various Christian denominations but
of non-Christian religious minorities - although David Wright's essay
is a necessary warning that the Kirk must not seek "national" status
at the expense of Christian character.

We who inherit this complex Reformed tradition and, more
important, live in the faith handed down through it to be rediscovered
in every generation, ought neither to be too elated nor too
apprehensive about the alterations to the political structures through
which some Scottish aspirations, but only some, can find expression.
Others depend on the mood of the people and not the powers of
politicians. This is not a revolution redefining our national character
and identity but an important stage in an evolution, some of whose

most important processes have been and will continue to be beyond the control of Governments.

Till halfway through the twentieth century the conclusion of an introduction to a book on these Reformed themes might have run something like this: we are the Church and people of Ninian and Columba, Knox and Melville, Henderson and Rutherford, the Covenanters and Carstares; of Alexander Duff and Thomas Chalmers; Norman Macleod and Robert Rainy; John White and George MacLeod. The very shape of that preceding sentence (less its last two names) echoes one I encountered years ago when researching the 1929 Presbyterian reunion celebrations and have no need to look up again. But would most of the names mean anything to an educated middle-class congregation of the modern Kirk, even to the average Scottish graduate able to satisfy the examiners in history, far less to the vast majority of the Scottish people today?

Of course not. But the lesson is not just that we have forgotten a lot of our national history, and that even the modern Church of Scotland can seem half-hearted about its history. The real lesson may be that we have lost our grasp of two vital priorities.

The first is that sense of the continuity of past, present, and future in national life - by which I mean not only life within Scotland but Scotland's inescapable involvement with the other British nations - which should provide the true perspective and sense of proportion for the new Scottish Parliament.

The second is even more important. It is our sense of what the Catechism, drafted without benefit of neutered language, calls "the chief and highest end of man".

That end is to glorify God and fully to enjoy him for ever: and that "fully" from the longer version of the catechism's first answer is surely the key to a deeper understanding of the place of the Reformed presentation of the Christian religion in our history and of the way the Church must keep re-forming itself for the future. See, for example, the reflections of Donald Smith on contemporary mission, Russell Barr on the parish system, and Stewart Lamont on the media world in which the Church is ill at ease but through which it must prepare the way of the Lord.

We have allowed Calvinism, Presbyterianism, and the Reformed tradition to be presented as "narrow". That is true only in the sense that Jesus warned his followers - as William Barclay translates Matthew 7:13 - to "go in by the narrow gate. There is plenty of room to go through the gate that leads to ruin." But beyond the narrow gate there is a fullness of life whose enjoyment is not only in worship and devotion but in the proper deployment of the human intellect and artistic imagination - as evidenced in the notable contributions of Tom Torrance and George Bruce, so authoritative in their very different fields, to this book.

The Realm of Reform, whether in Scotland or the universal Church, is no tightly-controlled unitary state of mind. It has many mansions and uses many talents. Only in one thing is it centralised: in the centrality of Jesus, the Christ and the author and finisher of our faith. As Barclay renders that passage from Hebrews, it is he "in whom our faith had its beginning and must have its end".

1   THREE PORTRAITS OF SCOTTISH CALVINISM

Views from literary, philosophical and political perspectives

William Storrar

Tom Nairn spoke for many of his fellow Scottish intellectuals when he remarked that Scotland would only be reborn when the last minister was strangled with the last copy of *The Sunday Post*! Personified here by the Kirk minister, Calvinism has certainly been perceived as a largely negative force in Scottish life in the 20th century. The term appears regularly in both modern Scottish literature and the contemporary media as a quick shorthand for all our national ills. As we enter the new millennium and welcome the new Scottish Parliament with a greater self-confidence about our national identity, it is surely time for a more nuanced reappraisal of the cultural role that Calvinism has played in modern Scotland.

We are now in a position to ask, *which* Calvinism are we dealing with when we hear the all too predictable verdict passed on the Calvinist bogeyman of Scottish culture? If Nairn made his now famous paraphrase of a French Revolutionary slogan in an essay entitled, *The Three Dreams of Scottish Nationalism,*[1] I wish to identify not one but three portraits of Scottish Calvinism for a timely re-assessment of his widely shared judgement.

In this essay, I am interested not in Calvinist religious doctrine as such but in the way in which a bundle of associated words - Reformed, presbyterian and Calvinist - is used as a cultural key to interpret aspects of our national experience in Scotland. The term 'Calvinism' will be used here as a portmanteau term for the many different and conflicting perceptions of the Reformed influence on modern Scottish history and culture. In reviewing the nature of this contribution, I shall argue that we need to distinguish at least three pictures of Calvinism in the 20th century gallery of our national imagination.

Two of these cultural portraits are well known to us. I shall describe them as *anti-Calvinism* and *secular Calvinism*. The third portrait, however, has been over-painted by the other two interpretations of Scottish Calvinism and now deserves its own title. I shall call it *civic Calvinism*, and seek to restore some of its all but forgotten features for public viewing. Before exhibiting the canvas of civic Calvinism, however, we have to strip away the layers of the other two, more familiar portraits in our mind's eye.

Anti-Calvinism - A Literary Portrait

The most influential portrayal of Calvinism in 20th century Scotland has undoubtedly come from the school of *anti-Calvinism* associated with the leading figures of the Scottish literary Renaissance in the inter-war years, especially Hugh MacDiarmid and Lewis Grassic Gibbon. In seeking to create a modern Scottish identity, such writers felt it necessary to break what they saw as Calvinism's deadlock on our national psychology, indeed our national pathology.

In particular, the figure of John Knox, has been painted time and again in modern Scottish literature as the embodiment of Calvinism's malign influence on national life. This leading Scottish reformer and colleague of John Calvin in Geneva is seen as the mad doctor whose experiment in national reformation created the Frankenstein monster of the "divided Scot". As the literary critic, the late Alan Bold commented:

> The divided Scots needed heroes and villains. Knox is probably the best-known villain and appeared as such in a play by Bridie, a meditative book by Fionn Mac Colla, the poems of Edwin Muir and Iain Crichton Smith, the stories of George Mackay Brown.[2]

Bold went on to quote a poem on Knox by Alan Jackson which put this verdict on the cultural impact of Calvinism succinctly:

> O Knox he was a bad man
> he split the Scottish mind
> The one half he made cruel
> and the other half unkind.[3]

For Bold, the situation was far more complex than this anti-Knoxian strain in Scottish literature would allow. Undoubtedly, he thought, the tendency of the Scottish consciousness to think in terms of "stereotypes and archetypes" was "encouraged by the Calvinistic tendency to see the world in terms of absolute good versus absolute evil".[4] However, replying to Jackson's accusation that Knox split the Scottish mind, he asserted that, "Knox did nothing of the kind though the identification of one man with all the ills of a nation is symptomatic of national uncertainty."[5]

With that last comment, we get close to understanding why this anti-Calvinism was so important for the construction of a modern sense of Scottish national identity in earlier 20th century Scottish literary and intellectual circles. Whatever the social and biographical reasons why such writers rebelled against the dreary Calvinism of private and public life, literary anti-Calvinism also had a political dimension. These anti-Calvinist intellectuals were engaged in a battle against Scotland as North Britain, with its deep ambiguities and uncertainties about what constituted Scottish identity in the age of empire.

As the historian Linda Colley has shown, the sense of British identity which emerged after the Union of the Parliaments in 1707 was constructed out of a shared sense of a common imperial, military and *Protestant* identity between Scotland and England.[6] In Scotland, that shared Protestant Britishness took on a Calvinist guise. The new British (and yet still Anglican) state had to guarantee the special place of the Reformed and presbyterian national Church north of the border as a condition of Scotland's entry into the United Kingdom. It is easy to see why the literary and nationalist struggle to assert Scottish autonomy in the 1920s and 1930s included such a vehement anti-Calvinism, given their real enemy, the British state. The Kirk and its Calvinist ethos, underwritten by the terms of Union in 1707, were seen as the embodiment of a false and reactionary national consciousness in Scotland – and with some reason.

By 1929, when the two major Presbyterian churches came together in a reunited national Kirk, official Protestantism had adopted an anti-Irish stance, calling for the Catholic section of the Scottish population which had originally emigrated from Ireland to be deported.[7] Presbyterians in the Church of Scotland, the United Free Church of Scotland and the Free Church all vilified the immigrant Irish community as racially inferior and 'a menace to the pure Scottish race' of Protestant North Britain – a racist denial of the inclusiveness of the Gospel and the pluralism of modern Scottish society. Whatever the decencies and achievements of that Protestant and British identity in Scotland, and there were many, the Kirk made a shameful pact with its most intolerant and anti-Catholic traits. Mercifully, the Unionist politicians of the period did not give in to repeated calls from the General Assembly for punitive measures by the government against its own citizens and the Kirk's own fellow Christians.

At the same time, the Kirk's prophetic commentary on the social evils haunting the Scotland of the Depression was too often reduced to moralising about the dangers of gambling and the cinema. No wonder that Tom Nairn could sum up over fifty years of this understandable anti-Calvinism with savage wit, by identifying the Kirk and the SundayPost as the tragi-comic faces of an oppressive North Britain. However, as so often with Hegel's wise owl of Minerva, Nairn's killer punch landed on the poor old minister just at the moment when this era of triumphalist, reactionary Calvinism was effectively over.

By 1970, the year Nairn penned his ministerial death sentence, the Kirk was already in serious institutional decline. In the 1970s, its membership would fall below one million on a seemingly relentless downward curve. Underlying this numerical decline lay the collapse of its social base in local community and family life; a loyal source of Kirk membership and churchgoing which had survived the urban, industrial era, right up to the 1950s. With the onset of 1960s permissiveness, the Kirk's historic marriage to Scottish society was already in deep trouble and by the time of the unfettered free market of the 1980s, it appeared on the rocks. Kirk members, so much a part of their wider society, were not immune from these profound social and economic changes. By the 1990s, they too worked and shopped on the once inviolate Sabbath. And their children and grandchildren showed little interest in belonging to the outdated 1950s world that the Kirk now represented to younger Scots. Ministers were to be spared strangulation at the hands of Nairn's Revolutionary Left only because they were fast becoming victims of capitalism's own moral and economic revolution.[8]

And yet there is another reason why the earlier 20th century strain of anti-Calvinism was losing its virulence, and even its relevance by the end of the 1970s. Alongside the Kirk's decline as a dominant British and Protestant institution in Scotland, was the parallel recovery of its own prophetic voice as an advocate of social justice and Scottish political autonomy. The post-war Kirk abandoned its pre-war racist and moralising social stance and became a robust advocate of the welfare state and government economic intervention, to end such pre-war horrors as slum housing and long-term unemployment.[9] This was in large measure due to the progressive intellectual leadership of the Kirk by the theologian John Baillie during the Second World War, and the willing response of a new generation of able ministers and members committed to post-war reconstruction at home and colonial independence abroad.[10] But the Kirk had not escaped from being the bully pulpit for an ethnic Protestant Unionism up to 1939, only to become the church choir for Labour's Socialism after 1945.

It was the Attlee Labour government that began the centralisation of power in Britain, with state ownership of Scottish heavy industries and welfare services, and the setting up of the London-based nationalised industries and welfare state. The Kirk protested at this centralising loss of autonomy in the post-war period and began to make its own case for the devolution of power and decision-making back to Scotland. It maintained its support for political devolution for over fifty years, from its 1940s critique of economic centralisation to modern, democratic expression of the historic Reformed doctrine of limited and popular sovereignty.

From such a perspective on the post-war Church of Scotland, we can see that anti-Calvinism's equation of presbyterianism with what it perceived to be a reactionary British Unionism had lost much its force. Certainly by 1988, when Mrs Thatcher delivered her famous Sermon on the Mound to a polite but hostile General Assembly, no one could doubt that the Kirk had incurred her wrath and attention because of its frequent public criticism of her policies in the 1980s, from the poll tax to her unyielding opposition to devolution.

Such was the sea-change in the Left's attitude to the Kirk in this period that the political magazine *Radical Scotland*, which had been launched with a front cover depicting Nairn's minister being strangled with *The Sunday Post*, could write an editorial revising its earlier stance and acknowledging the Church's contribution to the common cause of constitutional reform and social justice in the 1980s. Even Tom Nairn could be found writing a revisionist column for *The Scotsman* after attending the General Assembly in this period, in which he decided that a re-born Scotland might just spare a few of the more radical ministers!

So, anti-Calvinism was an important element in the first intellectual wave of Scottish nationalism from the 1920s up to the 1970s. Its typical biographical and ideological trajectory can be traced in the life of the poet Christopher Grieve. As "Hugh MacDiardmid", he deconstructed his presbyterian Sunday School teacher past on his way to becoming Scotland's Nietzschean superman. Grieve's poetic genius struggled to create a new linguistic and internationalist Scottish identity as an act of pure will, by inventing his own literary Scots and imagining Scotland's socialist independence. To re-invent Scotland, MacDiarmid and his contemporaries had to attack what they saw as the complacent, small-town Presbyterian world of ersatz Burns Suppers, Calvinist inhibition and North British, anglicised forms of Scottish identity. By the end of the 1970s, the rhetoric of anti-Calvinism no longer resonated with most Scots' cultural or historical experience. The Calvinist bogeyman was fast becoming a figure of straw. In response to a profound, secularising shift in Scottish society, a new generation of nationalist intellectuals began to paint a very different picture of Scottish Calvinism - a philosophical portrait of secular Calvinism.

Secular Calvinism - A Philosophical Portrait

By the time the first wave of cultural and political nationalism had reached its high tide in the 1979 devolution referendum (but not high enough to cross the infamous 40% barrier), Scotland itself was changing fundamentally from the presbyterian Langholm of Grieve's late Victorian and Edwardian youth. Younger generations could no longer recognise their country or their experience in the anti-Calvinist portrait of Scotland, painted as it was in the hodden greys and puritan blacks of a now receding moral landscape. Their Sixties world was bathed in technicolor lighting and dressed in psychedelic prints.

Typically, younger Scots from a Protestant background were now growing up with only the most casual contact with the Kirk. Presbyterianism rarely cast an oppressive shadow over their upbringing and outlook, certainly in Lowland Scotland. For some, like a Joyce McMillan or a Gordon Brown, it was even an acknowledged source of their humane and egalitarian values, to be carried into adult life when Sunday School and churchgoing had been left behind. But without the felt need to exorcise the anti-Calvinist demons of an earlier generation, some of them were now, paradoxically, open to a more sympathetic portrayal of Scottish Calvinism.

They had their own formative cultural and political landscape to inhabit and interpret. They were riding the second wave of cultural and political nationalism after the failure of the 1979 devolution referendum to deliver its promised Scottish Assembly, a formative event in their experience. For some of the post-1979 intellectuals at least, the Kirk and its Calvinist imprint on Scottish history offered a neglected and misrepresented cultural inheritance, a tradition ripe for critical retrieval if secular Scots were to understand their own modern history and identity. From this post-1979 perspective, these secular and sometimes nationalist thinkers began to paint a portrait of the Scottish Reformed legacy in the warm if unfamiliar colours of *secular Calvinism*.

By this I mean first the intellectual current among those critics who were seeking to retrieve the theological contribution of Calvinism to the cultural formation of contemporary, secular Scotland. Chief among such secular interpreters of Scottish Calvinism must be Craig Beveridge and Ronald Turnbull, freelance intellectuals with wide-ranging interests in history, psychology and philosophy. Their work is part of the cultural renaissance that rose phoenix-like from the ashes of the 1979 Scottish Assembly; a burst of intellectual energy in the 1980s associated with the early years of the journal *Cencrastus* and the *Determinations* series of books on Scottish culture edited by Cairns Craig. Their own two jointly written books in that series, *The Eclipse of Scottish Culture*, and *Scotland After Enlightenment*, are among the key texts for understanding the new school of secular Calvinism.

Drawing on the moral philosophy of Alasdair MacIntyre and the social theory of Pierre Bourdieu, Beveridge and Turnbull interpret the

Scottish Reformed tradition as a narrative of "internalised codes and dispositions" which have profoundly shaped Scotland's secular as well as religious history and identity. And so, secondly, at a deeper level, the term secular Calvinism refers to Reformed theology's deep imprint on secular Scottish thought and practice; to the extent that certain Scottish writers and philosophers can best be described in their originality and comparative distinctiveness as exponents of a secular form of Calvinism. The work of Beveridge and Turnbull is about secular Calvinism in both these senses: it is a more favourable cultural portrayal of Calvinist theology and practice by contemporary secular intellectuals; and it is an account of the secularised Calvinist doctrines to be found in modern Scottish philosophy and social thought.

Their first book, *The Eclipse of Scottish Culture*, argued that Scottish culture had too often been intellectually eclipsed by a dominant anglicising interpretation of Scottish history and identity, in which the native contribution to thought and letters was seen as inherently inferior to its proven superior south of the border.[11] In particular, Beveridge and Turnbull drew on the ideas of the North African writer Frantz Fanon about the internalised sense of inferiority of colonised nations; a verdict of inferiority not only imposed by the imperial power but also adopted by the colonised themselves, in their own attitudes to their own culture and identity. Beveridge and Turnbull applied Fanon's thesis on "inferiorism" to Scotland, and argued that many members of the Scottish intelligentsia, including leading exponents of what I have called anti-Calvinism, had similarly adopted an "inferiorist" interpretation of their own history and culture.

In particular, Beveridge and Turnbull contested the notion that the Scottish Enlightenment was only made possible in a barbaric, minister-ridden Calvinist country like Scotland because of the civilising influence of the Union with England after 1707. As an alternative interpretation, they argued that pre- and post-1707 Scottish traditions of philosophy, social theory, historiography, and, significantly for our purposes, Reformed theology were in the mainstream of European and Western thought. Indeed, Beveridge and Turnbull pointed out the key role played by theology in Scotland's intellectual internationalism. They sought to show, for example, how important 20th century Scottish Reformed theologians had been in introducing major works of continental philosophy to the English-speaking world.

In their more recent book, *Scotland After Enlightenment*, Beveridge and Turnbull have developed their critique of Scottish inferiorism into a full-blown counter-argument for seeing the Scottish Enlightenment as an inherently "Calvinist Enlightenment".[12] They go even further and suggest that a case can be made for two Calvinist enlightenments in the history of modern Scotland, not only around the mid-18th but also in the later 19th centuries. In defence of their own theory of twin Calvinist Enlightenments, they draw on recent scholarship which challenges the dominant view of the Enlightenment as a break with Scotland's Calvinist past. To that end, they quote the work of the historian David Allan to the effect that, "many major texts of the Scottish Enlightenment might in one sense be considered as extended Calvinist essays on the unruly passions of man."[13] Commenting on what they regard as "inferiorist" interpretations of Scotland in the 19th century, which see the country falling into kailyard decline after the golden age of the 18th century Enlightenment, Beveridge and Turnbull argue with a certain irony and *brio* in favour of the philosopher Alasdair MacIntyre's claim that it represents a second Calvinist Enlightenment:

Before the end of the [19th] century which began with the "demise", "disintegration" or "withering" of this [Enlightenment] culture, and saw Scotland sink into the mindlessness of tartanry and kailyardism, another generation of Scottish Calvinists had re-ordered intellectual discourses in ways arguably as profound and influential as the achievements of the previous century. William Robertson Smith would pioneer the sociology of religion; J.G. Frazer's work would establish anthropology; James Clerk Maxwell – now in Scotland inexplicably forgotten – would revolutionise physics. The story of what MacIntyre has termed this second Scottish Enlightenment … has yet to be written.[14]

With that last comment, we catch something of the sense of intellectual adventure as well as combativeness which characterise Beveridge and Turnbull's secular Calvinist perspective on Scottish culture – there are vast vistas which have yet to be mapped before we can even begin to appreciate Scotland's Reformed inheritance. In particular, the two centuries that book-end Scotland's Golden Age - the 17th and 19th centuries with their notorious Killing Times and Disruption - have to be re-discovered not as dark pages of obscure presbyterian dispute and "theological squalor" but as companion volumes in a series of Calvinist intellectual continuities with the 18th century Scottish Enlightenment.

Beveridge and Turnbull go further, and argue that 20th century Scottish intellectual history also represents an "Augustinian moment" where distinctively Calvinist themes, rooted in Augustine's more ancient anti-Pelagian theology of predestination, continue to reverberate in the approach of secular Scottish philosophers to public debate.[15]

Here, as so often in their work, they are deeply indebted to the Scottish philosopher and historian of ideas George Davie, perhaps the greatest influence on their post-1979 generation of nationalist intellectuals. Davie's book on earlier 20th century Scottish philosophy, *The Crisis of the Democratic Intellect*, demonstrates the continuing articulation of "the secular calvinist position", particularly in the thought of Norman Kemp Smith and John Anderson.[16] What Kemp Smith and Anderson offer is something different in the philosophy of the inter-war period, something Davie calls, "a sort of secularised version of the doctrine of original sin" to counter contemporary progressive notions of human perfectability.[17] With this example, as in so many aspects of their thesis, Beveridge and Turnbull are seeking to retrieve Calvinism from the dominant interpretative discourse of barbarism and to restore it to what they regard as its rightful and central place in Scottish philosophy and social thought.

Whose Calvinism? Which Scotland?

It is pertinent to ask why a generation of Scottish intellectuals like Beveridge and Turnbull, born into the second half of the 20th century, have been more favourably disposed to paint this sympathetic portrait of secular Calvinism. Why have they not been content to stick with the anti-Calvinism of an earlier generation of Scottish literati like MacDiarmid and Gibbon? One reason must lie in their different perceptions of the role played by Calvinism in either distorting or sustaining Scottish identity.

For the anti-Calvinists from MacDiarmid to Nairn, Scottish Calvinism was irredeemably tarnished by its association with the Presbyterian Scotland of reactionary North Britain. MacDiardmid's motto was, "Not Traditions – Precedents". Anti-Calvinism sought a radical break with what it saw as debilitating traditions of national identity sustained by the Kirk and the Kailyard (Nairn's minister and *Sunday Post*). Bolshevik Revolution and literary modernism served as better precedents for the new Scotland.

For the more recent secular Calvinists like Beveridge and Turnbull, a robust if unfashionable defence of Scottish Calvinism represents the recovery of native and yet European philosophical traditions. They see the retrieval of such traditions as essential to understanding Scottish nationhood and identity today. They see George Davie's philosophical appreciation of the presbyterian mind, as in his seminal book on the Scottish educational tradition, *The Democratic Intellect*, as a better key to understanding Scotland's past and present than the rhetoric of anti-Calvinism.[18] They see no biographical or intellectual reason to identify with Hugh MacDiardmid's compulsive need to demolish Calvinism, as in his self-creation of Scottish identity in *A Drunk Man Looks at The Thistle*.[19] In other words, *pace* MacDiarmid, secular Calvinists have proved more willing to look to Reformed traditions, not Revolutionary precedents, in order to understand Scotland's past and to determine its future.

Given this more flattering philosophical portrait of Scottish Calvinism by the secular Calvinists, it might seem that their work was a sufficient defence of the Reformed contribution to modern Scotland to spare the last minister from strangulation. However, inspired though its brush strokes have been in capturing the Calvinist mind behind the many faces of the Scottish Enlightenment, the secular Calvinist portrait has not done sufficient justice to one remaining feature of Scottish Reformed religion - its political dimension.

Civic Calvinism - A Political Portrait

With the advent of the Scottish Parliament, this political dimension merits a higher profile. The anti-Calvinist cartoon rightly caught the cultural ambiguities of Scottish Calvinism and the secular Calvinist panorama has highlighted its philosophical vistas. What is needed, finally, is a view of Scottish Calvinism that does justice to its constitutional significance for modern Scotland.

I call this perspective *civic* Calvinism because of its Reformed vision of Scotland as a *polis*, a political community best governed by the twin assemblies of civil society and the state. To see this third, political portrait of Scottish Calvinism in its proper light, one needs to understand something of the Church of Scotland's church-state settlement.

Unlike the Church of England, the Church of Scotland is not a "state church". According to its own constitution, the Kirk's national status is not conferred upon it by the civil power; nor does the state play any part in its internal government. The Church of Scotland believes that its sovereignty and independence in the running of its own affairs are directly conferred on it by Christ alone, the divine head of the Church. The state's duty is to recognise the Kirk's independence and national role, something which the British Parliament did in its 1921 Church of Scotland Act. The state is also given authority by God to rule in its own civil sphere, something which the Kirk in turn respects and acknowledges in its own constitution.

The historian William Ferguson has described the distinctive features of this constitutionally radical presbyterian theory of church and state, as set out in the Reformed Kirk's *Second Book of Discipline* (1578):

> ... it grappled with the problem of sovereignty and sought to resolve political-ecclesiastical conflict by claiming that the church was supreme in the spiritual sphere .... The Second Book of Discipline did not aim at theocracy, but rather postulated the "two kingdoms" theory of separate but co-ordinate jurisdictions.[20]

As so often, it is George Davie who has brilliantly identified the cultural importance of this political theory of Scottish Calvinism, where Scotland is to be governed through the separate but co-ordinate jurisdictions of General Assembly and Parliament. Referring to the critical decade of the 1690s when presbyterianism was finally confirmed as the polity of the Church of Scotland, after a century of opposition from a Stewart monarchy which favoured a more amenable episcopacy, Davie observes that the triumphant presbyterians were enthused,

> by the opportunity thus belatedly offered of realising their long deferred reformation ideal of a constitution finely balanced as between church and state: a constitution by which they would govern themselves as through the cooperation of a pair of mutually critical but mutually complementary assemblies, the one concerned with politics and law, the other with the distinguishable, but nevertheless inseparable sphere of ethics and faith.[21]

This civic Calvinist theory of *the separate but co-ordinate jurisdictions of mutually critical but mutually complementary assemblies* was always a constitutional ideal rather than a political reality in 18th and 19th century Scotland. Despite the guarantees of the Treaty of Union in 1707, the British state refused to respect the Kirk's claim to autonomy as a self-governing sphere. With its 1712 Patronage Act, Westminster imposed the hated patronage system of appointing parish ministers on the Church of Scotland, and maintained its grip through the civil law courts, causing the many presbyterian secessions which bedevilled Scottish church life from the 1730s to the 1840s. However, the Kirk did not abandon its civic Calvinist ideals in its constitutional struggles with the British state and these were finally vindicated when Westminster recognised the Church of Scotland's constitutional claims in 1921.

Whatever political frustrations it faced, the presbyterian constitutional ideal also made a fertile intellectual contribution to the emergence of modernity in Scotland. George Davie agrees with those scholars who argue that it was "the spiritual-temporal tension inherent in this two-kingdoms scheme of separate but co-ordinate jurisdictions between church and state which gave the Enlightenment in Scotland its distinctive character".[22] It was also in defence of this constitutional principle that the major national event in 19th century Scotland, the Disruption of the Church of Scotland, took place in 1843; when over a third of its members and ministers left the national Church in protest at state intervention in church affairs.[23] Again, Davie has described the events of the Disruption in the now familiar terms of what I am calling civic Calvinism:

> ... the Scottish nation was struggling to find a solution of the universal problems of the relation of theory to practice and of the few to the many by a restatement of the presbyterian idea of the two-kingdoms constitution in modern and popular terms.... equal in authority but independent of one another and, it was hoped, complementary, the one managing the temporal interests of the whole people as expressed in law and politics and the other the spiritual interests of the whole people as expressed in morals and faith.[24]

It should be remembered that until well into the 19th century, the Kirk's management of the people's spiritual interests included areas of national life which today are regarded as aspects of civil society and subject to state or voluntary provision, such as welfare and education. Given the overwhelming social problems of mid-Victorian Scotland, the break-up of the national Church, and the growing Catholic population, after the 1843 Disruption the General Assembly could no longer lay credible claim to being the national forum of Scottish civil society. We have already noted the unrepresentative and racist claims of the General Assembly in the 1920s when it presumed to speak for the nation. For civic Calvinism, however, the constitutional health of society still requires the co-ordinate jurisdictions of two assemblies, representing the autonomous but related spheres of civil society and the state. In an age when Scotland was seen as a Christian society, this meant the General Assembly and Parliament, whether the pre-Union Scottish Parliament or the post-1707 Parliament of Great Britain. But what, if anything, does civic Calvinism have to offer Scotland today, as a more pluralist society with its own modern, democratic legislature? Can we detect the constitutional features of civic Calvinism anywhere in the emerging face of Scottish politics in the 21st century? I think we can.

Amid all the proper excitement at the new Scottish Parliament, there is one related development which I believe to be of profound constitutional importance for the flourishing of democracy. Along with the campaigning of the political parties, perhaps the most significant political development in the 1990s was the mobilisation of

Scottish civil society in support of self-government. Active citizens and civic groups and institutions, unaligned to any political party, together made common cause for democratic renewal through a Scottish Parliament. More than that, such citizens and civic bodies realised that the Scottish Parliament would not deliver the kind of open, consensus politics or participatory decision-making they sought, unless it was surrounded by a democratic culture of active citizenship in civil society at large. Such a civic democratic culture needed its own national voice.

To that end, the Scottish Civic Assembly was set up as a national forum for Scottish civil society. Its aim was to debate the pressing public issues of the day and offer government a fresh civic perspective on legislation. Its authority was distinct from that of the elected legislative assembly of Parliament. It spoke with the moral authority of informed representatives of all aspects of civic life, from the voluntary organisations to branches of the economy and public sector, and including the churches.

Although the Civic Assembly was still very much in the first stages of development in 1997, the new Labour government and its consultative process on setting up the new Parliament recognised the importance of this civic dimension. It seconded a civil servant from the Scottish Office to work with the Civic Assembly on establishing a national Civic Forum. Whether any official Civic Assembly or Civic Forum recognised by the Parliament becomes more than just a consultative body for civic opinion remains to be seen.

However, with its vision of *the separate but co-ordinate jurisdictions of mutually critical but mutually complementary assemblies,* civic Calvinism offers a more radical vision of the Civic Forum's constitutional role in the politics of the 21st century. Active citizens of all beliefs and none might well look to it as a model of democracy in which decisions about our future are too important to be left to Members of Parliament alone, even Members of the Scottish Parliament. Would the new Parliament's legislation be better drafted, its debates more constructive, its spirit more consensual, if it had to engage in a necessary dialogue with its independent but companion Civic Assembly, whose only authority was the moral one of being informed and in touch with the realities and values of Scottish life, including those of the Reformed faith?

Much has been made of the fact that the new Scottish Parliament lacks a second chamber to correct its legislation. But that has never been the Scottish constitutional way. Rather than a bicameral Parliament, our polity since the Reformation has been that of a bi-polar constitution, with Scotland ideally governed by its twin national assemblies in church and state. On the eve of the 21st century, the political arena has gained its new democratic assembly in the shape of the Scottish Parliament. Is it not time that civil society also gained its own pluralist successor to the Kirk's General Assembly, and entrenched its Civic Assembly as Scotland's other national voice? If such a rival Assembly makes the new MSPs feel uncomfortable as they walk through the courtyard of the Kirk's General Assembly Hall to their temporary home, then the statue of John Knox can only smile down on them. Civic Calvinism would then prove his best and most enduring likeness.

[1] Tom Nairn, "The Three Dreams of Scottish Nationalism", in Karl Miller (ed.), *Memoirs of a Modern Scotland* (Faber: London, 1970), pp.35-54.

[2] Alan Bold, *Modern Scottish Literature* (Longman: London, 1983), p.8

[3] *Ibid.* [4] *Ibid.* p.9. [5] *Ibid.* p.8

[6] Linda Colley, *Britons: Forging The Nation 1707-1837* (London: Pimlico, 1994), see ch. 1, "Protestants", pp.11-54

[7] Stewart J. Brown, *"Outside the Covenant": the Scottish presbyterian churches and Irish immigration 1922-38, Innes Review,* vol. xlii (1991).

[8] Callum G Brown, *Religion and Society in Scotland Since 1707* (Edinburgh: Edin. Univ. Press, 1997), pp.158-176. See also William Storrar, "Understanding the Silent Disruption: A Response to David McCrone", in *The Future of the Kirk,* edited by D. A. S. Fergusson and D. W. D. Shaw, St Andrews Univ.: Theology in Scotland Occasional Paper No. 2, pp.21-26

[9] Donald C. Smith, *Passive Obedience and Prophetic Protest: social criticism in the Scottish Church 1830-1945* (New York: Peter Lang, 1987), pp.245-383

[10] Andrew Morton, ed., *God's Will in a Time of Crisis: A Colloquium Celebrating the 50th Anniversary of the Baillie Commission,* Edin. Univ. Centre for Theology and Public Issues Occasional Paper No. 31

[11] Craig Beveridge and Ronald Turnbull, *The Eclipse of Scottish Culture* (Edinburgh: Polygon, 1989)

[12] Craig Beveridge and Ronald Turnbull, *Scotland After Enlightenment* (Edinburgh: Polygon, 1997), pp.80-90

[13] *Ibid.* p.87. Quoted from David Allan, *Virtue, Learning and the Scottish Enlightenment* (Edinburgh: Edin. Univ. Press, 1993), p.203

[14] *Ibid.* p.90 [15] Ibid, pp.111-134

[16] George Davie, *The Crisis of the Democratic Intellect* (Edinburgh: Edinburgh University Press, 1986)

[17] *Scotland After Enlightenment,* p.118

[18] George Davie, *The Democratic Intellect* (Edinburgh: Edinburgh University Press, 1961)

[19] See Michael Grieve and W. R. Aitken, eds., *Hugh MacDiarmid: Complete Poems 1920-1976* (London: Martin Brian and O'Keeffe, 1978), Vol 1

[20] William Ferguson, *Scotland's Relations With England: a Survey to 1707* (Edinburgh: John Donald, 1977), pp.92,93

[21] George Davie, *The Scottish Enlightenment and Other Essays* (Edinburgh: Polygon, 1991), p.1

[22] *Ibid.* p.48

[23] Stewart J. Brown and Michael Fry, eds., *Scotland in the Age of the Disruption* (Edinburgh: Edinburgh University Press), pp.1-43

[24] Davie, *The Scottish Enlightenment,* p.42

2   THE KIRK: NATIONAL OR CHRISTIAN?

Dangers of a religious veneer

David Wright

Scotland's nationhood must increase, yet the national Church of the land seems doomed to go on decreasing. With a sense of timing that falls just short of genius (six months later and it would be truly millennial), Scotland gets its first parliament since 1707 - yet whether its proceedings will open with prayer is far from certain. One headline-hugging Churchman, leader of one of Scotland's smaller denominations, believes that the parliament should be a prayer-free zone. He is all for abandoning it to secularity - or should it be secularism?

That the question of parliamentary prayer is publicly contested is a measure of the largescale loss of a national role on the part of the Church of Scotland - as well as of other developments such as the variety of faiths that own some allegiance in our pluralist society. It has often been said that, in a Scotland without its own parliament, the Kirk's annual General Assembly has served as some kind of substitute, particularly in its coverage of national concerns. The arrival of a real parliament might therefore be felt as a threat to the self-esteem of the General Assembly. Yet the Assembly has been steadfastly committed to the cause of devolution, and the Kirk already had its parliamentary officer in post, well ahead of the elections. The use of the Church's Assembly Hall as the parliament's first, temporary, home might be viewed as altogether fitting: the Church's parliament-substitute gracefully makes way for the authentic article, and the national Church picks up not a little kudos in the process.

But no one is predicting a revival in the national Church's fortunes to accompany the heightened sense of national identity that the parliament is most certainly engendering. The Moderator of the day is sure to have a part to play in the ceremonial inauguration of the new parliament, the Kirk's Assembly Hall will enjoy hours of TV exposure, and the General Assembly itself in its temporary accommodation elsewhere will welcome Scotland's grateful first First

Minister at the earliest opportunity. Yet meanwhile the membership rolls of the Church will continue their sadly consistent decline, and the galloping de-Christianization of society will lose none of its momentum. Scottish nationhood is set for a glorious new flowering, but the colours will be increasingly those of a lustreless secular realm.

It would be faithless to exclude the possibility that intense concentration at all levels of public life on devolved government may promote rediscovery of the Church's signal contribution to Scotland's first experience of nationhood in the medieval centuries. We dare not lose hope that parliamentary rebirth may provoke sobering reflection on the moral and spiritual malaise of the Scottish people. Some preachers who catch the media's ear and eye may be trusted to speak a sensitive word in season on the perils of gaining the whole political world at the cost of losing our souls. Opportunities will abound for prophetic utterance from the Word of God, for dreaming dreams and seeing visions in the power of the Spirit. The weakness of the Church whose national status rings ever more hollow should safeguard us against triumphalism in the house of the Lord.

A new air of realism is discernible in the courts of the Kirk. The first editorial of *Life and Work* in this new parliamentary year called for "ditching the label of 'the national Church'" lest it nourish a nostalgia that obstructs essential change. The claim lacks credibility in some parts of the country, as congregations, services of worship and ordained ministers become increasingly thin on the ground - and these parts are bound to go on expanding. But the emptiness of the Church's inherited national status extends beyond the ever thinner stretching of resources and energies. It is glimpsed most starkly in the widespread disregard for the Christian faith in the public squares of Scottish society.

Nothing has revealed this dismissiveness more starkly than *The Scotsman*'s editorial on the morning after the House of Commons voted to lower the age of homosexual consent to 16. The opposition was put down to "bigotry, ignorance or religious belief" (a hybrid trinity!), insisting "contrary to the evidence, contemporary or historical, on an impossibly narrow definition of what is normal". So much for the consensus of all the Scottish Churches (with the possible exception of the maverick Scottish Episcopalians), here lumped together as "a minority afflicted by an imperfect understanding of Christ's love". My concern at this point is not with the substantive issue (it takes faith of supernatural proportions to believe that most Scots regard anal intercourse as normal!) but with the marginalization of the mind of the Churches, displaying on this question remarkable unity. They count for nothing but "religious inhibitions to which few these days subscribe", which must be laid aside together with cant and prejudice.

There is abroad a new intolerance that claims the high ground of equality and human rights but has decreasing patience with the beliefs of mainstream Christianity. Institutions of all kinds must have their mission statements, but woe betide the Church of Jesus Christ when it dares to be faithful to its Lord's foundational marching orders - to makes disciples of this and every nation. The Christian Church is nothing if not a missionary movement. A slogan like "Tell Scotland" goes to the heart of what the Church has to contribute to the new Scotland - what the Church will and must say that no one else can say.

It is one of the "Articles Declaratory" of the 1920s, commonly regarded as the nearest thing the Kirk has to a constitution, that talks so impressively of "its distinctive call and duty to bring the ordinances of religion to the people in every parish of Scotland". But in so doing it describes the Kirk as "a national Church representative of the Christian Faith of the Scottish people". What if "the Scottish people" no longer owns allegiance to "the Christian Faith"? More critically, what if the kind of Christian faith credibly attributable to any majority of the population is credally vacuous, driven by sentiment more than conviction, humanitarian under at best a religious veneer - does the Church of Scotland have a duty to be representative of that religion of universal niceness, barely recognizable as "Christian faith"? Is it constitutionally bound to play along with such a drastic reductionism in order to remain a nationally representative Church? This would be a new Babylonian captivity of the Church with a vengeance.

As I contemplate the resurgence of national self-esteem in Scotland - irrespective of whether the parliament turns into a launching pad for full independence - the prospect that fills me with greatest alarm is that of a Church of Scotland endeavouring to flow with the tides of national sentiment by dumbing down its distinctive Church identity. To put this fear at its sharpest: the Church may be tempted to seek to retain, or recover, its national character at the expense of its Christian character.

A Church that is no longer Christian may seem an absurdity, yet the Bible provides precedents and analogies galore, from ancient Israel, the covenant people of God, faced repeatedly by the prophetic threat of abandonment by God, to the salt that has lost its taste and is fit only for throwing away, the many the Lord will disown despite their proud records of religious activity ("I never knew you"), the Church whose light is at risk of divine extinction. Examples come readily to mind, within the twentieth century, of Churches so captive to sub-Christian cultures as to have fatally compromised their calling to be Christ's people. Let no national Church think that it is immune to such degradation.

My concern, then, in this chapter is with the peculiar temptations that may seduce a Church like the present-day Church of Scotland which remains national in name, and even remains proud of it, when the reality is a thing of the past. By this I simply mean that on a realistic assessment the Church enjoys the allegiance of only a fast-decreasing minority of the population. I am aware that on some measures, such as the nationwide network of parish Churches and the prevalence of expectations of Church funerals, and even perhaps the percentage of the population who were baptized as babies in the Kirk, the Church of Scotland appears still a national force in the land. I have no interest in selling the Kirk short, and I must be content to present my assessment rather than argue for it. The statistics are all too familiar, and inexorably discouraging.

But one comment is in order as we turn to the paper's main burden: reluctance or refusal to face up to the Church's minority existence almost certainly makes one more vulnerable to the temptations I will be speaking of. The fear or pride or piety that prefers something else to realism - whether it be nostalgia or idealism or optimism or uncritical generosity in measuring the strength of religion - is likely to induce a person to act, as far as changed circumstances allow, as though the Church still enjoyed general acceptance.

"As far as changed circumstances allow"; what if they allow a minister of the Church to function as chaplain of the local school only on condition that he conducts no worship that is distinctively Christian? - so that he cannot lead the children in celebrating at Christmas the human birth of the one and only Son of God? Or on condition that in any classes he teaches he conveys nothing about the uniqueness of the Christian revelation?

If ministers subject to such role restrictions confine their chaplaincy to promoting a general religious or spiritual awareness, they do so probably on the grounds of their responsibility as parish ministers to care for all the children in their schools - that is, on the basis of assumptions derived from the national status of the Church. But notice what has happened: in order to maintain this national role on the local level of the parish and its school, they have to this extent ceased to be ministers of the gospel, servants of the Word and sacraments of Christ.

The minority existence of the Church today is not merely numerical. It is determined also by the dominant pluralist assumptions of our culture which, for a variety of reasons ranging from high-minded tolerance to denial of any absolute truth, will not grant a privileged hearing to any creed. The possibilities surveyed above are already realities in some schools in some parishes in Scotland. They have become in effect no-go areas for ministers of the Kirk in their specific character as "stewards of the mysteries of Christ". Since most Church of Scotland ministers now in office were trained to serve in a national Church, with all that this implies, it is not surprising if some have succumbed to this particular reductionist temptation in order to retain a foothold in largely secular schools.

Sometimes it seems that it is the national Church which attracts the harshest intolerance - as though it is being made to pay for its privileged history. Its earlier dominant influence on our culture makes it fair game for scornful ridicule and tasteless satire to an extent that is not tolerated for any other religious community. Kicking the Kirk is a regular pastime for some of the chattering classes in Scotland's national newspapers.

The danger lies not in the denigration itself (although one sometimes longs for a columnist who could pass an elementary exam on John Knox and John Calvin) but in how Churchpeople respond to it. Relatively harmless (though far from admirable) is the flinch of affronted dignity, the recoil of outrage that the national Church should be so demeaned by cheap jibes and tawdry insults. Less common than a generation ago but by no means extinct, such a response springs ultimately from a proprietary spirit that believes the Scottish people owes the Church a living. Public respect is no less than the due of the nation's Church. As one of the "Articles Declaratory" puts it, "The Church and the State owe mutual duties to each other, and acting within their respective spheres may signally promote each other's welfare." Insisting legalistically that this is still in force can only trap the mind of the Church in an outdated time-warp. Living in the past is not good for the health of the Kirk.

Far more insidious a reaction is the quiet, perhaps half-unconscious, resolve never again to expose oneself or the Church on this or that unpopular tenet of faith, to soft-pedal the gospel which originally met with incredulity from Graeco-Roman gentiles and sounded deeply offensive to many Jews, to tailor the Church's teaching or service to what sceptics or humanists will bear in silence. We are so keen to be liked by the community, and especially by the opinion-formers. We lack the stuff that martyrs are made of, and so we will decline to enter the lists against the mocking taunts of the irreverent. If we still hold to any convictions that unbelievers might object to, we will keep them to ourselves. Accommodation is the order of the day.

The Church's ministry cannot for a moment ignore its social and cultural context. Changing moral norms may present challenges no less acute than the changing school scene. For example, there is no doubt in my mind that some of the pressure within the Church to revise its ethics of marriage and sexuality springs from a concern (or a fear) that the Church will otherwise find itself increasingly out of touch with society at large. From time to time this unspoken worry surfaces explicitly. Witness the extraordinary weight given in the General Assembly in 1994 by the convener of the Panel of Doctrine to the statistic that 99% of a certain age group had had sex before marriage. How unthinkable, so the implication went, that the Church of the nation should maintain unaltered its conviction that sex outside marriage was invariably wrong! Who wants to belong to such a tiny minority? How can it alone claim to be right?

Note the hidden assumptions here. One of them seems to allow consensus to determine truth; if such an overwhelming proportion of the population believes something, that must influence the Church's perception of truth. This may be called the Gallup-poll approach to truth. Another seems to reckon that nothing could be worse than for the Church - this national Church - to find itself marginalized by ever-widening forces of unbelief and immorality. Without doubt marginalization is a deeply painful experience for a body like the Kirk, creating crises of self-identity for many. Yet did not the Lord of the Church once say: "What will it profit a person (or a Church) to gain the whole world and lose its soul?".

More subtle to recognize for what they are will be the changing demands and expectations still addressed to the parish Church by people who are less and less comfortable with the Christian character of its ministry. Can a minister of the national Church refuse to marry a couple whose previous behaviour or present attitude gives no evidence of sympathy for the Church's understanding of marriage?

Funerals can be deeply dispiriting occasions when the bulk of those attending seem incapable of tuning into the right wavelength. Of course such services, especially funerals, may still be hopeful outlets for a pastoral gospel ministry (or do we kid ourselves, in our reluctance to face harsh reality?). But if we stand back a little, a clearer perspective may emerge. The energies of ministers are increasingly consumed by agenda set by others, and as the general level of Christian belief and awareness drops, they find themselves more and more servicing the sub-Christian requirements of a secular society.

Dividing lines are notoriously difficult to draw. The instinct that welcomes every request for a Church wedding or a Church funeral as a precious opportunity is laudable; after all, the minister will be in charge of what happens, will (s)he not? In fact, the subtly shifting pressures to play down the authentic Christian note are not so different from the changing expectations of chaplains in public contexts - hospitals, prisons, universities - to tone down the Christian in favour of the generally theistic or spiritual. Prayers may continue to be acceptable so long as they are not presented in the name of Christ or with a Trinitarian doxology.

Again, let us pause and reflect. These difficulties or temptations have their origin in the increasing mismatch between the Kirk's inherited national role, with its lofty sense of calling to serve all the people of Scotland, and the kind of service that alone the de-Christianized, or de-Christianizing, community will tolerate. The problems are undoubtedly more complex than those facing a minority Church in a pagan unevangelized world - although there are already elements of this in the Kirk's experience at the turn of the millennia. The Church's predicament is somewhat akin to that of Britain after the Second World War: she lost an empire and with it a sense of her role in the world. Adjustment to being at best "first among equals" in the new Commonwealth was inevitably painful.

There is a real risk that, without a realistic re-appraisal of its position, a national-minority Church ends up with the worst of all worlds - with neither the recognition and influence appropriate to national status nor the freedom of action and initiative indispensable for a minority body. Worst of all is the pathetic impotence that results from a rejection of the latter (perhaps with an emotive sneer at "sectarianism") in the deluded belief that the former still has cash value. This outcome was graphically illustrated in a report of Glasgow Presbytery's Education Committee in December 1994, recording deep perturbance over religious education in Glasgow schools:

The presentations showed two main strands in RE: Roman
Catholicism and a mixture of all the other religions. With
the latter category there seems to be very little interest in
the presentation of Christianity but much more interest in
some of the other religions. It cannot be right that RE
should marginalise the National Church (and the wider
Reformed Tradition) in an attempt to be all-embracing....

In the [Roman Catholic schools] there is a very close partnership
between priest and school and there is no problem over teaching the
dogma of the Roman Catholic Church. In the non-denominational
Schools the chaplains have to try to relate to pupils of all faiths and
no faith, thus they cannot operate in the way which is allowed in the
Roman Catholic Schools.

Whether or not this quotation still accurately summarizes the
experience of Catholic schools (the Catholic Church in Scotland has
had its own high-profile tribulations since 1994, fuelling the forces
of de-Christianization), some representatives of the national
Reformed Church cannot find it in themselves to envy their freedom
- even if allowance were made for the errors of the Roman faith. A
revealing article on denominational schools and public education in
Life and Work in September 1998 by John Stevenson, the general
secretary of the Kirk's Department of Education, placed a higher
premium on promoting tolerance than teaching Christianity. In his
view "the human quest for meaning, value and purpose in life" is the
fundamental ingredient in any religious education. Nothing should
be encouraged which might threaten social cohesiveness or breed
misunderstanding, distrust, suspicion or bigotry - as though these
were the inevitable results of teaching Christianity, let alone any
particular brand of it, as truth.

This is a large subject, and this essay is not the place to take it
any further. For our purposes it is sufficient to draw out the
implications of the policy enunciated by John Stevenson. In effect it
allows the Church of Scotland's sense of national responsibility to
override its calling to be the servant of Jesus Christ and his gospel.
The view of the Church's Education Committee gives a higher
priority to an open-ended, exploratory, personal search than to
"knowing something about Christianity". "Only educational factors
should determine the kind of school provision that is made." A
committee that propounds this approach is operating more within
the parameters of the country's system of public education than as
an agency of the Christian Church. It has succumbed to the

temptation to maintain the national role of the Church of Scotland at the expense of its Christian identity.

What has happened is that the "non-denominational" character of most schools in the public sector (that is, all but Roman Catholic schools) has been re-defined as "non-Christian", or perhaps "non-religious". At best they are now to be treated as "multi-religious", but even this is not sufficiently elastic, for religious education has to explore the beliefs of those who give non-religious as well as religious answers to pupils' questions. The most that can be said for this policy is its respect for the sensibilities of Hindus, Muslims, Jews, humanists, new-agers and wicca-paganists no less than of Scotland's Christians.

Paul, it is true, became all things to all kinds of people - but only so that he might by all possible means save some! Paul's ministry did not suffer from the submerging of the Christian message in some all-embracing multi-religious morass. At what point will the Church of Scotland recognize that faithfulness to its calling as the Church of Jesus Christ means that it can no longer relate harmoniously to people of all faiths and of no faith - without risking the offence of the gospel? Servicing the mixed multitude of contemporary Scotland will be perpetuated only at the cost of the Church's stewardship of the gospel. An inclusivism of theology or of practice that refuses to bear the cross - that is, that rules out ever suffering martyrdom for the name of Christ - must seem uncannily like a hollow imperialism afraid to face the real world after the loss of the empire.

The Church of Scotland's national network of parish Churches offers immense opportunities for a nationwide ministry of the gospel. Any other national role looks increasingly like dangerous self-delusion. If the national Church holds anything in trust for Scottish people it can only be the faith of Christ crucified and risen, not some all-encompassing consensus redolent of a pre-pluralist Britain. Failure to read the signs of the times, and to undergo the appropriate conversion, will increasingly hand the initiative not only to the Roman Catholic Church but also to new post-charismatic Church movements, to say nothing of a confident Islam and an assimilationist Buddhism. Not for them the quaint but pitiable self-induced identity crisis of a Church clinging stubbornly to national pretensions long after the tide of national favour has passed it by.

The issue hinges partly on the freedom of the Church. Critics of the particular form of state establishment enjoyed by the Church of England sometimes cast envious eyes north of the Border, at the Church of Scotland's combination of national recognition and status with unfettered spiritual freedom. The Kirk knows nothing akin to the Prime Minister's office's involvement in the selection of bishops, dependence on parliamentary legislation for important Church reforms or the monarch's position as Supreme Governor of the Church of England.

Yet the presence or absence of freedom is not solely a matter of constitution and law. Has the Church of Scotland cramped its own style by choosing to operate within limits that in practice restrict its freedom to serve Christ, "the King and Head of the Church"? How weighty a criterion in determining the ministries of the Church should be the maintenance of national unity or local harmony? Should truth - the truth of the Christian faith - play second fiddle to peace? "Woe to you when all people speak well of you!" (Luke 6:26).

In almost pontifical tones, the "Articles Declaratory" assert that this Church of Scotland "maintains its historic testimony to the duty of the nation acting in its corporate capacity to render homage to God, to acknowledge the Lord Jesus Christ to be King over the nations, to obey His laws, to reverence His ordinances, to honour His Church, and to promote in all appropriate ways the Kingdom of God". How magnificent this sounds! But how hollow it rings when measured against the real world of second-millennium Scotland! The Kirk may huff and puff, but efforts to breathe fresh life into this pretentious profession can only distract from the urgent task of revitalizing the Church's gospel mission at ground level. People who barely know who Jesus was can scarcely take their place in a corporate Scottish acknowledgement of his Lordship over the nations. The recent promotion of the "Articles Declaratory" in some circles as the bed-rock expression of the Kirk's sense of identity must reckon with their outmoded triumphalism. Like all such statements they betray the temper of the age of their composition. They have in some respects dated more damagingly than other much older documents that define the Church's identity.

Forecasts of the demise of the Church of Scotland within a generation are no more than artificial extrapolations from statistical decline. The Church retains institutional resources that must make it corporately one of the wealthiest organizations in the country. It also still owns deep-seated loyalties among at least the middle-aged to older sectors of the population. Survival in substantial size is not in doubt. But as what kind of body will it more than survive? Will it, in a vain effort to preserve its national reach, progressively lose its Christian bite? Not all the omens are set fair.

3 CALVINISM AND THE NEW MILLENNIUM

An exploration of myths, realities, and prospects

Donald Macleod

"Calvinism", wrote the late Ian Henderson, "is a handy term which people use when they wish to disparage anything in Scottish religion" (*Scotland: Kirk and People,* p.64).

He might have gone further. "Calvinism" is a handy term which people use whenever they wish to disparage *anything* in Scotland. It has been blamed for depression and alcoholism, the Highland Clearances, the disappearance of Gaelic folk-lore, the absence of great Scottish drama, and prevalent underfunding for the arts.

Behind this lies a belief that until very recently ours was a Calvinist nation. This must mean, at the very least, that the early Scottish Reformers were successful in their attempts to have their beliefs enshrined in law and that for centuries afterwards the nation's political and intellectual leaders were thirled to the philosophy of Geneva. In such a world the entire population was controlled by what Derek Thomson called *The Scarecrow*: "A tall, thin, black-haired man wearing black clothes" sweeping away the cards, taking the goodness out of the music, and lighting the searing bonfire of guilt in our breasts.

This of course is pure myth. There have been very few periods (and these themselves very brief) when anything resembling Calvinism was the dominant influence in Scottish life and culture. Even at the Reformation the Scottish Parliament refused to endorse Knox's First Book of Discipline. The nobility had no intention of handing back the ancient ecclesiastical lands to pay the stipends for ministers, build schools, and provide relief for the poor. Knox never saw in Scotland anything remotely resembling his vision of the Godly Commonwealth. Even a century later, men like Samuel Rutherford received only the most haphazard remuneration; and many parts of the country had no Protestant ministry at all.

The Melvillean Second Book of Discipline fared no better and for the duration of James VI's reign Scottish Calvinism was on the retreat. The King's schemes culminated in the passing the Five Articles of Perth in October, 1618, imposing on the Kirk medieval practices which were anathema to Melville and his associates - kneeling at Communion, private baptism, private administration of Holy Communion, episcopal confirmation, and observation of holy days. Dr William M. Campbell was fully justified in commenting that in his own lifetime Andrew Melville saw little result of his work except frustration (*The Triumph of Presbyterianism*, p.8).

Under Charles I, Calvinism was fighting for its very life; under the Protectorate of Oliver Cromwell it was treated as a spoiled child; and under Charles II and his brother James it was harassed and butchered in a reign of terror as cruel and focused as Hitler's Final Solution. Unfortunately the period was darker than the *literati* of Scotland could bear to look upon; the revisionist version of the story triumphed and the world is now assured that the Covenanting Holocaust was a legendary creation of the Cameronian imagination.

The Killing Times eventually gave way to the Glorious Revolution, but the bright hopes of 1688 were quickly eclipsed by the Act of Patronage of 1712. Within a generation it had its intended effect: secularising the Kirk by making it the plaything of landlords. Even Francis Hutcheson, Professor of Philosophy at Glasgow University and father of Scotish Moderatism, viewed the outcome with foreboding, predicting in 1735 that the sole study of candidates for the ministry would be servile compliance with the humour of some great lord who has many churches in his gift" (quoted by McCosh, *The Scotttish Philosophy* p.67). These great lords, usually educated in the South and affecting membership of the Church of England, quickly filled the pulpits of Scotland with sycophants more concerned with their fields than their flocks, more interested in fishing for salmon than fishing for men, and better acquainted with whisky than with the water of life. In that long century of Moderatism, men who preached total depravity or mentioned the doctrine of Grace were banished to remote rural hamlets or forced to eke out their days in village schools. The pulpits were for plagiarists of Tillotson and the disciples of Shaftesbury; purveyors at best of natural religion and Stoic morality.

Thomas Chalmers and Hugh Miller briefly stirred the waters: the former calling the Church back to a curious combination of the philosophy of Thomas Reid, the theology of Edwards, and the piety of Romaine and Wilberforce; the latter reminding her of the martyrs of the Bass Rock and of her historic right to choose her own ministers.

But even before Miller died, the tide had once again begun to turn. The ablest men in both branches of the now divided Kirk were dreaming not of great spheres of evangelistic labour but of academic preferment; and they were preparing for that not by immersing themselves in the thought of Calvin or Rutherford but by going off to the universities of Germany. Before anyone noticed, the students of "Rabbi" Duncan were regurgitating the views of Wellhausen and those of William Cunningham were preaching the Gospel according to Ritschl. Soon the various Churches were passing their Declaratory Acts, formally divorcing Calvinism and launching out on a great sea of theological pluralism. It is doubtful whether the twentieth century has seen a single Calvinist appointed as Moderator of the Kirk's General Assembly or (at the time of writing) as professor in a Scottish divinity faculty.

Where have all the "tulips" gone? The plain truth is, they were never there. There was probably only one period in Scottish history when Calvinism was really in control and that was between 1638 and 1649 when the Kirk was led by the great though diverse talents of Henderson, Rutherford, and Gillespie. Presbyterianism held the conscience of the nation, the nobility briefly cast in their lot with the Church, and the English Parliament was desperate for her help in defence of national liberties. Long before the movement could permanantly change the face of Scotland it was reined in by Cromwell's Ironsides and then crushed into the earth by Claverhouse's dragoons.

There were other later periods of relative affluence. William Carstares injected some of his own Calvinism into the Revolution settlement and the Treaty of Union found lodging for the Confession of Faith in one of its paragraphs (where it remained until 1921 when it was spirited away by the Articles Declaratory of the Constitution of the Church of Scotland in Matters Spiritual). In 1843 the Disruption moved the soul of the nation and produced Scotland's greatest-ever crop of Calvinist theologians, but even so it involved less than half of the Kirk's ministers, commanded the loyalty of few of the *literati*, and left unaffected huge swathes of the urban population.

How has it come about then that in the soul of every Scot there lies the belief that the reason for all his inhibitions and explanation for all his failures is that he spent his early infancy among Holy Willies, justified sinners, penitence stools, gloomy sabbaths, and "fragments of the philosophy of Geneva"?

Part of the reason is that Scotland sees its remaining Calvinist bodies though magnifying-glasses. We cannot shake off our fascination with the Free Church and the Free Presbyterian Church.

They are part bogey-men, part scarecrow, part dinosaur, and part Super Ego. Between them they receive as much media coverage as the Church of England, yet the total male membership of the Free Presbyterian Church is probably less than a hundred and the total strength of the Free Church only a third of the population of Inverness. It is not the monster that breeds the fascination; it is the fascination that breeds the monster.

Another reason is that even when Calvinism had no teeth, and political power and intellectual influence lay elsewhere, it did command the loyalty of considerable numbers of the grass-roots population. Moderatism, for example, never won the respect or affection of the people and during its hegemony the Evangelicals remained the "Popular Party". Bear in mind, of course, that in the eighteenth century many Scots also used Moderatism as an excuse to turn their backs on religion for ever. This stubborn grass-roots Calvinism was partly the result of the work of conscientisation carried out by such men as Rutherford and Dickson in the South-West during the seventeenth century; partly of the binding of the peasantry as a result of the Killing Times; partly a result of such revivals as the "Stewarton sickness", Kirk o' Shotts, Kilsyth, and Cambuslang, which kept the flame of Calvinist piety burning in Clydesdale from the early seventeenth to the mid-nineteenth century; and partly the result of the grip of the Secession on Scotland's farmers and artisans even in the days when Evangelicalism had been banished from Kirk pulpits.

I saw this phenomenon clearly in my own childhood in Lewis. In the 1940's and 50's many would have called it a Calvinistic island. Yet that Calvinism was clearly a matter of class. Nobody who was anybody was a Calvinist: not a lawyer or a factor, not a doctor or head teacher, not a prosperous business man or local councillor. Only those below, large in number but small in influence, were Calvinists: the crofters, labourers, weavers, and fishermen. The island was inhabited by Calvinists but run by Moderates and Humanists.

Such a community encouraged social mobility. There was an easy way upwards and outwards: education. This education owed little to Calvinism. It was neither planned, developed, nor delivered by Calvinists. Yet when many (particularly the most successful) looked back it was the Calvinism, not the schooling, that they remembered. The school made them choose between Latin and Gaelic, but it was the Calvinism they blamed for destroying the culture. The school told them nothing of Culloden or Clearance, but it was the Church they blamed for suppressing the history of their people.

It is remarkable how this Calvinism produced a kind of retroversive mind-set, using core elements in the despised legacy to attack the legacy itself. The exponents of this mind-set would say that Calvinism destroyed culture. That very Calvinism, however, had a highly developed liturgy of listening. Church was about going to hear God speak. He spoke, of course, through his servants the ministers or, sometimes, through his servants the elders; or even in the religious ceilidhs through anyone, male or female, possessed of the average verbal facility of the Gael. Such speech, particularly in Gaelic, was often profoundly eloquent. Even a hostile observer like the poet, Donald MacAulay, could describe the prayer in the local village meeting-house as a "liberating, cascading melody - my people's access to poetry" (*Gospel 1955*). From the minister in the pulpit and from the elder in the prayer-meeting there poured a ready sure-tongued extempore stream of consecutive thought, wide-ranging vocabulary, and vivid imagery.

It is no surprise that the art-forms which arose out of such a culture were primarily art-forms of the word: the novels of John Buchan and the Ettrick Shepherd; the Wagnerian prose of Thomas Carlyle; the poetry of Donald MacAulay, Derek Thomson, Iain Crichton Smith, and Sorley Maclean.

How much do these masters of words owe to the word-liturgies of their youth? And how can they claim as they sit among the trophies of their own imaginations that those imaginations were stifled by a grim, repressive Calvinism?

Whatever the answers, their talents have never been volunteered for the defence of the religion of their people. Reared in it and nurtured by it and *prima facie* well qualified to tell, they have used their art only to paint it in monstrous, infernal colours. To a degree not rivalled in any other tradition they have depicted indigenous saints as scarecrows and indigenous piety as neuroses.

So much for the past. What of the future? Calvinism no longer has even a titular hold of Scottish culture. It has long since disappeared from its former strongholds in Clydesdale, Fife, and the South-West. Like the nation's ancient language, it has been banished to the remote North-West; and even there it bears little resemblance to the vision of Henderson and Calvin. The torch is carried by a dwindling few. Today Scotland's Calvinists are fewer in number than its Gaelic-speakers.

What do these few have to offer the new millennium? The answer, strange though it may sound, is "an affirmative attitude towards the world" (Alister E. McGrath, *Reformation Thought* p.220). Reformed thought, building on that of Luther, is of course, reactive.

But what was it reacting to? Medieval Christianity - a Christianity which was unashamedly monastic. The religious went into seclusion. The irreligious stayed "in the world". This ineradicable human tendency to equate religion with asceticism has sometimes existed within Scottish Calvinism itself. The converted turn their back on the world, regarding all secular activity as at best a necesary evil, to be abandoned as soon as possible in favour of church and prayer-meeting. There was nothing wrong with the positive side of such a culture; certainly nothing wrong with a relish for Christian fellowship and a hunger for Christian teaching. What was wrong was that it became a rule for the Order - for example for "The Men" of the Highlands - forbidding involvement in social, cultural, and political activities. Even the man who was over-enthusiastic in his crofting was frowned on as earthy (*talmhaidh*).

Wherever such attitudes came from, they did not come from Geneva. As Abraham Kuyper once pointed out, "avoidance of the world has never been the Calvinistic mark, but the shibboleth of the Anabaptist" (*Lectures on Calvinism*, p.72). Luther's doctrine of the priesthood of all believers meant that no baptised person could get off the hook by arguing that he was a peasant, not a priest, a merchant, not a monk. The full rigours of the Christian ethic ("the counsel of perfection") applied to all believers in every sphere of life.

Calvin's doctrine of Common Grace confirmed this positive attitude to the world. Despite the Fall, man's reason could still operate efficiently and as a result even non-Christians were capable of outstanding achievements in politics, art, science, and other pursuits. (See *The Institutes* Bk.II Ch.I, 12-17.) Abraham Kuyper added yet another tier with his idea of co-belligerence: Protestant, Catholic, and Socialist could fight together in pursuit of common political ideals (McKentree R. Langley *The Practice of Political Spirituality*, p.137). This accords fully with St Paul's directive in Philippians 4:8 to support "virtue" wherever it is found.

Overarching all this is belief in Christ as King of Creation. He is Lord of the temporal order as well as of the spiritual. Every inch of the cosmos is his, and every sphere of human life is bound to operate to his standards. He himself, after all, was no ascetic. John the Baptist was, but not Jesus; and the Baptist model is not an option for the Christian. We belong not in the desert with the locusts and wild honey, but in Jerusalem with its teeming multitudes, its sins and its sorrows, and its endless moral conundrums.

At first glance, monasticism poses little threat as Scotland steps into the new millennium. But the first glance is deceptive. The mood of *ennui* and the appeal of asceticism are both alive and well and the world is going to need all the positive affirmation Calvinism can give.

The political domain, for example, is viewed with growing cynicism. While there is no shortage of candidates for the new Scottish Parliament, there are ominous signs that the political process itself is losing credibility and that, more and more, especially among the young, are disengaging from it. At is best, politics is the art of the possible. At its average, it is tainted with sleaze. At its very worst it corrupts absolutely.

But the consequences of political cynicism are too grim to contemplate. There can be no democracy without participation. Discourage it, and public life will quickly fall into the hands of hard-core activists, and freedom gives way to tyranny.

Part of the blame obviously falls on politicians themselves. They convey the impression of being unable to give straight answers to straight questions, more interested in style than in substance, and more adept at denigrating opponents than at formulating solutions.

It should not be beyond our wit to raise the level of political discourse. But something more fundamental is needed if governance is to command respect. The State, and with it the whole political process, needs metaphysical and even theological validation. It needs the kind of endorsement which Calvin gave it: "With regard to the function of magistrates, the Lord has not only declared that he approves and is pleased with it, but moreover has strongly commended it to us by the very honourable titles which he has conferred upon it.... if it has pleased him to appoint kings over kingdoms and senates or burgomasters over free states, whatever be the form which he has appointed in the places in which we live, our duty is to obey and submit" (*Institutes* Bk.IV, Ch.XX, 4,8).

It followed from this that Calvinism could never share in the negative Anabaptist attitude towards politics. Instead it insisted in the *Westminster Confession* (XXIII.II) that "it is lawful for Christians to accept and execute the office of a magistrate." It also insisted that our obligations to government do not depend on its religious or spiritual orientation: "Infidelity, or difference in religion, doth not make void the magistrate's just and legal authority" (XXIII.IV).

This positive affirmation of politics holds true despite the fact that Scottish Calvinism also led the world in its doctrine of civil disobedience. The work of men like Samuel Rutherford (*Lex Rex*) and Alexander Shields (*A Hind Let Loose*) was epoch-making in the development of democracy and found dramatic expression in the Sanquhar Declaration of 1680 when Richard Cameron disowned

Charles II, declared war on "such a tyrant and usurper", and protested against the succession of James as "repugnant to our principles.

These should not be taken as indications of a culture of civil disobedience. *In extremis*, the king could be defied; but only *in extremis*. Ordinarily, government was as honourable as parenthood. This why in 1649 the heirs of John Knox found it impossible to condone the execution of King Charles. There may arise occasions when it is right to shoot President or Prime Minister but they are as exceptional as those that justify shooting your father. See McCrie's *Life of John Knox*, p.226.

At the root of much of the contempt for government there lies contempt for the principle that politics is the art of the possible. That idea, it is often assumed, is pragmatic and cynical and totally incompatible with any kind of idealism. Calvinism has never held this view. In fact the idea that politics is the art of the possible is almost exactly identical with Calvin's own principle of accommodation, set forth repeatedly in his *Commentaries on the Last Four Books of Moses*. When God spoke to men in human words he was accommodating himself to human limitations; when he revealed himself in the flesh of Christ he was doing the same; and when he laid down laws for Old Testament Israel he constantly had to accommodate himself to "the rudeness of his ancient people". These laws often did not correspond to perfect equity or to God's own absolute standards. They were "accommodations"; adjustments to reality; examples of the art of the possible. The Mosaic law on divorce, for example, reflected not the ideal that "what God has joined together, let not man put asunder", but the sad fact that due to the hardness of the human heart marriages do break down. The law gives up on the attempt to prevent tragedy and focuses instead on limiting it. This agrees exactly with the position laid down by Lord Hailsham: "The use of the civil law to hold together parties who wish to live separately is almost always misguided" (*A Sparrow's Flight* p.412).

At the dawn of the new millennium, the new Scottish Parliament will find itself faced with the same problem as faced the God of Israel: the rudeness of their people. On a wide range of issues - divorce, abortion, liquor, gambling, homosexuality, and possibly even the sale of cannabis - it will have to practise the art of the possible. Calvinism will not criticise it for doing so. It will recognise that all authority - parental, political, and divine - has to accommodate itself to reality. Otherwise the law is made an ass.

In education too there are signs of a growing inclination to monasticism. One form of this is the Roman Catholic insistence on separate denominational schools. This is driven by the understandable concern of the Catholic bishops to control the education of Roman Catholic children, though their Church's stautory membership of local education committees gives significant influence over the schooling of other children too. The theological concerns are not quite so clear. These schools obviously offer a marvellous opportunity for indoctrination in Roman Catholic belief, morality, and practice but their ultimate justification must be the perception that Catholicism is a total world-view and that education can only take place in that context.

More recently, the tendency to educational monasticism has begun to assert itself among conservative Evangelicals, some of whom have set up such bodies as the Highland Schools Trust. In contrast to Catholicism, this is a parent-led movement and to some extent understandable. Christian parents in non-denominational schools are weary of classroom denigration of the Bible, contempt for the doctrine of creation, endorsement of trendy ethnic religions, and revisionist anti-Protestant versions of Scottish history. Above all they are fed-up with euphemisms which brand destructive immoralities as merely "alternative lifestyles".

On the face of things Calvinists would, of course, support Christian schools. Knox's vision was of parish schools which above all gave instruction in religion. The original 3-Rs were reading, writing, and religion. But that was in a one-faith community which was happy that its schools, and indeed its universities, should teach the Protestant Reformed religion. What happens when society fragments and the one national religion is replaced by a collection of mutually contradictory faith communities?

The problem first faced Scottish Calvinism after the Disruption of 1843. Community education was immediately fragmented as parish schools sacked Free Church teachers and victimised Free Churh children. In the short term, the new Church had no option but to set up its own schools. It saw at once, however, that this offered no permanent solution and it set its heart on a State system.

For various reasons - prominent among them the effect of the West Lothian Question in reverse, English MPs having a decisive say in Scottish affairs - it took almost thirty years for a State system to materialise. Through the years of debate the Free Church was clear as to its own ideal: Scotland should have schools that taught the Bible and Shorter Catechism. It was equally clear that indoctrination was wrong. State schools could not give preference to one faith over others. Nor could the Catechism be pressed on children against the wishes of their parents.

What then was more important - State schools or Shorter Catechism schools? The Free Church with remarkably little hesitation opted for the former, agreeing that Parliament should not make any detailed provision for the teaching of religion.

That is not the same thing as saying that religious education should have no place in a national curriculum. Religion is inextricably bound up with every other subject in the timetable. How could one teach history or literature while banning all reference to religion? Besides, religion is a core element in universal human experience, so that someone who is ignorant of religion can scarcely claim to be educated at all. It seems to me fully consistent with the principles of Knox and Chalmers to support a form of State education which involves every child in the community and has, as one of its outcomes, children who have a well-informed, critical, and tolerant awareness of the great faiths of the world.

Religious instruction, of course, is the task of the faith communities themselves. Taxpayers' money should not be used to produce good little Catholics or Muslims or Presbyterians (or for that matter good little Humanists). The task of instructing its own children is going to be one of the major challenges facing the Church in the new millennium.

Other voices call for a retreat from science. One is the voice of the Fundamentalist, invoking once again the distinction between believer and unbeliever and between regenerate and unregenerate. Modern geology and biology are fatally flawed (so runs the argument) because they are the products of unbelieving men. We must opt instead for so-called Biblical Creationism with its insistence that the earth is a mere 6000 years old, notwithstanding the fact that many of the most reverent exegetes of Genesis see nothing in its early chapters to fix the age of the earth.

But the proscription of a scientific hypothesis simply because it was first proposed or discovered by an unbeliever is totally at variance with the spirit of Calvinism. The equations of Einstein cannot be be dismissed merely because he was a non-Christian. His genius was God-given, as was that of James Clerk Maxwell, the Christian without whose earlier work Einstein's would not have been possible.

Less noticed than the Fundamentalist but posing a far greater threat for the long term is the orchestrated challenge to science by the heirs of Romanticism: the nebulous but powerful coalition of environmentalists, New-Agers, new Pagans, anti-nuclear campaigners, naturists, and animal rights' activists who wage constant war on oil exploration, the internal combustion engine, fertilisers, power stations, motorways, airports and animal laboratories.

More recently a third anti-science voice has been heard, speaking ever more insistently. It is that of those, particularly Roman Catholics, who want the whole field of reproductive biology declared off-limits to science. This group is totally opposed to experiments on embryos, deeply uneasy about genetic research, and haunted by the nightmare of human cloning.

In the last analysis what secures the future of science is neither logic nor theology but basic human need and deep-seated human instinct. Our very nature impels us to fell trees and invent wheels. It also impels us to live in cities, and urbanisation immediately demands technology. This is not a matter simply of energy and transport. Public health and clinical medicine would be impossible without electricity, chemical factories, and radiology, a product of sophisticated nuclear research.

But science is more than a product of human necessity. It is divinely mandated. Humans have been made in the image of God, appointed vice-gerents of creation, directed to subdue their environment and ordered to fill the earth. This last is not simply a repetition of the command to "be fruitful and multiply" (Gen. 1.22). It is concerned with human expansion over the whole face of the earth, into every field the eye can see and across every barrier that obstructs our path. The human race was never intended to remain in Eden. From where they stood the First Pair could see unknown rivers and unexplored lands which fired their imaginations and fuelled their need to know. The divine word makes it our duty to move over the horizon. Our God-imaging nature impels us to move to the edge and live on expanding frontiers. We can never be content not to know. Once we stumble on the wonder of the atom we cannot close the door on further enquiry. Once we discover the gene we can never rest till it answers all our questions. Once we step on the moon we can't help thinking of Mars. That is no *hubris*. It is not a yielding to the temptation to be "like God" (Gen. 3:5). In this case, it is refusal of the knowledge that is ungodly.

Human beings live a two-fold pilgrimage, neither part of which is destined ever to end. One is the journey to the knowledge of God. The other is the journey towards knowledge of the world, sharing in God's own knowledge of his creation. Both are mandatory; and they are intertwined.

God has not declared any part of his creation a no-go area for science. Macrocosm and microcosm are alike legitimate fields of enquiry. Astro-physics and micro-biology, weather systems and sub-atomic particles, are equally within its domain. We cannot draw back from nuclear power because of the risks: we must make it both safe and efficient. Nor can we simply proscribe genetic enhancement and cloning. We have to find methods of research which are ethically acceptable. We can never say, we must hold back unless there is good reason to go forward. We must always say instead, we must go forward unless there is compelling reason to hold back.

But this not to say that science should be self-regulating. It manifestly should not. Eventually, of course, it is accountable to God. It is subject to the Ten Commandments. This means that it itself is not God ("Thou shalt have no other gods before me"), that it must be scrupulous with the Truth, and must have the highest and most comprehensive regard for the sanctity of Life. It also means paying homage to the "first and greatest commandment": love.

That is the main line of accountability, although modern man may not think so. But there is also an accountability to the community: an obligation to weigh the social cost of all research and development. The community has no right to hand science and technology over to unbridled academic and commercial interests. In the very nature of the case a great deal of modern science is remedial. We live on an earth which, described theologically, is "cursed". It brings forth "thorns and briers", not simply of itself or by direct divine retribution but by man's fallen inefficiency and spoliation. It resists our attempts at cultivation and kicks back in natural disaster and disease.

In such a world, science has to prioritise and the basis of such prioritising can lie only in Calvin's observation that the end for which all things were created was "that none of the conveniences and necessities of life might be wanting to men" Genesis p.96). Calvin clearly had no hair-shirt approach to the cultural mandate. Science is to minister to man's convenience as well as his necessity. It must, however, be the convenience of the many rather than of the few. Those who lack necessities have fewest conveniences. The biggest indictment of science is that it has too often been driven not by compassion but by greed. It has forgotten its primary remedial function and gone where the commercial rewards are greatest, pouring far more resources into lucrative human reproduction programmes that into Parkinsonism and malaria, and devoting far more research to inter-ballistic missiles than to the food-production problems of Africa. It has looked to advance the interests of those above, not those below. But in the last analysis that too was a decision made by society, not by scientists. The curse has been fulfilled through our own actions.

What of the *fear* that often underlies our suspicions towards science? The Fundamentalist worries that research may throw up something that contradicts Scripture. The Roman Catholic worries that we may upset the delicate mechanisms of nature. Greenpeace worries that we may release some uncontrollable genie into the atmosphere.

The answer to all such anxieties surely lies in Christ himself. He is the Truth and we pursue the truth fearlessly in all disciplines because we are confident that we can never come across truth that contradicts the Truth. Fear of the truth, whether in history or cosmology, is unbelief. Faith is absolutely sure that the stamp of the divine Logos, the face of God's love, lies on the whole of creation. The quest for laws and causes and explanations derives from that. We look for system, not chaos (for system even in chaos) because the worlds were framed by the word and Word of God. We look for benign and benevolent system because we know that God is love. If there is in God no un-Christlikeness at all, then scientists can go about their tasks confident that the universe contains no booby-traps. The tragedy is that we so often use our knowledge to create our own booby-traps. Even then it is not the knowledge that kills, but what we do with it.

What of Calvinism and the arts? Some of the stories about Highland converts burning their bagpipes and breaking their fiddles may, just possibly, be true. More seriously, there has been a tendency, as we have seen, towards Presbyterian monasticism, reducing contact with "the world" to a minimum, and sometimes, as in the case of the Free Presbyterians, placing an ecclesiastical ban on such things as "concerts and soirées". But such excesses are far from peculiar to Calvinism. Virtually every religion on earth has fallen into the trap of erecting ridiculous taboos; and Roman Catholicism has gone even further than the Free Presbyterians, insisting that spiritual perfection can be found only in a monastery.

Art, like science, will survive whatever men do to it. It will survive because even in its fallenness the human race retains imagination, a sense of beauty, and an irrepressible urge to express itself.

But there are still deeper reasons for the durability of art. God made man in his own image and that means that we are made in the image of the supreme "Makar", who placed the first human pair in a garden and filled it with "every tree that is pleasant to the sight" (Gen. 2.9). The trees were not there because they were useful. They were there because they were beautiful; and so long as they were beautiful they had a right to be there.

Calvinism can never allow that redemption means detachment from creation. It is through the universe of landscape, seascape, and skyscape that God reveals his glory. Irreverence towards it is therefore irreverence towards him; and that can never be a product of redemption. On the contrary, redemption is the restoration and renewal of the divine image. If anything, therefore, it should enhance artistry and creativity rather than inhibit them.

A culture such as ours, to which art is virtually sacred, will probably be more amused than impressed with its endorsement by Calvinism. But there is more at issue than mere endorsement. There is the question, for example, of the accessibility of art. Calvin did not, like Luther, use the phrase "the priesthood of all believers", but he certainly endorsed the idea. There could be no élitism in the Church. Equally there can be no élitism in the arts. Genevan church music, for example, was not for expert musicians and choristers. It was for the people. All were to sing, none merely to listen.

In modern Scotland there is substantial Government patronage of the arts. Too much of that, however, goes to the top galleries, orchestras, and ballet companies which cater for an élite. Their very prowess should enable such institutions to finance themselves. By contrast, too little goes to those struggling to learn and to the remote provincial areas of the country. Is it too much to ask in the new millennium that every child should be taught either to paint or to sing or to play an instrument? Is this not the answer to the constant complaint that we produce so few great artists?

Is art limited to the beautiful? And if so, what is beauty? On the face of things, Calvinistic art might be expected to be severe and restrained: Puritanical, I suppose. But this is more an *a priori* theory than a matter of historical reality. John Milton's work was often gorgeous and full of conceits. Bunyan is hardly restrained and simple. There is no reason to set the alleged Calvinist penchant for simplicity over against the Celtic genius for embellishment. Highland Presbyterian churches were often the only ornate buildings in their localities - more ornate, paradoxically, than the sanctuaries of Saint Columba.

But the more important point is that when it comes to judging truth and beauty we are not at liberty to make self-contained human judgments. The first art critic was God himself: "God saw that it was good (Gen. 1:25). Serious criticism must still ask, consciously or unconsciously, "What would God think".?" Otherwise we have nothing but *De gustibus non disputandum*: no real objective difference between Mozart and the Sex Pistols.

This cannot mean that art is limited to painting pretty pictures. *Hamlet* is not pretty, nor are Goya's paintings of war in Spain; nor many of Picasso's portrayals of the lot of women. Yet we can be confident that in God's judgment they are truth, and truth prophetically highlighted, as surely as St Paul's description, almost unbearable to read, of contemporary civilisation in the first chapter of Romans.

Of course it may be insurmountably difficult to ascertain what God does think and unwarrantably arrogant on our part to claim to know. The attempt must be made nevertheless. Presumably if we can be so sure what God thinks of the present Government we can have some idea what he thinks of the novels of Hemingway and the poetry of e.e. cummings (Edward Estlin Cummings).

But maybe not! Criticism of government is to a large extent moral criticism. It focuses not on style but ethics. It dispenses praise and blame (mainly blame): politicians are wrong when they ignore those at the bottom of the social pyramid and wrong when they exacerbate the plight of single mothers.

Literary and artistic criticism, we are told, is entirely different. A good novel is a well-told story with rounded characters, a fascinating plot, proper proportion and emphasis, authentic dialogue, and a lucid, energetic, and economical style.

But is it? Calvinism (and indeed all Christian traditions) insist that we must subject art not only to aesthetic but also to moral judgment. We would not, after all, even contemplate judging New Labour on its politics alone, ignoring accusations of sleaze and cronyism. Why should we treat art differently? A "great" film might, for example, glorify racism, homosexual promiscuity, anti-Semitism, paedophilia, adultery, treason, and the exploitation of women. Is the critic to ignore all these and commend the film (or novel) simply for its artistic brilliance? To do so is surely to argue that great art can be wicked. If so, at what level are we to "enjoy" it? And would a humanist critic be equally willing to set moral and theological judgments aside if he were reviewing a novel built around the assumptions of Calvinism?

None of this is a mandate for censorship. Scottish Calvinism has more often been a victim of the censor than his abettor. Buchanan's *De Iure Regni apud Scotos*, Rutherford's *Lex Rex*, and Gillespie's *Dispute against English Popish Cermonies* all had the distinction of being burned by the public hangman. None of these gentlemen, admittedly, was much in advance of his age when it came to toleration; but it was an Assembly in which Rutherford and

Gillespie both played influential roles that gave us one of the greatest statements of liberty in the English language, in the Westminster Confession (XX.II). "God alone is Lord of the conscience, and hath left it free from the doctrines and commandments of men."

No man needs to ask another man, "Permission to speak, sir?" Freedom of expression is an inalienable human right.

Calvinism, said B.B. Warfield is primarily a vision - a vision of "God in his majesty". He is real. He reigns. He is Christ-like. Whether that vision, with the principle of *kenosis* at its very heart, can survive in Scotland the continuing onslaught of the Counter-Reformation, the ethnic religions, and institutionalised humanism remains to be seen. But some of us, certainly, will cherish it. He's got the whole millennium in his hands.

SOME BOOKS REFERRED TO

J. Calvin *Institutes of the Christian Religion*, tr. Henry Beveridge, London, James Clarke, 1962

J. Calvin *A Commentary on Genesis* Edinburgh, The Calvin Translation Society, 1847

J. Calvin *Commentaries on the last Four Books of Moses*, four volumes, Edinburgh, The Calvin Translation Society, 1852-55.

W.M. Campbell *The Triumph of Presbyterianism*, Edinburgh, The Saint Andrew Press, 1958

Lord Hailsham *A Sparrow's Flight*, London, Collins, 1990

Ian Henderson *Scotland: Kirk and People*, Edinburgh and London, Lutterworth, 1969

A. Kuyper *Lectures on Calvinism* (original lectures given in 1898, published by Eerdmans, Grand Rapids, 1961)

M.R. Langley *The Practice of Political Spirituality: Episodes from the Public Career of Abraham Kuyper 1879-1918*, Jordan Station, Ontario, Paideia Press, 1984

D. MacAulay, ed. *Nua-Bhardachd Ghaidhlig: a Bilingual Anthology*, Edinburgh, Canongate 1976, includes poetry from Derek Thomson, Iain Crichton Smith, and Sorley Maclean

A. McGrath *Reformation Thought: an Introduction*, Oxford, Blackwell, second edition 1993

J. McCosh *The Scottish Philosophy: Biographical, Expository, Critical*, New York, Carter, 1875

T. McCrie *Life of John Knox*, Edinburgh, Blackwood, fifth edition 1850)

S. Rutherford *Lex Rex*, Edinburgh 1644, most recent reprint by Sprinkle Publications, Harrisonburg, Va. 1982

A. Shields *A Hind let Loose*, Utrecht 1687, reprinted Edinburgh 1744 and Glasgow 1797

B.B. Warfield *Calvin and Calvinism*, New York, Oxford University Press, 1931

4   IS THE KIRK STILL RELEVANT?

Home truths about influence as a national institution

Johnston R. McKay

I began to write this on the day a committee met in Edinburgh to choose whom to nominate to be Moderator of the 1999 General Assembly of the Church of Scotland. He will be the Moderator who welcomes the new Scottish Parliament and who will speak for the Kirk at the start of the new millennium. But for the second year running there was no reference in the half-hour "Reporting Scotland" to the announcement of the Moderator-designate's name.

There are some who will see this as evidence of the increasing secular pressure on broadcasters to ignore news about the Church. There may even be some who see it as evidence that Moderators-designate are less colourful, charismatic characters than once they were, and of less interest to the media. Both opinions may be correct. But to stress them too much would be to obscure something much more serious for the Church of Scotland: that to the national life of Scotland the Church of Scotland *as an institution* is increasingly irrelevant; and so, to the nation's media, the Kirk seems only to be newsworthy when it offers a juicy scandal involving a minister or provides an easily stereotyped controversy to report.

Clearly there are still several hundred thousand people who derive spiritual value, personal comfort, and a sense of purpose from the worship of the Church of Scotland Sunday by Sunday, and there are sick, old, lonely and bereaved people who are grateful for the Church's concern. Clearly for many the worship of the Church of Scotland and its pastoral care are not irrelevant. However the Church of Scotland *as a national institution* reflected in the debates of the General Assembly or through the pronouncements of the Assembly's committees is increasingly irrelevant both to public policy-making and to the development of society.

I first visited the General Assembly as a schoolboy in 1956 and it is an extremely illuminating exercise to compare the amount of coverage given by the Scottish broadsheets to the General Assembly in that year with the coverage in 1998. In 1956 the Assembly lasted ten days and every day there was at least a full page of coverage, whereas last year there was less than half a page on any day of the week-long Assembly and hardly any reporting of the business on Saturday and Sunday or the closing Friday. That comparison may reflect the fact that in 1961 the membership of the Church of Scotland was nearly 1,300,000 and in 1998 it was half that, and that newspaper coverage of the General Assembly is very likely to be a mirror of public interest in it. It may also reflect the historic refusal by the General Assembly to arrange its business and debates at a time which encourages media coverage. As those in the media are constantly told by Assembly managers, Assembly business is run for the convenience of the Assembly and not the media - though it is a little irritating to receive complaints from the same managers about lack of adequate coverage.

However the decline in press coverage, despite the best endeavours of the Kirk's press office (which in my experience tends to present itself more as a public relations department than a point of contact for press enquiry) may reflect a crisis in the calibre of the Kirk's leadership which, with some fine, notable exceptions, bears little comparison with the leadership of the Church forty years ago for intellectual ability, political acumen, and theological insights. The point can be made simply by listing some of those who were Assembly conveners then, most of whom still had twenty years of Assembly service to give: Archie Craig, Charles Warr, Archie Watt, Nevile Davidson, John Kent, W.M. Campbell, Roy Sanderson, Leonard Small, George Reid, Tom Torrance, Hugh Douglas, and George MacLeod. Were these giants or is it only in comparison with the present leadership of the Church that they seem so?

To use the word "irrelevant" in the sense that I have used it of the Church of Scotland today is, I fully admit, pejorative and subjective. There are many who will disagree with me, though most of them view the institutional Church from a position where their own welfare is inextricably linked to forecasts of the institution's significance and survival. That too tends to encourage a rose-tinted subjectivism.

There are, however, two other senses in which the word "irrelevant" can more dispassionately be used of the *constitutional* position in which the Church of Scotland finds itself as it vacates its Assembly Hall to give a temporary home to the new Parliament.

In the years leading up to the union of the Church of Scotland and the United Free Church enormous care was taken to ensure that nothing was done which implied that the Church's freedom in matters spiritual was a freedom "granted" by Parliament, for the U.F. Church had insisted from the moment discussions started in 1909 that the spiritual freedom of the Church derived from Jesus Christ and could in no way be either protected or restricted by Act of Parliament. The U.F. Church could not acquiesce in any procedure which required Parliament to be asked to declare the Church free in matters spiritual, for that would have been giving Parliament a role to which the U.F. Church could not agree. On the other hand, if the two Churches united on a basis which did not have parliamentary approval there could have been challenges to the Church's right to do what it did. The compromise solution which was brilliantly proposed by C.N. Johnston (later Lord Sands) in a memorandum of 1912 was this: that the two Churches would draw up a statement of their agreed position and that Parliament would then be invited to endorse this statement as a true account of the situation and repeal any Acts which contradicted it.

The relationship between Church and State envisaged was described during the debate on the second reading of the Church of Scotland Bill in the House of Commons by Sir Arthur Steel-Maitland, who had been a member of the Church of Scotland committee since the negotiations began: "It is a new type of relation which we have in mind - not a Church that is in any way set up by the State or drawing its authority from the State, but a Church which has got religious influences which are quite outside the State but which as they operate in men's minds are a fact that the State takes note of and recognises and, in so far as it is a Christian State, also approves."[1]

In other words the Church of Scotland has a relationship with the State, and the passing of the Scotland Act has done nothing to alter that relationship. But it is a relationship recognised by the Westminster Parliament. Thus the constitutional position of the Church of Scotland is with the Parliament which has devolved most matters Scottish to the new Parliament, but with which the Church of Scotland still has a formal relationship. It is, for example, the Government at Westminster which advises the Monarch about the appointment of her High Commissioner to the General Assembly.

As the focus of political debate and decision-making in Scotland increasingly centres on Holyrood, one wonders whether the constitutional relationship of the Westminster Parliament will not seem increasingly irrelevant to the life of Scotland.

A second area of political irrelevance for the Church of Scotland relates to the new Parliament itself.

The Church of Scotland cannot expect, because of its status as the National Church, to be accorded any special position within the life of the new Parliament. Or, to be more precise, some will expect it, but they will be disappointed. In this connection I recall Dr Andrew Herron, as clerk of Glasgow Presbytery, fulminating at a proposal by the first convener of Strathclyde Region, Geoffrey Shaw, that the inaugural act of worship to mark the new region should take place in a church other than Glasgow Cathedral, with the then Archbishop Winning as preacher. Twenty-five years ago it was possible for Andrew Herron to use the status of the National Church to get his own way. But that status, it seems, will cut very little ice with the new parliamentarians.

Three years ago I produced a television programme about the impact a new Parliament would have on the Church of Scotland. Two things struck me as I researched the programme. The first was that, although the Church of Scotland had supported devolution since the 1940's, there had been no thinking whatsoever done on the impact which a devolved Parliament would have on the Church of Scotland. At the time I found this incredible, but have since reflected that within the Church of Scotland there is a serious division between those who consider and make proposals on political and constitutional matters and those who are guardians of the Kirk's constitutional position. Perhaps if some of those who see themselves as guardians of the Kirk's constitutional position had not in a mood of patronising haughtiness gone off to play golf on the days when Church and Nation matters were under discussion, the Church of Scotland would have been more ready to prepare for the effect of devolution on its constitutional position.

One of the most significant and influential reports of the Church and Nation Committee to the General Assembly on the issue of a Scottish Parliament was submitted exactly ten years ago.[2] This report stated: "The Church of Scotland can only make a distinctive and effective contribution to the government of Scotland if it grounds its position in its own historical and theological convictions as a national Kirk within the Reformed tradition."[3] It quotes Lord President Cooper:[4] "The principle of the unlimited sovereignty of Parliament is a distinctively English principle which has no counterpart in Scottish constitutional law" and contrasts that English principle with "the Scottish constitutional tradition in both its secular and religious streams of thought and practice" which has consistently favoured a "limited" rather than an "absolutist" notion of sovereignty.

Historically this meant that the ruler was seen as subject to the law and consent of the people.[5] The report concluded that "it is not possible to resolve the question of the democratic control of Scottish affairs and the setting-up of a Scottish Assembly apart from the fundamental shift in our constitutional thinking away from the unlimited or absolute sovereignty of the British Parliament towards the historic Scottish and Reformed principle of limited or relative sovereignty."[6]

All of this was given more popular and pithy expression in a speech in the General Assembly on the report when the Revd MacKay Nimmo of Dundee summarised the 1320 Declaration of Arbroath as saying effectively to Robert the Bruce: "Awright, you're the King, but if you dinnae dae whit yer tellt, yer on the buroo", and in the frequently quoted words of Canon Kenyon Wright at the first meeting of the Scottish Constitutional Convention: "What happens when that other voice we know so well says *We say No and we are the State*? Well, we say Yes and we are the people."[7]

One of the most consistent opponents of devolution both inside and outside the the Church of Scotland, the Very Revd Dr Andrew Herron, described the 1989 Church and Nation report as providing "what might be called a theology of Scottish nationalism." He adds: "But even accepting it as such, I find it remarkable that after consistently calling for an effective form of devolution for the past forty years it has taken us until now to discover that we have a good theological foundation for our position - I should have expected the theological position to have been laid forty years ago, rather than that we should have erected the structure and then after nearly half a century found we had a foundation for it. This is surely justification *ex post facto*."[8]

Of course it is nothing of the kind, and it was mischievous of Andrew Herron to claim that it is. The justification for the attitude of the Church and Nation Committee was expressed in the theological reflections on sovereignty of George Buchanan (*Dialogus de Iure Regni apud Scotos*) in the sixteenth century and Samuel Rutherford (*Lex Rex*) in the seventeenth. Dr Herron was carrying his antipathy both to the Church and Nation Committee and Scottish devolution too far in suggesting that the theories propounded by Buchanan and Rutherford were unknown to a succession of Church and Nation Committees and conveners, or that *reminding* the General Assembly of them was discovering a foundation forty years after erecting a structure.

Reformed theology has always been suspicious of giving people power, not because Christians should be particularly suspicious of people with power but because Christians should be suspicious of *themselves* when they have power. We are all tempted and liable to use power for selfish ends. We are all likely to abuse power for our own purposes.

This view is based on an analysis far deeper than any prevalent cynicism about politicians. Reformed theology has always taken the view that the right exercise of power orders our common life, specifies society's goals, and distributes society's wealth; and so to refuse to share in power means avoiding sharing fully in the life of the community.

However the doctrine of Original Sin requires us to be sceptical of all political endeavours. As John F. Kennedy once famously put it, "All politicians have to cope with the inherited blunders of Adam and Eve," It is therefore appropriate that in the light of the insights both of the theological doctrine of Original Sin, and its constitutional expression in the doctrine of limited sovereignty, it has been decided that there should be a code of conduct for members of the Scottish Parliament.[9]

While it is right that any code of conduct for MSPs should concern itself with the behaviour of MSPs, any code should go beyond the negative and the prudential and should be widened to ensure that it reflects the conduct of Parliament as an institution, in its dealings not just with civic society but with individuals.

The consultative steering group on the Scottish Parliament identified several "key principles" which should govern the working of the new Parliament.[10] These principles are that:

- The Parliament should embody and reflect the sharing of power between the people of Scotland, the legislators, and the Scottish Executive.

- The Executive should be accountable to the Parliament and the Parliament and Executive should be accountable to the people of Scotland.

- The Parliament should be accessible open, responsive, and develop procedures which make possible a participative approach to the consideration of legislation and the scrutiny of public policy.

- The Parliament in its operation should recognise, as far as possible, the need to allow equal opportunities for all.

If these principles, which I would imagine gain widespread support, are to be put into effect in the working of the new Parliament, then they must be reflected not only in a regulatory, behavioural code for MSPs but in a code which reflects the way the Parliament will operate *as a Parliament*. This might well be regarded as Parliament's side of an agreement, covenant, compact, or contract with the people, who have asked it to exercise the sovereignty which lay with them.

The second thing which struck me as I researched the programme *The State of Faith* was the unanimity of those to whom I spoke that the Church of Scotland should have no pre-eminent position within the new Parliament because of its past status. We spoke to politicians from all parties and a variety of Church representatives; and while most were prepared to admit that the Church of Scotland might be the "lead" Church in a relationship with the new Parliament, this was conceded because of the Church of Scotland's numerical strength and historical contribution, not because of any national status it was perceived to possess.

It is clear that those preparing for a Scottish Parliament expect it be even-handed not only as between Christian denominations but as between different faiths. In an ecumenical multi-cultural Scotland, the traditional status of the Church of Scotland as the *national* Church is irrelevant to the role which the communities of faith can play.

This makes it all the more clear that if the Church of Scotland is to have an effect and an impact on the new Parliament it will be on the basis of the quality of its submissions, not the significance of its status; on the grounds of its intellectual and political wisdom, not its historic and constitutional position; because of the respect in which it is actually held, not the reputation it is supposed to have. So the quality of the leadership of the Church of Scotland is a crucial factor; and the quality of the Kirk's leadership is, to put it mildly, open to question today.

In the discussions leading up to the union of the Churches in 1929 a great deal was made of the principle of "the national recognition of religion". During these discussions it was argued that there were other means than through an "established" Church that effect could given to the national recognition of religion, which gave a place to Christian communities other than the Church of Scotland. When the heir to the Throne has said that he would be happier to be described a "Defender of Faith" rather than inherit the title of "Defender of *the* Faith", might it not be possible for Scotland's Parliament to affirm its recognition of the place of *religion* within civic society? Might such a recognition not affirm the value of tolerance, respect, and understanding in religious terms which give religious leaders rather more moral authority than they presently possess when asking for a less strident confrontational form of political debate in the new Parliament?

That view, however, is not likely to commend itself to the former Moderator of the General Assembly who, on an annual moderatorial visit to BBC Scotland, told management and programme-makers that faiths other than Christianity were tolerated in this country; but only tolerated.

In arguing the case for a Scottish Parliament in 1974 the late John P. Mackintosh wrote that the "pervasive Scottish consciousness arises from the existence, ever since 1707, of some of the traditional carriers of nationalism, the institutions which have kept such feelings alive in parts of Europe which have endured centuries of alien domination. First, Scotland has retained its own Presbyterian Church with its General Assembly in Edinburgh, the nearest thing to a Scotish Parliament."[11] John Mackintosh taught me at Glasgow University about political institutions and constitutional law and his early death was an enormous loss to the public life of Scotland and the irrepressible social life of humanity! He may have been right to say that the General Assembly is the closest thing Scotland has had to a Parliament since 1707, but the claim does not amount to very much, because the General Assembly is neither elected nor representative of the nation and for most of its time it debates issues which would be of little interest to a Parliament and less to an electorate. John Mackintosh was right, however, to hint that this is how the Assembly has been perceived when he adds: "The General Assembly is commented on in the media, especially when it deals with social and semi-political issues."

I have already drawn attention to the reduction in Assembly coverage by the broadsheets, but BBC television and radio still devote a considerable amount of time and money to coverage. The question arises, however: if coverage has continued because the General Assembly has been perceived (both within the BBC and among its audience) as a substitute for a Parliament, what will happen to that coverage when the "real thing" is elected?

The changing nature of the Assembly itself is already raising the question for the broadcasters.[12] Debates in the Assembly are rarely now, if ever, the dramatic set-piece occasions they once were. Speeches have more in common now with management presentations than political oratory. And even the area that John Mackintosh identified as inviting most media comment, the work of the Church and Nation Committee, has changed considerably in the course of the 1990's. Under two successive conveners, the Revd Andrew McLellan and Dr Alison Elliot, the Church and Nation reports and the debates on them in the Assembly have been characterised by a desire to achieve consensus and for the avoidance of confrontation. That is not to say that the approach of the committee has become less inclined to be critical of the Government of the day, but the style of presentation and the choice of wording have been more inclusive than under the two previous conveners, the Revd Maxwell Craig and the Revd Norman Shanks, both of whom gave the impression of believing that only by the expression of extreme opposition to government could the Church be true to its convictions.

It has to be said, however, that their convenerships coincided with the Premiership of Mrs Thatcher (as she then was) when it was much easier to justify outright opposition to government as an expression of Christian conviction than it was under either Mr Major or Mr Blair. Nonetheless it is true to say that there was a lot less "knee-jerk" reaction by the Church and Nation Committee in the 1990's than there was in the 1980's.

If debates even on the Church and Nation report are less confrontational and more managerial than ever before, and the quality of what is contained in the *reports* is seldom brought out in the *debates*, then it will be necessary in the years to come (especially when the General Assembly inherits from the Scottish Parliament an entirely different form of conference chamber from the one it handed over) for BBC Scotland to consider how it can effectively reflect religion and life in Scotland.

This has been a constantly revisited area of discussion between the Church and the BBC, and at different times I have been on either side of the discussion, as a member of the Kirk's Board of Practice and Procedure, as convener of the religious advisory committee of the BBC, and latterly as editor of the BBC's radio coverage and producer of its television coverage of the General Assembly.

In recent years on television I have tried to introduce an increasing emphasis on the work of conveners of Assembly committees and the issues facing the committees, partly because this reflects what is now the stress within the work of the Assembly itself, and partly because it affords the opportunity to make use of a more varied range of pictures than debates within the Assembly Hall provide for a medium which relies on a range of pictures. It is likely that in the opening years of the millennium this emphasis will be continued and extended.

One of the most treasured pieces of symbolism in the Assembly Hall is that the gallery occupied by the Lord High Commissioner is within the Assembly Hall but not part of it, reflecting the freedom greatly cherished by the Church. Those arranging the meeting of the Assembly in 1999 had to find some way of continuing this symbolism within the Edinburgh Conference Centre. On the only other occasion when the Assembly met outside the Assembly Hall on the Mound (apart from a day's journey to the Bute Hall in 1990 to mark the 300th anniversary of the restoration of Presbyterianism) the failure of those advising the Duke of York, later King George VI, threatened to mar the proceedings which marked the union of the Church of Scotland and the United Free Church in 1929.

The Assemblies of the two Churches were to meet separately and then to come together in Edinburgh's Annandale Street Hall. It was decided that the Duke should enter by the front door of the hall and make his way through the Assembly to a temporary throne. Immediately the great John White sent a message to say that this must not happen, but that the Lord High Commissioner should enter by a side door. However those arranging the Assembly were told that, despite the message from John White, the Duke would enter by the front door, where a military band would be playing. John White then informed the Palace of Holyroodhouse that "the last word was with the Church of Scotland and I, John White, have spoken it."[13] He went on to demand an assurance from the Purse-bearer that the Lord High Commissioner would enter by a side door, or there would be no Lord High Commissioner present at the Assembly. When the situation was described to the Duke of York he agreed to do as the Assembly (or at least John White) expected. Thus symbolism triumphed.

While the symbolism preserves the separation of Church and State, the exchanges between High Commissioners and Moderators in recent years have emphasised that the two come from similar worlds. When she was High Commissioner in 1994 and Dr James Simpson was Moderator, Lady Marion Fraser referred in her speech to the two of them being brought up together in the Giffnock area of suburban Glasgow. In 1998 Lord Hogg and Professor Alan Main shared reminiscences of their upbringing in Aberdeen. And in 1993 Lord Macfarlane of Bearsden brought the house down by suggesting that his newly-born grandson might have been named after one of the Moderator's chaplains, the minister of St Giles', Gilleasbuig Macmillan. But he added: "Those who could pronounce his name couldn't spell it, and those who could spell it couldn't pronounce it."

Those exchanges do not just reflect the polite pleasantries of exchanges between the Throne gallery and the Moderatorial chair. They hint at something which has always been central to the Church of Scotland's understanding of the relationship between Church and State within the realm of reform: that Church and State are two aspects of one reality. This was observed by Professor Gordon Donaldson - as it happens, not a member of the Church of Scotland but of the Episcopal Church - at the end of his study of various themes in Scotland's religious history, when he reflected on the famous words of Andrew Melville to King James VI: "There are two kings and two kingdoms in Scotland, and in Christ's Kingdom, the Church, you, the head of the State, are neither a king nor a lord but only a member."

In practice, said Gordon Donaldson:[14]

> it proved impossible to separate the two kingdoms; it proved impossible to separate Church and State.... The simple fact is that all along a simple conflict between Church and State makes nonsense. The conflicts surely must at best have been between the Parliament and the Assembly, between the Council and the Assembly, perhaps even between the Council and the ministers; it certainly makes sense to speak about a conflict between the King and the Assembly, just as there can be a conflict between the King and the Parliament. But a conflict between the King and the General Assembly was no more a conflict between Church and State than a conflict between King and Parliament was. Parliament and Assembly did at times consist very largely of the same personnel, and certainly the same individuals could sit and vote in both; were they entitled to have their say in ecclesiastical affairs as members of the one but not of the other? If you ask, who composed the Church, the answer is, the people of the country; and if you ask, who composed the State, you get the same answer.

In the secular, multi-cultural society which is Scotland, it would be wrong today to say that the same people composed the State as composed the Church. It would be just as wrong for the Church of Scotland to claim, either because of its past position or its present relationship with the Crown-in-Parliament, some superior position in relation to the Parliament which will meet in Holyrood. But the Church of Scotland will betray its inheritance if it abandons the historic Reformed stance that the realm is indivisible in the sight of God.

[1] Parliamentary Debates, June 22, 1921, p.1446

[2] Reports to the General Assembly 1989 p.144

[3] *Ibid.* p.145

[4] *Ibid.* p.146

[5] *Ibid.* p.147

[6] *Ibid.* p.149

[7] *The People say Yes*, Kenyon Wright 1997, p.269

[8] *Minority Report*, Andrew Herron 1990, p.206

[9] What follows is based on work done for the Church and Nation Committee on codes of conduct, and I readily acknowledge the assistance given to me by Colin Mair and Roy Wilkie of the University of Strathclyde.

[10] CSG 98 (60) Annex B

[11] *New Statesman* Sept 29, 1974 reproduced in *A Diverse Assembly: the Debate on a Scotish Parliament*, Lindsay Paterson, 1998

[12] It is interesting to observe that the perceived reduction in the coverage of the General Assembly by the BBC is greeted with loud complaints whereas there has never been any protest at ITV's minimal coverage.

[13] *John White*, Augustus Muir 1958, pp.262-63

[14] *Scottish Church History*, Gordon Donaldson 1985 pp.236-37

5   VIA MEDIA

Reflections on the Infomation Revolution

Stewart Lamont

The medium is the message, declared Marshall McLuhan, the Canadian academic who became something of a guru in the 1960's with his views on the media. His theory was that the greatest revolutions in human society have not occurred through changes in political leadership but when the means of communication have changed.

Thus it has mattered little for the structure of society whether kings were replaced by prime ministers, presidents by juntas, and czars by politburos. The real changes occurred when railways came, or a trade route opened up, or a new means of communication became available. One of his books was entitled *The Gutenberg Galaxy*, because the first Gutenberg printing press in Germany roughly coincided with the dissident movement led by Martin Luther which grew into the Reformation. Without the printing press, Luther's sermons and pamphlets would have had limited circulation and taken much longer to spread around Germany if he had been confined to preaching his way around Germany on horseback. Without the Bible printed by this press in the common language of the people, his listeners would have lacked the foundation stone to set up a coherent system outwith the medieval Catholic Church.

The point is a simple one. Luther's message would have come to nothing without the new medium with which to spread it. The medieval Church controlled all the conventional means by which ideas were shared, and had the power to enforce conformity by suppressing heresy - as it had done with earlier movements which challenged its control, such as those of Wycliffe and Hus in the preceding centuries. By burning the opposition (as in the case of Hus) it tried to snuff out the dissent. But after printing was invented, in order to stop the ideas from spreading it was necessary to find and destroy all copies of the work, not simply the author. Perhaps the best illustration of that is provided by William Tyndale, the English

Bible translator, who was caught and executed in 1525 but whose translations were preserved and became the backbone of the Authorised Version when it was published in 1611.

It had taken one and a half millennia of Christian history for this development to happen. The original Christian Church, in order to disseminate the Scriptures, had to rely on papyrii, which were laboriously copied by hand, then bound into the more user-friendly form of a codex. Lacking a central focus for its organisation, communication in the early Church was much more difficult. It survived initially after the rising of 70 A.D. in Judea had been crushed and Roman reprisals created colonies of Jewish refugees around the Mediterranean. The Gentile Christians linked by Paul and his letter-writing deputies were able through years of persecution to leave tangible legacies of faith, but the actual means of dissemination were primitive. They remained so for 1500 years. The medieval period saw enormous power concentrated in the papacy. Since books had to be copied by hand in monasteries, and in Latin, there was not much chance of a free market in ideas. The new Reformed religion relied less on the performance of the sacraments for its appeal and more on words - the words of the sacred Scriptures and the words of the preacher who expounded them. As a religion it was therefore ideally suited to the era of the book, which reigned supreme as a means of communication for over 400 years until the middle of the nineteenth century. Newspapers existed but they were for the élite, priced beyond the means of the ordinary citizen.

In Scotland the Reformed Church, the established form of religion, promoted this emphasis on literacy through its parish schools. While it has become fashionable to use "Calvinist" in a pejorative sense for some aspects of this time of Protestant ascendancy, there is no doubt that it resulted in a much higher level of literacy among the working class, then largely rural. Robert Burns in his poem *The Cottar's Saturday Night* may be accused of sentimentalising the practice of Bible-reading in the rural working-class home, but no-one has claimed it was an invention.

This legacy of literacy persists in some curious ways. Scots have still one of the highest levels of newspaper readership in the world. There is also no doubt that the internationally famous writers whom Scotland produced during these 400 years - Burns, Scott and Stevenson among them - were products of this word-centred Presbyterianism. Another example not so well known as Burns is the Cromarty stone-mason Hugh Miller. During the ten years of the Church-State conflict in the mid-nineteenth century, culminating in the Disruption, those on the side which eventually became the Free Church were championed by *The Witness*, a newspaper edited by Miller, who was a gifted polemicist. The lesson was not lost on Dr Archibald Charteris, the leading Church of Scotland minister who founded *Life and Work* in 1879.

Come the twentieth century after telephones were invented, radio waves discovered, and newspapers acquired mass circulations, nothing disturbed this positive attitude towards the media by Scots Presbyterians. Perhaps this was because the emergent new forms of media were sympathetic to the Reformed faith and rarely hostile to it. Newspaper editors were often Kirk elders and devoted much space in their columns to respectful coverage of Church affairs. The first director-general of the BBC was the son of a Free Kirk (later U.F.) manse. John Reith's mission to inform and educate the listener was high-minded and, as he saw it, simply an extension of his religious principles. He also saw no difficulty in recruiting a Church of Scotland minister to run the Scottish end of the BBC operation. The Revd Melville Dinwiddie was plucked from the pulpit of St Machar's Cathedral in Aberdeen and was BBC Controller Scotland until he retired in 1957.

The fact that Reith is revealed to be a bullying prig in Ian McIntyre's definitive biography (mostly from Reith's own diaries and memos) is not the business of this chapter. My concern is to demonstrate the mutually supportive attitude which existed at this time between the media and the Reformed Churches in Scotland.

When the print media began to be overshadowed by the new broadcast media it was natural that "men of the Word" would find it a natural habitat in which to work. The Revd Ronald Falconer, a Scot brought up partly in New Zealand, was an Aberdeen graduate who became a minister in Coatbridge before joining the BBC. He was later picked to head the BBC's religious broadcasting in Scotland and ran a highly successful operation from 1950 to 1971. This was partly due to his assertion that religious traditions were different in Scotland and his refusal to allow BBC religion in Scotland to become a region of a London-controlled BBC. But it also rested on picking churchmen who had a facility with words to be his star performers. Professor William Barclay and Hugh Douglas became the best known; and, since this was still a period in which the Church of Scotland enjoyed a prominent position in society, it was natural that both were from the Kirk.

It is worth pausing at this point to see where this Via Media has taken us in the Realm of Reform. The Scotland to which Falconer broadcast midway through his twenty-year BBC headship was very different from that of today. Its values were closer to the *Sunday Post*, its politics largely Tory - that party had a majority of the popular vote at one point in the 1950's - and its religion was predominantly Presbyterian. As an illustration of how much things have changed I could take two stories. The first concerned the sustained campaign and front-page treatment which the *Scottish Daily Express* (under the editorship of Kirk elder Ian McColl) gave to the proposal in 1957 that the Kirk might consider adopting some form of episcopacy. In 1998 the same newspaper carried no report at all of Church unity proposals which involved taking in bishops, and which at the General Assembly were nodded through for further discussion with scarce a murmur of dissent.

The intervening years have seen many changes in the Kirk. Women ministers, once a "controversy", now attract few headlines, except when they are involved in scandals such as the Angus case in 1998. In 1983 the Kirk even opened the way to admit a convicted murderer to its ministry. However, the abiding trend lies not in sensational stories but in the anonymous legions who have left the Kirk. In 1961 the Kirk's adult communicant membership stood at nearly 1,300,000, a substantial proportion of the adult population. A generation later it stands at about half that. Yet that generation has been shaped by the media which (as I have argued) were well-suited to, and packed with, practising Presbyterians. What went wrong?

The first answer must be that not only in etymology, but by very nature, media are pluralistic. They constantly demand new material, new faces, and are ideally suited to looking over the garden fence, where of course the grass is always greener. Radio and television killed off music-hall comics, not because audiences would not go to see them at their local theatre, but because the performers could not get away with keeping the same act and material for years on end. The long lists of scriptwriters who appear in the credits of today's star comics are testimony to the insatiable demand of the new media for new material.

Religion perhaps could keep up with such demands but only if given protected status or budgets whoch would enable its productions to appear as novel. Even then there are deeper reasons why the new manifestations of media are ambivalent at best and subversive at worst where religion is concerned. Where there is choice, there is freedom to choose and it is no coincidence that two of the last advanced societies to embrace television were Israel and apartheid South Africa (the latter having Ronnie Falconer advise on religious broadcasting.) The broadcast media can be used to dominate in a totalitarian way, as in Orwell's *1984*, but in general tight control is counter-productive, as in pre-perestroika Russia.

The second reason why broadcasting did not produce the goods, as far as bolstering the position of religion in Scotland, is intrinsic to broadcasting itself. By its very nature it is mass media, and must regard the world as its audience. It must therefore, to be successful, be pluralistic or secular as far as religion is concerned. It cannot assume that the audience is either captive (for it is not, especially with the proliferation of channels and stations available at the turn of a switch) or that it shares the same values and beliefs. Thus it opts for a neutral approach, offending none where religion is concerned.

The charters of both BBC and commercial TV companies provide for programmes of a religious nature and these continue, but tenor and content are now of a much more "neutral" stance towards the Churches. Falconer was regarded, by himself and the Kirk, as the Kirk's man at the BBC. His successor, Ian Mackenzie, also a Church of Scotland minister, paddled fiercely in the opposite direction, even employing a Jehovah's Witness on his religious department staff. Kirk traditionalists did not assuage Mackenzie's mood at this period, and criticised every attempt to break with tradition.

If they had taken the longer-term approach they would have seen that it was inevitable that the privileges of the past would not be maintained. Faced with such grumbles, BBC management reacted in the same way as when faced with pressure-groups such as that of Mrs Mary Whitehouse. They simply adopted a more pluralist approach and defended this as being even-handed.

This approach means that (as with politics) each ideological system must be given an airing. This approach, vigorously pursued by Sir Hugh Greene, director-general in the 1970's, effectively ended the kind of privileged access for Christianity which Reith had in mind. Thus neither the nature nor reality of mass media, whether pluralist or secular, made good news for Churches fighting to keep their influence in an increasingly secularised society. There are those who may regret this and long for a return to Reithian norms, but these are simply not attainable with the nature of modern mass media. Nor are they desirable, since they would require a totalitarian régime to control them.

My argument is simply that pluralism has not happened because of an influx of Asian Muslims to Britain. It has happened because in a free society mass media will tend to break down dominant cultures into pluralistic ones. The mistake we sometimes make about mass media is to assume that they have a mass audience, like Churchill's radio broadcasts during the war. The reality is that, apart from occasional sporting or soap opera events, the nation no longer sits down for the same programmes and wakes up to be able to discuss them with their family at breakfast or their colleagues at work. In the typical family Dad may watch football on one TV set while Mum watches her favourite soap opera on another. In her bedroom their daughter listens on headphones to a CD of the latest pop sensation and her teenage brother surfs the Internet in his room. They inhabit the same house, but different worlds. The pluralism which the mass media have delivered to them has led to cultural fragmentation.

Before considering the effects of this on the Reformed Churches, it is worth reflecting on the fact that all this has happened in one generation. In thirty years the pace of change has not simply increased but accelerated. This exponential explosion in media and cultural change has been dubbed "Future Shock" (by Alvin Toffler) and its single most influential factor is the Mighty Microchip.

This tiny and inexpensive piece of silicon has provided the technological changes in the media which have in turn led to the immense social changes. I can offer a personal perspective on the technical changes within the timespan of my own career in the mass media. When I began as a BBC producer in 1972 there was no colour television in Scotland and video cassette recorders had yet to be invented. We recorded music at 15 inches per second on quarter-inch magnetic tape and 2" video tape. Film cameras held ten minutes of film which required elaborate lighting and expensive processing. Now domestic camcorders can produce broadcast quality images and digital machines give high-quality music reproduction with no tape at all. As for newspapers, I used to type my weekly *Herald* article and deliver it to be reset in hot-metal process. Now it goes from computer down a phone line straight into the newspaper computer without touching paper until it is printed.

In less than thirty years the technology, working practices, and - most pervasive of all - the diversity of choice in media have been revolutionised. It is a revolution not only comparable to the invention of the printing press, but it has brought about far greater changes in far less time.

The Reformed Churches find themselves ambivalent about these changes. On one hand they were a kind of Reformation, taking control from the "priesthood" who controlled what we read and watched and put it in the hands of the people. However, when many churchmen saw what the people wanted to watch and read they were not so delighted and began to see the media as a threat to moral standards. On the other hand, there were those who saw the new forms of media as an opportunity for the Church to make its message heard in new ways by people who would not be likely to encounter it in a church pew.

This ambivalence is reflected in the way that Church people in Scotland view the media. Over the years I have given a large number of talks to church groups and found that invariably they view the media as a threat to Christian values and are hostile. Yet with few exceptions they read and watch a great deal of media, even the newspapers and programmes about which they complain!

Beneath this reaction is the misplaced assumption that somehow it can all be adjusted and the old values reinstated, if only someone would assert control over the beast. The fact is that the genie cannot be put back in the bottle and the Churches must live with this ambivalence and cultural fragmentation, and what is now called "post-modernism".

It used to be called "the permissive society", but even that sounds as dated as a Mary Quant dress. Personally I prefer the term *information revolution* since this conveys the momentous nature of the change but is morally neutral. That does not mean that I am morally indifferent to many of the consequences, but it means I accept them as facts about which Christians can do little.

Although most Churches had ceased to exercise the kind of power over what people could say and do which they once had, Christians standards and morals were still the "official" ones in society. In 1959 Lonnie Donegan had to record an alternative version of his hit record *The Battle of New Orleans*, replacing the term "bloody British" with "bloomin' British". However the "swinging sixties" soon put that kind of conformity under pressure. At first those who rejected the old ways went cautiously as each new "outrage" produced protests and calls for heads to roll. Those who held the axes (and purse-strings) noticed that outrages resulted in an increase in public curiosity. The control grew slacker and the pace increased. The first F-word pronounced on television, the first nude love-scene, the first homosexual kiss.... The head of Channel 4, Michael Grade, decided to make it his policy to promote "gay" programmes in order to give alternative sexuality equal treatment.

The "battle" had been lost. The way to deal with the new reformation is not to wind the clock back, even if that were possible, or to redouble the ferocity and purity of our views as happened when the Jesuits produced the Counter-Reformation as a reaction to the fragmentation of the medieval Catholic Church. That kind of fundamentalism, whether Roman Catholic, Protestant, or Islamic, belongs in the dustbin of history. Rather the answer lies in trying to utilise the new situation to the benefit of Christianity.

At first this looks a promising area. There will always be a place for books, magazines, and programmes made about Christian topics. The new technology means that desktop publishing, digital equipment, and cameras with microchips enable these to be executed to top professional standards at a fraction of previous costs. The terrestrial broadcasters will now take programmes from independents, both in radio and television.

However it is not apparently all that easy, as recent years have proved. The world of publishing has been in turmoil for more than a decade with takeovers and mergers and many of the small publishers have found it difficult to survive. While there have never been so many glossy magazines, this has simply underlined the difficulty of a Church publication commanding loyalty in such a competitive market. As for independent productions for broadcast, it has not been so easy for outsiders to gain access. "Sweetheart deals" with former staff and budgets driven down in a buyer's market by the duopoly of BBC and ITV have meant that many "indies" find themselves making wedding videos to make ends meet.

It is against this background that the Church of Scotland communications empire is experiencing difficulty in making the transition to the new situation, despite having been a trailblazer in many of its ventures, for example the video unit and the more recent Church of Scotland web pages on the Internet. There are internal reasons for some difficulties, but the fact that it is losing money heavily, despite having competetent staff and doing all the right things by embracing new technology, does not encourage optimism. The publishing arm was heavily dependent on the (now) outdated William Barclay Bible commentaries, the magazine circulation is spiralling down, and the video unit does not seem to get a foothold into enough broadcasting work to generate income. The professionally presented

Internet pages are dependent on external funding and in addition are subsidised by being produced at volunteer rates.

I am reluctant to draw conclusions, except that the day of the in-house media unit is perhaps over for the Church and that it will need to go the way of privatisation for its media units. This is anathema to some, not simply because it has negative political connotations for them but because it means surrendering yet another bastion of control. Churches and their clergy feel that they must have control of the message. They will call in a plumber to fix the church drains but they would not consider asking a journalist or a PR professional to arrange the way their message is presented. That seems too big a reform for a Reformed Church in which so many ministers have learned to think of themselves as professional communicators because they climb pulpit steps every Sunday.

Some would argue that a faith commitment is necessary to work in Church media, but I have never subscribed to that argument. Since media work is more craft than art, and programmes must be more than a vehicle for the beliefs of the producer, the "committed" person can sometimes be more of a liability than an asset. I remember being interviewed by one such person who reacted to one of my answers by saying :"You can't do that!". To which the only reply is "I just have". We do not forbid agnostic surgeons to perform operations on Christians and can no doubt trust agnostic journalists to write fair articles on religious topics.

In addition to its centralised media enterprises, the option exists for the Kirk to make use of the many opportunities at local level which the information revolution has brought. Local radio stations are often delighted to receive news items and the 30-day licence provided by independent local radio provides an opportunity for churches to run their own local radio station for a month, as happened in Glasgow in recent years during Advent.

More and more churches and manses now have e-mail addresses and this is another area in which the local church can play an educative role. Evolving Bible classes into groups which surf the net in search of biblical and religious material is perhaps one way. Another idea concerns the provision of music in church. Many rural or "urban priority area" churches lack an organist and resort to cassette tapes for hymns, but the clunking of cassette changes or spooling to find the right band can be eliminated with a PC with CD-ROM which will instantly give digital quality at the tap of three digits.

At the moment the big-screen projected TV is still expensive but digital technology will soon make this cheaper and the images sharper. This would enable churches to show professionally made films or the parish pilgrimage to the Holy Land re-edited from the session clerk's camcorder. This would have the advantage of reassembling the fragmented audience which home video has created into a visible faith community. My own church is ideally suited for such a set-up if we can get the money for the equipment but there is still a problem. A dominant central pulpit sits on the back wall which would act as a screen. Perhaps there is a parable here!

So far I have not mentioned the bigger option of launching Christian media outlets such as satellite or cable channels. These tend to be a peculiarly American phenomenon spawned by the less regulated TV system in the USA. Their style is a curious amalgam of old-style hotgospelling with modern sales technique. Not all are as extreme as Jerry Falwell or as corrupt as Jim Bakker. In 1984 I met a Franciscan nun in Birmingham, Alabama, Mother Angelica, who ran a very appealing TV station featuring programmes in which she mixed orthodox Roman Catholicism with homespun homilies. However in the main the tele-evangelists, with their emphasis on the cult of personality, money-gathering, and apocalyptic theologies, belong to the realm of cults rather than mainstream religion.

The laws governing broadcasting in the United Kingdom do not permit TV stations to proselytise or appeal for money in the American manner but could not prevent a consortium of Churches putting up programming of a Christian nature on a satellite. However it is not as easy as that. In recent years an attempt to launch a Christian TV channel (Ark II), seeking support from mainstream Churches, ran into funding difficulties. Perhaps, like the American tele-evangelists, this is not our future but our past dressed up in modern technology.

Prophecy about where it is all leading is not easy, especially in such fast-changing times. Two of the most interesting reflections about the way the world is going, in my view, come not from the Reformed faith but from the Jesuit order. Although both are now over a generation old, Teilhard de Chardin's synthesis (in *The Phenomenon of Man*) and Ivan Illich's analysis (in *Tools for Conviviality* and other works based on his work in Latin America) hold out a vision which is neither Protestant not Catholic but radical and optimistic about a new type of Christianity arising from the ashes of the old order which is fast disappearing.

Along with the information revolution other changes have occurred in the last thirty years in the way the world is run. The nation-state is beginning to give way to larger groupings within which frontiers are less defined. Mobility within the United Kingdom and more widely within Europe has led to a less static society with less attachment to traditional loyalties in Church or State. The multinational company is now the major player in many key industries but lacks accountability to the nation-state.

This is not an entirely new scenario. There are some parallels with medieval Christendom - but I leave the reader to decide which is the multinational which lacks accountability! However the difference beteen modern Europe and medieval Christendom is that Christianity was regarded as essential and was thus imposed. In the centuries following the Reformation, as tolerance grew, "essential" became "necessary". Now it is optional.

When John Knox led the Scots Reformation in 1560 he did so as a man of impeccable European credentials. The bulk of his active life had been lived furth of Scotland. He expected that the Scots Parliament would deliver to the Kirk a powerful and controlling status; and when it did not, preferring a fudge in which Mary Queen of Scots kept much of her power, he grew angry and frustrated, sidelined till his death in 1572.

Yet the Kirk was able to use the status which was accorded to it to develop a prophetic role in society. There are fears that the new Scottish Parliament of 1999 will do something similar about the recognition of religion, preferring an even-handed approach that will not exclude Roman Catholics, many of whom voted for the party which delivered the Parliament. When the Churches themselves cannot agree very much in ecumenical terms, it is unlikely that the new Scottish State would want to fish in that pond. More likely, it will opt for the neutrality of a secular Scotland. When that happens, as with the information revolution, there is no use thinking that the tide can be turned back. The Churches must go with the flow and adapt to the radical new role of being a minority in a media age. The message is to use the medium.

6 MISSION AND REFORM

Faith, Church and structures for the future

Donald Smith

The Christian Church cannot by definition have a Reformed Tradition, though there can be a tradition of reform or a reforming tradition. Emphasis should always fall on the ongoing process. In itself Tradition - that which is passed on - can only in any core sense be what the Church has received through Christ and the Apostles. Much else is given through the Holy Spirit but can equally be changed and removed through the Holy Spirit.

So much is truism. But many questions arise about the contexts and the dynamics of change and reform. These are what the Church rather inadequately describes as "mission", which is the relationship in any period or society between faithfulness to the Gospel and responsiveness to contemporary needs and circumstances.

Viewed in that light Church history, not least in Scotland, becomes less a matter of denominational conflict and more an issue of the struggle for reform. This struggle is not the possession of one period or one denomination but a recurring theme. Moreover the conflicts involved are not primarily between opposing Christian groups but about the ways in which society at large both offers opportunities for reform and frustrates its fulfillment through political, military, economic and cultural pressures.

With a very broad brush one might identify the following reform movements, though the examples are more important than any particular historical schematisation.

Celtic Mission and Reform

Scotland's apostolic age brings a new faith which is also applied culturally as a reform of existing religious practice. The Celtic Mission is a response to the conditions of a post-imperial world in which margins are required to become centres till a new order is shaped.

Monastic Mission and Reform

This medieval movement encompasses not just the "great houses" of the monastic orders but the institutionalization of the parish system in Scotland. Together these efforts constitute the Church's response to and also struggle with the feudal system.

Medieval Urban Reform

The growth of towns through the medieval centuries requires a different response including friaries, hospitals, alms houses and collegiate burgh kirks. The first universities should also be seen in this context.

The Sixteenth Century Reformations

As late medieval Catholicism struggled to keep pace with the rapid social, intellectual and economic changes of the century after 1450, radical Protestant reform set a new agenda which was then paralleled by systematic Catholic reform. All of this took place in the most difficult social and political circumstances Europe had experienced since the collapse of the Roman Empire.

Evangelical and Pietistic Reform

The nineteenth century brought an explosion of religious energy and activity begun in the pietistic and evangelical movements of the eighteenth century. The context was principally urban and these movements were responsive to the phenomena of industrialization and large-scale migrations of population. Colonialisation and missionary expansion also moved in tandem. Considerable conflict was engendered between secular and religious aims yet the two forces were often also seen as complementary.

Modern Reform

In European terms the most significant reforming movement of the twentieth-century has been post-Vatican II Roman Catholic Reform. Globally however parts of the world church are experiencing the kind of growth associated in the nineteenth century with industrialization and urbanization. A large part of this growth is in the form of independent evangelical and pentecostal churches which also reflects nineteenth century patterns in Northern Europe at least.

At the centre of these movements is the attempt to align Church as an expression of Gospel with the structures and needs of contemporary society. When this is not achieved the Church stagnates and simultaneously generates fringe or counter-church movements which seek to rediscover and express a missionary relationship. Conflict and even oppression may be generated in the process and such struggles are usually complicated by the relationship between the Church and its social context as external and often secular influences are brought to bear on both sides.

This relationship between Gospel and Society is well summarized by the Scottish historian Rosalind Mitchison in a telling comment about the Church's difficulties in sixteenth-century Scotland:

> Cumulatively the effect was that the Church had by 1550 ceased to be an institution effectively presenting the image of a spiritual life to the mass of the laity, or receiving participation and loyalty from laymen.[1]

Undoubtedly the situation was more patchy than this suggests but the impetus for reform - Protestant and Catholic - lies in such analysis. As indicated above this analysis is consistent with simultaneous and very different attempts at reform. It is also predictable that the final shape of institutional reform in Scotland had as much to do with secular factors as it had to do with the missionary impulse. It is often forgotten that John Knox died bitterly disappointed that his agenda for radical reform had been frustrated by the Scottish noblity's distinctly limited appetite for a Christian society.[2]

Reform then is not the possession of any single denomination or of any one ecclesiastical style. But can any common characteristics of missionary reform be identified across denominations and historical movements? The attempt at least is worthwhile and I would begin by outlining four important trends or aspects.

1 Authentic Witness

Missionary reform brings to the fore aspects of the Christian Gospel which have been neglected or obscured, and testifies to their importance through living demonstration. In this way reform does not reduplicate itself in carbon copy but creates fresh patterns of emphasis and new combinations of the diversity-in-unity which is evidenced in the New Testament... Authenticity to the Gospel through a lived rather than a theoretical witness are the hard-to-define but always necessary components.

2 Response to Social Change

Missionary reform is not achieved through detached ecclesiastical inspiration but in response to social needs and opportunities. Some understanding of changing historical conditions is therefore essential to the process and forms part of the stimulus towards the recovery of authentic witness.

3 Prophetic Vision and Leadership

Though missionary reform is inescapably social in its origins and effects, the role of inspired leadership is a vital one. This may be a historiographically unfashionable perception but religious change is effected by the influence of people on people and collective movement normally occurs when some individuals are able to influence significant groups of people. Clearly without gifted individuals Christianity quickly succumbs to social and ecclesiastical inertia.

4 A Secular Framework or Concordat

Missionary reform cannot be successful on a large scale without influencing secular structures. Reform often generates conflict with secular authority but at some point conflict has to be converted into a degree of cooperation if social impact is to be achieved short of theocracy. The framework may be a minimal one of mutual tolerance, but some form of shared understanding of the church-society, sacred-secular interface is essential. This may be inimical to both sides of the equation during a heroic or pioneering phase of missionary reform but becomes increasingly accepted if reform is to be sustained beyond the early impetus.

The contemporary situation of the Christian Church in Scotland clearly presents the need for missionary reform to close the gap between church and social change, but it can also be argued that the contemporary situation also provides the opportunity. The dominance of secular modernism has slipped and Western European society as a whole demonstrates a new openness to spirituality and religion, though not necessarily to Christianity. This cultural pluralism is a missionary opportunity if the Church is prepared to recognize pluralist tolerance as a framework within which the sacred-secular relationship can operate. Such a framework or concordat is a necessary component of reform. Accepting a pluralist framework for mission is not the same as embracing a relativistic approach to theological, philosophical or social truth, but an acknowledgment that the starting point is a pluralist context.

Pluralism has two further advantages to offer Scottish Christianity. It is firstly an environment in which the Church can shed the institutional image of "big brother" and "teacher knows best". By and large the twentieth century Scottish Churches are seen as the embodiment of an outdated paternalism which has been comprehensively rejected by the Scottish population and is still actively resented. Secondly, openness to models of association between religion and culture in the Scottish context positively foregrounds Christianity if the Church can be creative in the way it uses the rich resources of the past. The reinterpretation and reapplication of Celtic missionary models is a case in point.

Taking forward the general characteristics of missionary reform, what specifically might constitute such reform in the contemporary Scottish context? This question will be considered under the headings of Public Worship, Word and Sacrament, Membership and Discipleship, Authority and Structure.

PUBLIC WORSHIP

The worship of the Church is its core missionary activity, since without worship evangelism and social action fall apart . When "para-church" organisations and instruments lose touch with the public worship and fellowship of the Church they become secular organisations with religious labels.

For the Church to achieve missionary reform in Scotland its worship must be public and open to everyone. This may seem an obvious or unnecessary point, but as the Scottish Churches withdraw from many of their historic buildings there is a danger of privatization.

In addition there is clear evidence of the domestication of church buildings, particularly Protestant and Independent churches, through the installation of carpets, light-fittings and windows modelled on the scales and standards of a private home.[3] The message given out is that the worship activity is for an in-group which is "at-home" and comfortable in the church space.

The issue of public visibility and access does not rest solely on owning a uniquely dedicated building, though this remains a very effective way of achieving these goals. Shared use of a public building not owned by a congregation is also compatible with access and openness.

Openness needs also to be a feature of the lay-out and use of a public worship space. Cluttered spaces give out messages of constraint and offer no room for incomers to find their own place within the worship event without physical or psychological pressure. Equally points of access and welcome need to be designed in such a way as to be genuinely open and not dependent on certain codes of behaviour - forms of acknowledgment and recognition for example - which do not apply to other public situations and are therefore only user-friendly for the insider group. The purpose must always be to remove any unnecessary barriers between the worshipper and the content of public Christian worship.

WORD AND SACRAMENT

Over a period of centuries the content of Christian worship in Scotland has become tailored to different denominational traditions and increasingly divergent from contemporary culture. No area of activity is more clearly in need of missionary reform.

The resources of Word and Sacrament remain at the core of what the Church has received from Jesus and the Apostles, but the manner in which these are deployed is currently governed more by what church institutions perceive as the needs and rights of their concept of religious authority than by faithfulness to the Gospel.

The New Testament understands the good news of the Kingdom of Heaven in the context of a visible communion which expresses the nature of that Gospel. It is evident that Communion/Eucharist/Mass is the defining sacrament and one which should be celebrated regularly and frequently in the life of any Christian community. Anything less is not only a departure from what has been given to us by Jesus and the Apostles but a curious arrogance. How can the Church sustain its life without this means of grace - the gift of Christ's body and blood and the sharing of a table fellowship at which Jesus himself is the host?

This leads to an equally fundamental point. Communion/Eucharist/Mass should be a public celebration open to everyone regardless of age, class, race, gender, sexual orientation, membership, profession or baptism. Communion is supremely an evangelical witness and to experience inclusion is converting. To be invited by Christ is the beginning of the Christian journey; those invited to share the table may not understand the full meaning of communion but every guest has a place.

Western European society at the end of the twentieth century is characterized by spiritual search and by existential emptiness amidst material plenty. Post-modernism requires a semiology of grace, and it is already present at the heart of Christian Tradition in bread and wine. To set up barriers and make exclusions is to be counted among those who have the keys to the Kingdom of Heaven but leave the gates locked.

Communion/Eucharist/Mass defines Christian fellowship, uniting worship, community outreach and social action. It is the vital accompaniment to and underpinning of preaching because it is a living demonstration and embodied form of the Kingdom which the Word seeks to build. The Church which cannot unite men, women and children around the Lord's Table is in danger of becoming at best half a Church and at worst a sham.

MEMBERSHIP AND DISCIPLESHIP

The major problem with the above analysis is that the self-definition of most Christian Churches in Scotland is linked to sacramental demarcations. This takes a variety of forms all of which have long historic roots. It is therefore important to examine these different models of "membership" and "belonging" before suggesting ways in which they could be brought together in harmony with Gospel models of worship and mission.

1 The Church as Public Institution

In this model church and society are closely linked and people are related to the institution by mutual ties of obligation and service. This model, of which The Church of Scotland "Auld Kirk" is an example, can only function as a "stand-alone" form when the majority of people within a given community accept some association or attachment to the institution.

2 The Church as Voluntary Association

In this model individuals and/or households choose to associate themselves with a church and voluntarily support it through attendance and financial contribution. The voluntary church is likely to have a confessional basis to which members subscribe, though socio-cultural motivations for attachment may in reality be as strong as credal ones. The United Presbyterian Church and its Secession predecessors are examples of this model while also sharing some characteristics of 3 below.

3 The Church as a Community of Disciples

In this model, whatever additional forms of membership or association apply, religious commitment through baptism, creed, and/or confession is the primary benchmark. The Free Church of Scotland set out after the Disruption of 1843 to re-create a National Church on this model. The Roman Catholic Church is also based on this model though it is qualified by a strong commitment to the concept of a Christian society. Where the majority of the population or of a grouping within the wider population adheres to Catholicism the Church also has the character of a public institution, but a minority Roman Catholic Church is liable to the dangers of exclusivism and ghettoisation. It is interesting to note that the Free Church of Scotland began with a strong commitment to Thomas Chalmers' ideal of a Christian Society but became increasingly denominationalised as a membership organisation.

This analysis is summary rather than exposition but indicates three sometimes overlapping models of being Church which have considerable influence in Scotland. It is my argument that contemporary missionary reform must draw on all three models if it is to make an adequate response to social change.

1 Through its public worship the Church should remain a public social institution offering religious services to whoever in the population desires them. These services should include:

- Communion/Eucharist/Mass open to all without restriction
- A service of blessing for a new-born child
- A service of blessing for a civil marriage
- A service of thanksgiving and commemoration for the dead
- A service of blessing and healing

Such services should be couched in simple non-technical language. All services are offered in the name of Christ but should be sensitive to the different backgrounds and experiences from which people may come.

2 Churches should maintain and actively recruit to computerised lists of friends/supporters/members who belong by voluntary association to the network of those in sympathy with the Church's provision of religious services and with its charitable endeavours across society. Such lists should be specific to individual churches or groups of local churches operating together. The voluntary

association model is a sound basis for fundraising, publicity and the management of normal operations.

An important feature of this model is that people may actively support more than one church. In addition the degree and kind of support will be their choice, since no conditions should attach to belonging to the network other than willingness and commitment expressed through voluntary work and/or financial donation.

The services provided by the Church under 1 will provide one means of recruitment to 2.

3 The public worship of the Church, and the voluntary network with its wide community links are the contexts within which the Church's call to discipleship can be grounded. They are twin expressions of the open invitation to everyone to travel on the journey of Christian faith and to grow in community as disciples.

The journey of discipleship should be nurtured and encouraged through:

• Opportunities for prayer and meditation in addition to the regular public services.

• Lifelong Christian education with provision for children, young people and adult learners.

• Experience of local, national and international paid and/or voluntary service.

People should be free to join, leave and rejoin the journey of discipleship according to choice, need and opportunity within their own lives but there should also be clear publicly acknowledged staging posts or milestones as follows:

• Baptism either as an infant within the context of family commitment or as an adult or young adult with profession of faith.

• Confirmation of Baptism through an act of commitment and profession of faith

• Christian marriage

• Christian funeral service

It is also suggested that the initiation milestones should be publicly advertised within some kind of national framework, and that such a framework should relate to the seasons of the Christian year. Initiation groups could for example meet across Scotland in a cycle culminating in Easter baptisms and professions. This would be integrated within adult education programmes and would allow for enquirers who did not wish to make a public commitment at that juncture.

The only institutional regulation required for this process would be that Baptism should precede confirmation. At the other milestones the choice of making a specifically Christian commitment or expression should rest with those involved under the guidance of normal pastoral counselling. Records should however be kept under all four categories.

It will of course be argued that this pattern is too complicated and that congregations as presently constituted could not sustain these interrelated models. However that is to put the cart before the horse. The church must reform and restructure according to Gospel faithfulness and missionary need. Modern society operates in a complex way and the Church's response must match contemporary conditions.

Clearly existing churches and clergy would need to operate in groups deploying employees and volunteers, lay and ordained, in team structures to meet the challenge. There is considerable evidence that the Scottish churches already know that this is the way they need to operate but are struggling to find the right frameworks within which to achieve the necessary changes.

AUTHORITY AND AUTHENTICITY

The issue of authority is often raised within churches as a means of blocking change and reform. Unless, it is argued, there is a single agreed source of religious authority there can be no basis for changes which may disrupt or bypass existing lines of ecclesiastical demarcation. The political equivalent of this stance fostered conflict and social stagnation in Northern Ireland until the Good Friday agreement of 1998, designated by the Scottish Churches as a Year of Hope in the approach to the third millennium of Christianity. It is significant that the demand for irrefutable external validation is always more rigorously applied to proposals for change than to the status quo.

Authentic witness has already been cited as a prime characteristic of missionary reform. Could the idea of authentic witness in this wider context usefully extend or qualify the idea of authority with its apparent implication of a single external means of validation?

Christian authenticity is derived from a number of factors which can only be recognised or identified through a cumulative process of trial and confirmation. This process is a function of many different people and groups operating in different parts of church structures and sometimes on the margins beyond them. There is a need for mutuality, reciprocity and co-operative affirmation, founded on the open acceptance that no single party has privileged access to external authority whether that is defined as resting with Scripture, Church Tradition, the Holy Spirit or a combination of the three.

Authenticity does not supplant authority since the goal or focus remains that which we have received from Christ and the Apostles, but it grounds authority in the Christian life. The long hard route to authenticity cannot be short-circuited with integrity. The primary mark of Christian authenticity is the making and the formation of Christian disciples, but its characteristics would include table fellowship (sacramentally and socially), prayer and spirituality, mutual care, engagment with the wider community, and growth in understanding and commitment. The experience of such authenticity which is the living demonstration of the Christian gospel can shift understandings of authority. It is in itself a process of missionary reform which paves the way for ongoing renewal.

Only the influence of the Holy Spirit, expressed through Scripture, Sacrament and the experience of the Church past, present and future, can aid the Church's progress towards the authenticity embodied in the person of Jesus, whose hands, arms, ears, eyes and lips we seek to become. Many different styles of devotion and many different kinds of church organisation have a contribution to make to such missionary reform in contemporary Scotland.

STRUCTURE

If these are the goals and parameters of missionary reform,what are its institutional means? The challenge is considerable: to achieve sustainable reform in a complex situation of diversity-in-unity and unity-in-diversity. At the same time missionary reform must balance the globalisation of Christianity with the need for local identity and roots. Globally and nationally Christianity must also be open to inter-faith dialogue and influence while sustaining a passionate commitment to its own spiritual distinctiveness.

By definition this will not be achieved by any single organisation or network but there is equally a need for liason.cooperation and conflict resolution. Who structurally in the Church in Scotland can tackle such an agenda? Each important piece in the present ecclesiastical jigsaw will be examined in turn.

The Roman Catholic Church in Scotland

Since the nineteen-sixties the Roman Catholic Church has set itself an ambitious reform agenda. Some have argued that the charismatic papacy of John Paul II has stalled aspects of this agenda but the changes are substantial and ongoing. Most importantly the concept is of a pilgrim Church whose journey is not end limited by anything other than Gospel faithfulness.

Nonetheless Roman Catholic ecclesiology is not attuned to some features of the kind of missionary reform outlined in this article. Experience suggests greater local flexibility in Scottish Catholicism than sometimes presumed, but the internal dynamic of Catholicism requires that the Vatican II process be taken forward before other agendas can be fully addressed.

Action of Churches Together in Scotland

Established in 1990, ACTS has already proved an invaluable forum for dialogue and cooperation with a significant and useful base at Scottish Churches House. However it can be argued that the main strength of ACTS - the inclusion of the Roman Catholic Church - is also its greatest weakness as a primary instrument of missionary reform in any structural sense. Moreover, while ACTS can stimulate local change and development there is inevitably tension between a locally-grounded agenda and the ownership of ACTS by the participating denominations at national level.

Despite this ACTS will continue to be one very helpful route for reform which brings together mainstream churches and a range of national Christian agencies in its membership. The ACTS network would be greatly strengthened in its effectiveness if the independent churches and fellowships could be brought into some form of association enabling dialogue and cooperation.

Scottish Churches Initiative for Union

SCIFU offers a potentially very fruitful framework for structural and missionary reform involving the major Protestant denominations in Scotland. Such a framework need not lead to full structural union in the medium or even long term if it can enable local initiatives to have a recognised frame of reference and encouragement for structural change. This is clearly the intention of the partners in the Initiative.[4]

The Church of Scotland

Irrespective of its minimal constitutional status, the Church of Scotland has by reason of its size and geographical distribution a major role to play. It can be a prime mover of missionary reform or its greatest obstacle. The Church of Scotland's problems include inward-looking congregationalism, sclerosis at presbytery or regional level, and organisational gridlock at national level where an impossibly large General Assembly retains nominal authority while struggling to control and failing to co-ordinate a plethora of quasi-independent committees and bureaucracies.

Nonetheless the presbyterian constitution of the Church of Scotland provides for missionary change and reform in the face of socio-ecclesiastical inertia. If the Church of Scotland were to actively engage with the Scottish Churches Initiative for Union as an instrument of reform much could be achieved.

Independent Churches

The independent and evangelical fellowships have grown in overall numbers in Scotland over the last decade though it is arguable that some at least of this growth has been a product of transfers from other churches. The independent nature of these fellowships has also been qualified by increasing networking through organisations such as the Baptist Union of Scotland, the Evangelical Alliance and the "There is Hope" campaign. These local church fellowships have an important role to play and their involvement in cooperative ecumenism can be justified both as a means of influencing the overall missionary agenda and of self-development. The national networks of these fellowships should be encouraged to enter into dialogue and cooperation with ACTS.

National Christian Agencies

The role and scope of national organisations such as Christian Aid, Scripture Union, the Iona Community and the National Bible Society of Scotland have increased in Scotland over the last twenty-five years. It was noticeable at the Scottish Christian Gathering, held by ACTS in the Scottish Exhibition and Conference Centre in Glasgow in 1997, that a lot of the energy and sense of collective Christian endeavour was generated by the presence of forty such agencies. In a complex and specialised society organisations devoted to particular themes and specific areas of mission can achieve progress which slower moving church structures cannot easily emulate.

It is however important that such organisations and the wider Church keep in close contact and influence each other. Unless the independent agency is to become in itself a form of church, relationships with locally rooted worshipping communities are a vital anchor. The existing national agencies vary widely in their constitutions and purposes but a significant proportion are now associate members of ACTS.

It is clear from this review that several potential and complementary routes for missionary reform exist in Scotland today. The Scottish churches may not have crossed the missionary Jordan but neither are they languishing in Egypt. Yet the motivation for reform remains an imponderable, dependent ultimately on a spiritual shift in consciousness which cannot be prescribed though it can be fostered and appropriately channelled. Without this strong underlying impulse visionary and prophetic leadership is diverted into individual rather than collective routes.

Christian disciples live perpetually "between the times", anticipating the Kingdom of God but working within the constraints of earthly reality. There are glimpses, illuminations and moments of fulfilment, but Gospel and World, Gospel and Church, co-exist in an often uneasy tension.

Missionary reform is therefore a struggle in which disappointment is inevitable, and over which the temptations of aggressive conflict and despairing disillusion always loom. But missionary reform is also a struggle which brings fulfilment now: it is an integral part of the Christian vocation which refreshes, renews and instructs. The impulse to reform and the inevitable failure to achieve such reform completely is part of the death-and-resurrection experience to which Jesus calls his followers.

On the eve of the twenty-first century I have no doubt that Christianity will find new fulfilment in Scotland through faith, hope and love. As long as we can have the grace to recognise God's grace as the truly motivating impulse of all reform and mission, the Church can cross another Jordan without fear of drowning.

[1] Mitchison, Rosalind *Life in Scotland* (London, 1978) p.21

[2] For recent discussions of the Scottish Reformation see: Cowan,Ian B. *The Scottish Reformation* (London, 1982) and Wormald, Jenny *Court, Kirk and Community* (London, 1981). For the more biographical point on Knox himself see Ridley, Jasper *John Knox* (Oxford, 1968) and Smith, Donald *John Knox House* (Edinburgh, 1996).

[3] See, for example, "Report of the Consultative Committee on Artistic Matters" 14/2 in *Reports to the General Assembly* (Edinburgh, 1998)

[4] See "Report of the Committee on Ecumenical Relations" 23/14-23/40 in *Ibid.*

7   THE PARISH: PAST, PRESENT, FUTURE

Old boundaries and new horizons

Russell Barr

The concept of the parish and the importance of parish ministry has been a fundamental part of the life and ministry of the Church of Scotland. Following the Reformation in Scotland, the reformers adopted the parish system as the best practical way of expressing their theological understanding of ministry. John Knox and his colleagues held that the purpose of the Church was to attend to both the religious and public needs of the people of Scotland. They believed Scotland to be a nation under God and the parish system proved attractive to them in turning that belief into action. A Kirk Session and congregation was established in each parish with responsibility not just in explicitly religious matters, preaching the word of God or celebrating the sacraments, but in the provision of education, law and poor relief to the people of that locality.

The persistence of the parish system as the basic model of ministry in the Church of Scotland from the time of the Reformation to the present day, and the considerable efforts which the Church of Scotland makes to maintain and defend it, suggests that in the minds of many no significant changes have taken place in the social or ecclesial landscape of Scotland that would prevent the continuing practice of ministry as envisioned by the reformers in their adoption of the parish system. In fact, however, significant changes have taken place in the social and cultural landscape of Scotland, in the way society is organised, in the provision and administration of education, law and poor relief, in the way people live their lives and in their expectations. What consequences do these changes have for the Church? How have they affected the practice of ministry? Does the parish system continue to serve the Church well as its basic model of ministry or has the time come for it too to be embraced within the realm of reform?

In April, 1993, the Presbytery of Edinburgh inducted me to be the minister of the congregation and parish of Cramond. I was given a call signed by members and adherents of the congregation inviting me to be their minister. The Presbytery Clerk also gave me a note with details of the parish boundaries. One does not need to have any local knowledge of the Cramond area to discern that several of the boundaries have been decided in a purely arbitrary manner and pay little attention to any sense of neighbourhood or community or to the natural movement of people towards shops or schools. Although the boundary to the north makes use of the obvious geographical feature of the river Forth, other boundaries to the south and east of the parish consist of an imaginary line drawn along the centre of one road and down the centre of another. As the history of the origin and development of parishes reveals however, this arbitrary arrangement of boundaries was not the original intention.

The first historical records of what came to be known as parishes date from the early twelfth century.[1] Landowners and noblemen felt charged with the spiritual care of their people. These landowners built a church and appointed a priest to carry out religious duties. A piece of land was set aside for a cemetery and the district served by this church and priest was called a parish, its boundaries normally coinciding with the landlord's estate. The priest was supported by teinds, a system which provided the incumbent with a percentage of the rents and produce of the land. The rise in favour and influence of the monasteries proved to be to the detriment of the parish structure. When a landowner wished to add to the revenue of a monastery, he would attach one or more parishes under his patronage. For example, in 1178, the Abbey of Arbroath was founded and provided with endowment by attaching to it thirty three parishes. (Kelso Abbey had 37 parishes attached, Holyrood Abbey 27, Paisley Abbey 29) This resulted in monasteries like Arbroath becoming the nominal holders of parochial appointments. In practice, the spiritual care of the parish was neglected and in many cases the parish priest was robbed of his revenue and left impoverished.[2] What is beyond dispute however is that come the Reformation in Scotland when the monastic system was swept away, the reformers such as John Knox recognised the potential of the parish system as the basic unit of church life. John Burleigh notes that until that time the parish church could well be described as the "Cinderella of the ecclesiastical institutions of the Middle Ages, most of all in Scotland".[3] But following the reformation the importance of the parish structure in Scotland came to be realised as a means of ensuring that each community was provided with a minister and Kirk Session to attend to the spiritual care of the people and also to administer poor relief and provide education.

In contrast to the description of the Cramond parish boundaries, the original parish structure developed around natural communities and this practice continued in Scotland into the nineteenth century. At that time the pressure for change proved irresistible when major developments in agricultural and industrial practices led to the movement of large numbers of people into the towns and cities. However the change brought about by these social pressures was not to question the viability of the parish structure as a model for ministry but to create new parishes out of the old *quod omnia* parishes which had existed until that time. In order to meet the need for places of worship in the developing towns and cities of Scotland, chapels of ease were created to supplement the existing parish churches.

One figure who played an important role in the development of these new chapels of ease was Thomas Chalmers, one of the leading evangelicals of the 19th century. Following his experiences in the Tron Parish in the centre of Glasgow, where he had been appointed minister in 1815, and in which he had created an imaginative scheme of poor relief involving the city authority and local businessmen, Chalmers took up the case for church extension in the city areas. He proposed to create *quoad sacra* parishes where there had been chapels of ease and to persuade the government to build new churches. Although as many as forty-three were built in the Highlands, nothing was done in the cities and so evangelicals like Chalmers set about raising the money themselves. Many new church buildings were created and in 1834, the General Assembly passed the Chapels Act which gave these new churches parish areas *quoad sacra* status. However the Chapels Act was declared illegal by the civil courts and after the disruption of 1843 the Act was repealed. Following the Disruption however, the process of church building continued as the newly created Free Church built churches in many of the existing parishes of the established church. After the union in 1929 between the Church of Scotland and the United Free Church, the parish system was extensively rearranged so that each minister and Kirk Session was given a territorial area of responsibility. Although the provision of education and poor relief had passed by that time from the responsibility of the church, the concept of the parish as a model for ministry was not called into question. While many of the inconsistencies and idiosyncrasies of present parish boundaries are undoubtedly a left-over of that union, the situation is now far beyond a simple redrawing of boundaries and the time has come to examine the continuing viability of the parish system itself.

The Reformed theology of ministry is Christological and has always affirmed the principle that there is only one ministry, that of Jesus Christ, who was sent by the Father into the world to fulfil God's purpose for humanity and the world. From this starting point, the Reformed tradition concludes that the Church has no independent ministry of its own but is called to participate in the one ministry of Jesus Christ. On the day of Pentecost, the Holy Spirit was poured out upon all the believers. With this in mind, the continuing ministry of Christ is not the duty or responsibility of any one individual but is a responsibility shared by the whole people of God. All who have been brought into the Church through baptism are called to exercise the different gifts of the Spirit with which they have been blessed in the one ministry of Christ.

In order to ensure that this baptismal ministry can be faithfully developed and sustained, the Church of Scotland has argued that two distinct but related ministries may be identified, namely the ministry of kerygma or proclamation and the ministry of diakonia or service. While the Church believes that these two ministries are not exclusive of one another, that those who primary task is *kerygma* are not excused from the demands of *diakonia*, it has nevertheless argued for the distinctive contribution which each makes to the one ministry of Christ.[4] "The Scottish Reformers emphatically rejected the mediaeval understanding of ministry as primarily or exclusively that of priests who had received a 'character *indelibilis*' through the sacrament of orders and took their place in a hierarchically structured ministry. Instead with a strong theological reaffirmation of the priestly ministry of Christ, in which the whole Church participates as a Royal Priesthood, the Reformers stressed the importance of a lawful ministry, properly constituted."[5]

Christological in essence and corporate in nature, the Reformed doctrine of ministry is founded in the one ministry of Christ and involves the whole people of God. In adopting the parish structure as the basic unit of ministry, the reformers sought to give practical expression to that theological understanding. Authority was invested in a Kirk Session made up of minister and elders and together the

Session sought to address the religious and social needs of the people of a particular community. The minutes of many Kirk Session meetings indicate the extent to which a session was involved in every aspect of parish life. While the persistence of the parish system from the time of the Reformation until the present day indicates the strength and importance of the parish structure to the Church, it also suggests that it offers the same opportunities for the practice of ministry as it did then. From my experience of ministry in three different parishes, it is clear to me that that is not the case. While the parish minister may continue to have a certain public profile within a community, the practice of ministry tends to be confined to specifically religious matters like the conduct of parish funerals. To an even greater extent the role of the eldership is now largely confined to the internal life of the congregation and there is little understanding or expectation of the public role of eldership.

The changes which we are witnessing within the life of the Church are a result of the significant changes which have taken place in the social, cultural and ecclesiastical life of Scotland, changes that have radically altered the pattern of family and civic life in Scotland and which continue to have major implications for the practice of ministry. On one level these changes are described by the secularisation and politicisation of public life in Scotland and the fact that the provision of education, social security and law are now the responsibility of local and national government. Where once the Church exerted considerable influence, it now finds that its teaching has been marginalised from much of the main stream of public life. Even on the subject of many moral and ethical issues, the Church finds that its voice is one of many competing to be heard. On another level however the suggestion is now being made that we are witnessing a significant change in the cultural condition of Scotland, a change that has significant implications and offers important opportunities for the ministry of the Church.

This cultural change has been described in sociological terms as the move from modernity to post modernity and the issue was addressed in a brilliant paper presented by Professor David McCrone to a conference held in 1996 at the University of Aberdeen to discuss the future of the Kirk.[6] In seeking to clarify his use of terminology, McCrone argued that the term "post-modern" conveyed nothing of its meaning other than the fact that it followed something else, in this case "modern". By modern McCrone intended to name the cluster of social, economic and political systems that had developed in the western world during the period of the Enlightenment and in particular from the 18th century onwards. The characteristics of modernity include scientific rationality and a belief in the predictability and control of nature, industrialisation and an organised labour force built on the economic principles of capitalism, the political development of the nation state with associated implications for citizenship, the development of social and political movements as class-based and male-dominated and a clear identification of the relationship among state, nation and society.

In contrast to the characteristics of modernity, McCrone identified the characteristics of post-modernity as "a profusion of styles and orientations without any possibility of identifying deeper reality. It (post-modernity) celebrates pastiche and irony and is eclectic in style."[7] According to McCrone, this profusion is evidenced in the prevailing scientific belief in the erratic and unpredictable quality of nature, in the market-led economic forces of consumerism, in the development of the idea of limited sovereignty, in the emergence of single issue political or pressure groups that cut across the old class or gender boundaries and in the disassociation of the ideas of state, society and nation. It is McCrone"s conviction that these social changes had profound implications for the Church, not the least of them being the role of faith as a means to explain the meaning and purpose of life.[8] To support his thesis, McCrone noted that while the traditional secular and religious systems have lost, or are at least losing, their power to persuade and mobilise, there is a proliferation in what he described as lower case politics with a variety of single-nterest pressure groups concerned, for example, with environmental issues, and lower case religion with individuals or groups concerned with issues of spirituality.

The implications of McCrone's thesis for the future of the Kirk were briefly developed at the conference by Dr William Storrar. Examining the life of the Church intellectually, institutionally and politically, Storrar argued that the Church of Scotland exhibited all the hallmarks of a typically modern institution with its bureaucracy and its centralised methods of planning, finance and administration. He believed that one of the more pertinent insights of McCrone"s analysis was to demonstrate that the Church of Scotland is not alone in suffering this fate as a modern institution, that a similar pattern could be traced in for example the trade union movement, and that it is essential to reframe the various challenges facing the Kirk in terms of its wider social and cultural context and in primarily post-modern terms.

McCrone's analysis brought the role of the parish as the basic model for the Church's ministry into sharp relief. Although the parish predates the period of modernity as described by McCrone, the manner in which the parish system has been maintained and defended by the Church of Scotland is typical of the bureaucracy of a modern institution. Most notably in an annual reminder to congregations, the General Assembly affirms "its support for, and belief in, the full-time ordained Ministry, working as part of the whole people of God, and serving, through the parish system, as essential to the life and work of the Church".[9] It is the assumption on which that "annual reminder" is based that I want to call into question, namely, that the parish continues to allow for the practice of ministry which led to the parish structure being adopted by the reformers in the first place. Manifestly it does not. Where once there was stability in terms of the family unit, now we witness constantly changing patterns of family life and domestic arrangements. There was once a day when for many people the Church was their principal source of information and opinion on a whole range of issues; now the revolution in information and communication technology leads to a deluge of news and opinion. Stability and continuity of employment has been replaced in many sectors of the workplace by part time or short term contracts. There are countless sports and leisure options for people to enjoy and parents are often faced with juggling the competing demands of Sunday School or mini-rugby.

All of this points to what we recognise as the fragmentation of public life and the privatisation of common values. Christian faith is no longer a matter of public truth in Scotland but has become a question of private opinion. The parish system was never intended to minister to this kind of social situation. Although the word of God continues to be preached and the sacraments celebrated, the richness of the Reformed doctrine of ministry that embraced both the religious and public needs of a community of people is no longer addressed by the parish structure. Where once the social and cultural situation at the time of the Reformation led to the parish system being adopted and then to being reformed during the 19th century, now the changing situation of the late 20th century is at last calling into question the continuing viability of the parish system as the one model of ministry considered essential to the future life and missionary activity of the Church.

Through its creation of various forms of specialised or others forms of ministry, there is a sense in which the Church of Scotland has already recognised the limitations of the parish system. Ministries such as hospital, university or industrial chaplaincies or community ministries are now well established as part of the life and witness of the church in Scotland and such positions were created in response to the changing social, industrial and cultural patterns of life. That being so, it is even more curious that in its official pronouncements, and in the prioritising of its financial and human resources, the Church of Scotland continues to hold to the parish as the one model of ministry essential to the life of the Church.

One possible explanation is offered by Robin Gill. In his book *Beyond Decline*[10] Gill argues passionately that the continuing adherence to what he describes as "mediaeval parish boundaries"[11] must be changed if the Church is to engage in effective ministry in Scotland or in England. Gill concedes that while in rural areas the traditional parish may continue to be meaningful in defining community, that same case cannot be argued with any integrity with regard to the significance of the parish in the towns and cities of Great Britain.[12] He further argues that in a general context of membership decline, there exists the curious tendency for local congregations to reinforce their parish boundaries, even in situations in which such boundaries are quite meaningless.

This would certainly be the case within the Church of Scotland where in many Presbyteries, the organisational matter of boundaries has been drawn into the disciplinary procedures of the court.[13] Gill's analysis of the situation in both Scotland and England does not lead him to conclude that the church should abandon its claim to be a national church nor its commitment to serving the whole people. Rather he considers it important for churches to think geographically at a central level but to recognize that the perspective must be on "natural communities rather than on inflexible geographical areas."[14] It is in this context that we must seek to understand the development of the hospital, university, industrial and other such chaplaincies and ministries now established as recognised forms of ministry within the church. In many respects the medical, nursing, administrative and ancillary staff of a large general hospital represent as much a natural community of people as that embraced by the concept of the traditional parish.

That being so, it is not surprising to hear full time hospital chaplains describing their ministry as much in terms of their relationship with the hospital staff as with the patients. Defined in terms of community rather than fixed lines on a map, the hospital is one example of a contemporary "parish". Might not one of the large American style shopping malls be considered another? I live near to the Gyle shopping centre on the west side of Edinburgh, itself now part of a much larger industrial estate. Each day tens of thousands of people come to the Gyle to work, to shop, to meet for lunch or a cup of coffee. Music and other forms of entertainment are often provided, there are crèche facilities, in short, shopping malls like the Gyle have become a focal point for a great deal of community life. Although the church does not recognise them as such, they too are further examples of a contemporary "parish".[15]

In a report to the 1998 General Assembly of the Church of Scotland, the concept of a "maxi-parish" was proposed.[16] This proposal has arisen out of discussions first sponsored by the Scottish Episcopal Church and including the Church of Scotland, the Methodist Church, the Scottish Congregational Church and the United Reformed Church. Recognising that the different main stream denominations in Scotland have all experienced a period of numerical decline in recent years, the purpose of the proposed maxi-parish is to provide the church with an administrative structure that will encourage every congregation to function more effectively in its witness and outreach to the wider community.[17] The maxi-parish is defined as "a designated area, recognised by the local people as a definable community in which geographical and sociological factors are taken into consideration. Generally speaking, it would be the area of a sizable town and those surrounding areas which focus in on it. The area would have within it a number of church buildings, which are referred to in this report as worship centres, in that the building indicates the focus of a worshipping community. The area cannot be so large as to make administration and management unwieldy. In major cities several maxi-parishes could be identified. Ideally there would be no more than seven worship centres in a maxi-parish".[18]

Given the somewhat cumbersome designation of "maxi-parish", the report in fact touches upon many important issues. It acknowledges that the present structures and patterns of church life and ministry are no longer serving the church well. At a time when denominational loyalty is being eroded, the fact that the proposals are ecumenically based is to be welcomed, so too the continuing geographical commitment to minister to the whole people of

Scotland. Most noteworthy of all however is the recognition that no single model of ministry can serve as a blueprint appropriate for every aspect of contemporary Scottish society and that diversity in practice should not just be tolerated but actively encouraged at the local level.

If these indicate some of the strengths of the report, there is one major flaw, namely, that it puts the structural cart before the ministerial horse. Having established what are described as defining principles, namely that a united church will be a missionary church, that there will be continuity with the past and adaptability to changing circumstances, that a united church will maintain and protect the greatest possible degree of diversity at local level, and that the question of authority would be addressed at the local and not at the central level, the report then addresses the question of ministry. It affirms its belief in a typically reformed doctrine of ministry, that the one ministry of Christ is shared by the whole people of God, that some are ordained in order to equip the ministry of the whole people, and that it falls to "all the followers of Christ, not just the tiny minority of those who are ordained, who are charged by Christ to be salt to the world, light to the world, and yeast to leaven the whole lump of dough".[19]

Having thus stated its theological understanding of ministry, the report then describes the different patterns of ministry that have developed among the partner churches. The concept of the maxi-parish emerges out of this description but in such a way as to suggest that it is an attempt to find a compromise, that is, an administrative and bureaucratic arrangement that will accommodate what each denomination has been doing in the past and into which everyone can neatly slip without making significant changes. Such existing non-parish forms of ministry as hospital, university or prison chaplaincies, and the possibility that one might be included as a worship centre, are significant by their absence. And there is no acknowledgment of the challenge and opportunities presented by the likes of the Gyle shopping centre nor of the virtual community created by the Internet. The traditional model of the parish continues to dominate and with it all the assumptions about ministry which the concept entails.

Given the long and protracted history of ecumenical discussions in Scotland, and in particular the important but ultimately limited achievements of the Multilateral Conversations, the conservatism of the maxi-parish proposal is understandable. But the maxi-parish proposal will not do what the authors of the report hope it will do, namely, create a church that is renewed in its worship and missionary activity. And it will not do it because although they have described the different forms of ministry embraced by the partner churches, they have not articulated a theology of ministry appropriate to the present social and cultural context of Scotland. In the same way as the reformers adopted the parish system from the monastic tradition because it proved the most attractive way of turning their theology of ministry into practical action, so the question of ministry needs to be addressed first. Only then can the issue of turning that theological understanding of ministry into appropriate practice be properly addressed and appropriate administrative structures proposed.

Do we still hold to the reformed understanding of the corporate nature of ministry? Does our understanding of the purpose of ministry continue to embrace both the public as well as the religious needs of people? Have we the imagination to move from static model of the geographical parish to develop new flexible models of ministry in response to the changing social and cultural context of Scotland?

I ask these questions because of my conviction that the fundamental question facing the Church is the theological question about ministry and the ways in which our belief in the one ministry of Christ exercised by the whole people of God can be turned into practical reality. The reformers adopted the parish system from the monastic tradition because it suited both their theological understanding of ministry and the social and cultural context of their day. Scotland has changed, however, and continues to change, politically with the prospect of a new parliament at Holyrood, socially with a multi-ethnic population, culturally with all the characteristics associated with an individualist and consumerist society. Given these changes, I believe that the reformed commitment to a corporate and public theology of ministry remains a worthy one, not least because it guards against the prevailing individualism of contemporary culture and the temptation to reduce the Christian faith to questions of personal salvation. As well as inviting men and women to follow him, Jesus preached good news to the poor and freedom to the oppressed and at a time of important new political initiatives in Scotland, it will be more important than ever that the Church's ministry continues to address these matters. The question then becomes what new models of ministry can be developed which remain true to our theological commitment and responsive to contemporary society?

Flexibility and diversity will surely be important characteristics in the future life of the Church with an emphasis on local structures and initiatives. This will have inevitable consequences for many of the old denominational boundaries which have become increasingly irrelevant to the Church's worship and theology and detrimental to its mission. I believe that one key element of this process will be the reform of the traditional parish structure. As a model for ministry it embraced both the corporate and public aspects of ministry that were so important to the reformers. The parish structure has served Scotland's church and people well but new models are now needed to address the realities of life in twenty first century Scotland. The task of developing these new models is one worthy of a reformed and a reforming Church.

[1] John Dowden, *The Medieval Church* p.11

[2] A brief but helpful article on the historical development of the parish system is written by A I Dunlop in *A Dictionary of Scottish Church History and Theology* p.644

[3] J.H.S. Burleigh, *A Church History of Scotland* (London: Oxford University Press, 1960, p.53)

[4] Panel on Doctrine Report to General Assembly of the Church of Scotland (Edinburgh: Saint Andrew Press, 1985, p.144)

[5] Duncan Forrester, *A Dictionary of Scottish Church History and Theology* p.566

[6] David McCrone, *Theology in Scotland: Occas.Paper 2* (St Andrews: St Mary's College, 1997, p.11)

[7] *Ibid.* p.15   [8] *Ibid.* p.16

[9] Committee on the Maintenance of the Ministry Report to the General Assembly of (Edinburgh: Saint Andrew Press, 1998, p15/17)

[10] Robin Gill, *Beyond Decline* (London: SCM 1998)

[11] Gill suggests that in urban communities, where social boundaries are much more likely to be determined by ethnic or cultural factors rather than geographical ones (*ibid.* p.115)

[12] *Ibid.* p.116

[13] Superintendence Committee, Presbytery of Edinburgh, Minutes (Edinburgh: Presbytery Office, July 1993)

[14] Robin Gill, *Ibid.* p.116

[15] Perhaps the "virtual community" of cyberspace might also be another example of a contemporary parish, a place where people meet for business and for pleasure in order to exchange news, views and information?

[16] Committee on Ecumenical Relations, Report to General Assembly (Edinburgh: Saint Andrew Press, 1998, p.23/14)

[17] *Ibid.* p.23/17

[18] *Ibid.* p.23/28

[19] *Ibid.* p.23/21

8   REFORMING INHERITANCE

Ethic, pioneers, Guild and manse

Lorna M. Paterson

"Do bold things in a quiet way"
(Thomas Dunn English in *Betty Zane*[1])

In their volume *Sermons and Battle Hymns: Protestant Popular Culture in Modern Scotland (1990)*,[2] Graham Walker and Tom Gallagher suggest that Scottish Protestants are characterised by "a cultural pride in practical achievement, [a capacity for] rigorous intellectual and theoretical argument, a disposition to self-examination, and a concern for moral issues."

In many ways these characteristics are, arguably, exemplified by the contribution made, from first to last, by the Church of Scotland's women at home and overseas and by the on-going influence and outlook of the Church's women's organisation, the Guild (formerly the Woman's Guild). Moreover, the Protestant ethic, so described, is surely central to the core beliefs and mores of the decent, caring, civilised, modern society which we would wish comtemporary Scotland to become under the guidance of its new Parliament.

The early Church of Scotland laid down the tradition of, in Christopher Harvie's words, "the Presbyterian Buchananite doctrine of limited sovereignty". This view was confirmed in the Report of the Kirk's Church and Nation Committee to the General Assembly of 1989 where there appear these statements:

> Fundamental to the Biblical view of the state embraced by the Reformed theological tradition is the notion of of the legitimate but limited sovreignty of earthly governing authorities within the absolute sovereignty of God in his providential and redemptive rule over human affairs. It is therefore consistent for a Reformed Church and tradition shaped by such a theological understanding to favour a constitutional theory and practice based on the principle of the limited or relative sovreignty of the state. According

>to such a constitutional principle the state's sovreignty is
>not absolute but relative to the fundamental sovereignty
>of God, expressed within human society in fundamental
>law and the sovereignty of a people accountable to their
>Maker.

The Scottish constitutional tradition, in both its secular and religious streams of thought and practice, has consistently favoured just such a "limited" rather than an "absolutist" notion of sovereignty. Historically, this meant that the ruler was seen as subject to the rule of law and consent of the people..... In the Scottish constitutional tradition political sovereignty lay ultimately in the people and not the state.

Many of these "people" who "stepped forth as champions of the reformed cause and doctrine" were women: like Helen Stark of Perth who has the honour of being the only woman martyr of the Scottish Reformation, being drowned for blasphemy in childbirth; or Margaret Stewart, the young highly supportive second wife of John Knox, who married him despite considerable public criticism and hostility, notably from Mary Queen of Scots herself; or the famous Jenny Geddes, the kail-wife who, as her memorial in the Moray Aisle of the High Kirk of Edinburgh (St Giles') testifies, "struck the first blow for freedom of conscience which after a conflict of half a century ended in the establishment of civil and religious liberty": or the Cameronian Isabel Alison who, it was alleged, had "dared publicly to criticise some of the harsh treatment to which Covenanting sympathisers had been subjected"; she and Marion Harvie of Bo'ness, tried for similar offences, were hanged in the Grassmarket of Edinburgh in 1681. The stories of these fearless women and many others are fully recounted by the Revd D.P.Thomson, in his survey *Women of the Scottish Church.*[3]

In the eighteenth and nineteenth centuries we find that Christian women were in "a strange position in relation to a field of (missionary) service." In her account of the varied achievements of the Scottish churches now united in the Church of Scotland: *Vision and Achievement,*[4] Dr Elizabeth Hewat quotes from what she describes as a "pathetic article" in the Missionary Magazine of 1797: "Why," a female reader asks, "are females alone excluded from all ostensible share in these labours of love?" Dr Hewat's feisty response, still pertinent to-day, was, "There is, however, one contribution by women that the Church has never been averse for long to receive, their money.... but the gift of money without responsibility for disbursement or administration cannot for long satisfy adult minds". She goes on to recount that in 1821 there was formed in Lanark a Ladies Auxiliary Society, a forerunner of what was ultimately to become the Women's Foreign Mission of the Church.

At a time when opportunities to participate actively at the cutting edge of the Church's outreach were few, it was the growth of Empire and the spread of the Church's foreign missions that gave many women the opportunity to distinguish themselves and give outstanding service. It was in the Empire and elsewhere overseas that many Scottish churchwomen first developed public reputations in their own right.

There was, for example, the great Annie Small, who after pioneering work among Muslim women and girls in Poona, was forced back to Scotland by ill-health, only to become the first Principal of the Women's Missionary College, St Colm's (now in an exciting new phase as the international centre for the Scottish Churches' World Exchange). There was the redoubtable Mary Slessor of Calabar where, Dr Hewat writes, the position of women was "probably nowhere in the world lower than it was there, before the coming of the missionaries". To that land Mary gave "a life of unique, pioneering service" in which perhaps her most notable achievement was pressing the case for training Africans in industrial work; this led to the founding of the Hope Waddell Institute. Marion Scott Stevenson, the "Beebee Nyamacheki" of Kenya, so-called because that title was supposed to mean "one who possesses many cheques" - others say it means the "thin one" - in 1907 went out to Kikuyu to assist Mrs Minnie Watson with work amongst the women and girls there. In her biography *A Saint in Kenya*[5] written by Mrs H.E. Scott, she is described by the Head of the Alliance High School for boys thus: "her love of Christ and the overwhelming desire to carry out the work He had given her to do amongst the Africans of Kenya were, of course, the source of all her power. Her ability to carry out to the end any piece of work she had once begun, coupled with ability to read character in the teachers whom she chose to help her, and the skill in technique which she developed through her own experience in teaching, were the factors which brought about her success". Then there was Helen Wilson, Bible teacher and nurse, of Ichang in China, whose greatest work, despite nearing retirement, was her care of the 20,000 refugees whom she saw on a visit to Rennie's Mill camp in Hong Kong where she helped to establish a clinic in a small rudimentary bamboo hut, with little equipment. From there the work grew as nurses worked to control the widespread malnutrition and the enormous problems of tuberculosis.[6]

An outstanding woman in the twentieth century, whose neglected story deserves to be told is Mary Bruce of Caithness. Mary was the Lady Superintendent of Buckhaven High School who was persuaded to go out to Kenya to become Principal of the recently founded first secondary school for girls - the Alliance Girls High School at Kikuyu. The pre-independence settler government was not convinced about the value of secondary education for African boys, let alone girls, nor indeed were many of the parents of gifted girls convinced of its value. However, supported by some of the more enlightened civil servants and by the churches, Mary Bruce, with an able young staff, made this school academically an equal to the more famous boys' school. It was here that girls were educated who went on to become Kenya's first civil servants, lawyers, doctors and other leaders in the new Kenya.

All these women and countless others like them were motivated by their Christian faith, nurtured in the Protestant faith of the Church of Scotland.

So too were a multitude of women whose calling was to change the social conditions of women at home rather than abroad. In this category I would highlight Louisa Hope, a promoter of female domestic education and of the training of nurses in the latter part of the Crimean War. She was an evangelical who "during the Disruption crisis, shared her family's prominent commitment to the the Church of Scotland. The Church subsequently became the vehicle through which she advanced many of her educational ideas.... in 1849 the Church called for the creation of female `schools of industry' and in 1852 Louisa Hope played a leading part in the establishment of the Scottish Ladies Association for Promoting Female Industrial Education. This was an influential society, composed largely of wealthy women associated with the Church. Its object was to encourage the instruction of working-class girls in appropriate domestic and industrial skills and Christian beliefs and it sought to persuade upper-class women to promote such a prgramme in their localities." (*New Dictionary of National Biography*).[7]

Two women who also did much to advance women's education, and did so from a Christian conviction borne of the ministry of the great Free St George's Edinburgh, were the sisters Louisa and Flora Stevenson (after whom the Primary School in Comely Bank to-day is named). They were early members of the Ladies' Edinburgh Debating Society which "allowed a group of gifted young women to develop their interests and self-confidence to the point where they, individually and collectively, could make a significant impact on the community of their day" (Dr Tom Begg in his history of Queen Margaret College: *The Excellent Women*).[9] Quoting Josephine Butler he goes on: "The movement for the Higher Education of Women was colouring the horizon during all the earlier years of the Society's life, and the furtherance of the Cause frequently occupied its attention". Louisa and Flora were supporters of the movement for women's suffrage, Louisa being one of the first two women to obtain election to the Edinburgh Parochial Board where, writes Margaret Bryant in *The Unexpected Revolution* "she devoted herself specially to the nursing arrangements in the Poor-house".

At the Debating Society in January 1885, she "criticised the operation of the Poor Law, and "her argument had a strangely modern note". Her particular concern was the dilemma of allowances to deserted wives who were left without any support. Louisa also served on the Board of Managers of Edinburgh Royal Infirmary where a male sceptic, with whom she served, and who had been strongly oppposed to the idea of women on such Boards, had been compelled to change his mind, concluding that "Miss Stevenson was the most useful member the Board had had during all the twenty years he had been a manager". Louisa was a particularly able woman and a sound business and financial manager and she was ideally suited to the duties of Honorary Treasurer of the School (the Edinburgh School of Cookery), a position which she fulfilled for no less than fifteen years. Moreover, she was a gifted public speaker with a "naturally beautiful speaking voice" and she was precisely the kind of woman who could tackle the barriers of prejudice and ignorance while giving rise to the minimum of offence and opposition. Incidentally, it was a committed Christian woman who was the real leader and driving force behind not just the successful establishment of the Edinburgh School but also the movement to establish district nurses to care for poor women in their own homes - Christian Guthrie Wright - from the Scottish Episcopal Church tradition.

While Louisa was busy in these arenas her sister Flora was also making an important contribution to the women's cause by becoming a member of the Edinburgh School Board in 1873 and, eventually, its first female Chairman. She, too, was ahead of her times in advocating a fair balance in the education of boys and girls. In a long

letter to the *Scotsman* in 1876 about the slowness of the Edinburgh
Board to introduce cooking in its schools she observes: "By all means
let the girls of this generation be trained to be good 'house-mothers',
but let it not be forgotten that the well-being of the family depends
equally on the 'house-father'." In 1903 Flora received an LL.D. from
the University of Edinburgh and three years later, Louisa was awarded
a similar doctorate.

Another "household name" whose "faith was built into the fabric
of her life" was the great Elsie Inglis, the distinguished doctor
commemorated in the maternity hospital in Edinburgh which bore
her name until its closure in the early 1990s. Even in the thick of
war, (she led one of the all-female medical units to go to Serbia in the
First World War where her team of Scotswomen were known as
"the little grey partridges"), she always carried her book of daily
devotions as part of her personal survival kit and goes on to describe
how, outwith her war duties, she ran her own practice which included
a small hospice for women; acted as surgeon at the Bruntsfield
Hospital for women; lectured on midwifery and established a medical
school for women. (She was also a founder member of the Scotish
Women's Suffragette Federation.) All these activities, combined with
socialising and regular church attendance meant that each day was
very full.... Elsie's main concern was for the poor families in her care
and she was a dedicated and much-loved doctor, giving practical help
in imaginative and often unconventional ways. For example, a written
prescription might not specify pills but require the patient to eat
regular meals, go to bed early and take an interest in the church![6]

What a champion she would have been to-day for the campaign
on the issue of domestic violence against women! As a young medical
student in Glasgow, after visiting the homes of the poor she wrote,
records her biographer, Margot Lawrence: "...when I have the vote I
shall vote that all men who turn their wives and families out of doors
at eleven o'clock at night, especially when the wife is ill, shall be
horse-whipped. And if they make the excuse that they were tipsy, I
should give them double. They would very soon learn to behave
themselves."[7]

A close friend and associate of Dr Inglis, motivated by the same
Christian conviction, was Dame Helen Mackenzie or, as she was
popularly known, Lady Leslie Mackenzie. Described as "one of the
truly great Scotswomen of the early twentieth century... the work
nearest her heart was that in connection with Public Health", for
which she was appointed CBE and also received an LL.D. from

Edinburgh University. She had a superb record of achievement not only in connection with the health of school children, but also in the promotion of mental health care and rural district nursing. She also promoted women's education, one of her particular campaigns being for the extension of day and evening continuation classes for young women. Her membership of various bodies included the Woman Citizens' Association, "where she stressed the widening opportunities for women and their duties as citizens" (*New Dictionary of National Biography*)[8], the East of Scotland Provincial Committee for the Training of Teachers, governor of both the Royal Institution for Deaf and Dumb Children, and the Royal Scottish National Hospital for the permanent care of the mentally handicapped, and the council of the Edinburgh College of Domestic Science, becoming Chairman of the latter from 1943-45. Her interest in social work, especially the problems of female factory workers, led to her becoming secretary of the industrial section of the National Union of Women Workers and also of the Edinburgh branch of the Industrial Law Committee. Ever a believer in what to-day would be called the "hands-on" approach, Dame Helen was no mere figurehead either.

In 1902, she and her husband, on behalf of the royal commission (Scotland) on physical training, "conducted a pioneering investigation into the physical state of Edinburgh school children. Dame Helen organised the study which involved the examination of 600 children drawn from four schools designed to enable comparisons between middle and working - class areas of the city. She was present while her husband (the first medical inspector of schools at the local government board for Scotland) checked each child and she wrote down his findings. On the basis of their study they projected that almost thirty per cent of children in Edinburgh were severely malnourished".[9] Their work led to a revolution in Scottish schools, including the medical inspection of all children and the provision of free meals for the children of the poor. In a relatively few years ailments such as rickets, scabies, ringworm etc., which had spelt misery for thousands of Scottish children, were almost eliminated.

So far as the Church itself was concerned, perhaps the woman who did most to persuade the General Asembly to recognise the validity of the ordination of women in the Church of Scotland was Mary Levison (née Lusk). A respected theologian, she had to face not only theological opposition to the ordination of women, but also the complex procedural processes of the church courts. Her story of "frequent frustration but ultimately complete success" is fully documented in her book *Wrestling with the Church*.[10] There Mary tells of how, following graduation, she became involved with the work of the Girls' Association whose most "distinctive achievement was the support of our own missionaries, both financially and personally through correspondence and intercessory prayer". From 1948 to 1950 she was its Central President and therefore its representative on the Church's Women's Foreign and Home Mission Committees where she "could not help but be aware that missionaries and deaconesses were needed", these being the two avenues of service which the Church offered to women at that time. Mary had earlier qualified as a Deaconess of the Church of Scotland and it was through the Order of Deaconesses that she gave her main service to the Church although she was, in time, ordained as a minister.

The Order of Deaconesses had been founded in 1887/88 to offer an avenue of service in the Church, specifically for women as part of a woman's movement, by the Revd Dr Archibald Charteris, Professor of New Testament in the University of Edinburgh and Moderator of the General Assembly in 1892. And this brings me to the second section of this essay about the Guild.

Dr Charteris was ahead of his times in recognising that there were "vast untapped resources among the women of the congregations of the Church". In 1887 he was given General Assembly approval for his visionary scheme for the organisation of women's work which was for "the formation of a Woman's Guild to be organised in three grades:

1 The Guild, open to all women engaged in the service of Christ (which is what it still is to-day, with the option, too, that men may now also be members - as a few are);

2 A higher grade of Women Workers in congregations;

3 A still higher grade of Deaconesses (now also open to men and called the Diaconate), trained in an Institution set up for that purpose, and set apart by the Presbytery at a religious service."

The first Deaconess and National President of the Woman's Guild, Lady Grisell Baillie, was "set apart" in 1888.

The full account of the Guild's first hundred years is to be found in *Out of Silence*[11] written by Mamie Magnusson as part of the Centenary celebrations of 1987. That brief, but highly readable, summary of the life and work of the movement shows what a significant force it became for Christ and His Church, involving, at its peak in the 1950s, over 160,000 women in the congregations of the Church. It offered them a marvellous training ground: in public speaking, leading meetings, organising events, giving practical service, offering worship which could be different from the more liturgically focussed worship of a church service, and, above all in understanding and developing their faith, the better to serve the One "Whose we are and Whom we Serve" as the Guild's motto still puts it.

Over the years, as part of its Christian commitment, the Guild became, and still is, an influential body within and beyond the Church. In 1969 it was one of the founding members of the Women's National Commission, a government - funded body set up to advise it on a whole range of matters affecting the lives of women. One of the few Christian women's organisations represented there, the Guild has the privilege of membership to this day and most recently has been represented at the Fourth World Conference on Women, held in Beijing in 1995, and has contributed to the consultations about such current issues as violence against women, the plans for the new initiative for young people: *Millennium Volunteers* and, most importantly, the coming Scottish Parliament.

The Guild is also a part of the Church of Scotland which has not feared to address change and adapt to the times, however unpopular that might have been. The establishment of its Young Wives and Mothers' Groups (now Young Woman's Groups) in the 1950s was a conscious attempt to bring younger women into its membership and address their particular needs. Another innovation which attempted to take account of the more issues-centred interests of younger women, educated in a different way from their mothers and grandmothers, was the introduction at the end of the 1980s of an annual Discussion Topic. The purpose of this was to raise informed awareness of topical issues, to bring a Christian mind to bear on them and to take such practical national and local action as seemed appropriate. Helpful in the preparation of study material for some of these were the Church's own Committee on Church and Nation, its Board of Social Responsibility, the Women's National Commission and the independent Christian "think tank": the Jubilee Centre in Cambridge. In the last decade or so topics covered have included family debt and credit, homelessness, women and poverty, faith and the arts and faith in the family. As an example of action taken I cite the study of homelessness which led the Guild to be a founding supporter of *The Big Issue* in Scotland and to promote and interact with the Bethany and Rock Trusts in Edinburgh; the Scottish Churches Housing Association and Women's Aid centres in various parts of the country.

The Guild's most recent attempts to change and to appeal to a wider spectrum of modern women did not command universal acceptance and are well documented in the research report into the organisation and its future: *20:20 Vision*[12] by Jane Gray. The slight change in name and more flexible structures outlined in a revised Constitution, which the General Assembly of 1997 approved, while not going far enough for some, signalled that change is very much a part of the Guild's continuing agenda.

Many women would say that they owe much of their own personal, cultural and intellectual development and growth in faith to their membership of the Guild. Significantly, several of the Guild's local and national leaders went on to become elders, and, in a few instances, ministers of the Church of Scotland but the vast majority of its members saw the Guild as giving them a role and an avenue of service to the Church rather than ordination to its courts. The projects for which, over the years since 1969, the Guild has raised over £1m, have engendered in members an awareness of the wider work of the church which is second to none, an understanding of the wide scope of the work of the Church, a concern for a whole range of issues which are approached from a sense of Christian compassion and an unrivalled commitment to the Church and, fundamentally, to its King and Head, Jesus Christ.

Without exception, the Guild's National Presidents (now Conveners) were, and still are, able, committed women of strong Christian character derived from a rich devotional life, and with gifted leadership skills. To these inspiring women the Church of Scotland owes more than it realises. Their stories (until 1987) are well summarised by Mamie Magnusson (and perhaps the decade since then will also one day be written up). However, I hope none will take offence if I single out for particular mention, because of her relevance in the context of this esssay, Maidie Hart from Bridge of Weir and ultimately, Edinburgh and Dirleton. From the "indefatiguable vigour and intellectual drive of her presidency" in the Guild Maidie gave further service to the Church in a variety of ways, most notably as a delegate to the fifth Assembly of the World Council of Churches in Nairobi. But the significant factor for this article is that in 1977 she founded the Scottish Convention of Women, which drew together in common purpose women from a wide range of organisations, or none, from across Scotland. Although now defunct, SCOW provided the seeds of the new Women in Scotland Forum.

Many of the women who came to leadership in the Guild were, almost inevitably, the wives of ministers or "ladies of the manse" as the traditional description has it. Their influence, indeed the influence of the Scottish manse, is something that also deserves attention.

I am privileged to write from personal experience on this subject. As the daughter and grand-daughter of ministers and now the wife of one, my whole life has been spent in a manse and looking back down sixty years I can truthfully say that I would not have had it otherwise!

Despite the frustrations of (until now) living in large, cold houses, of scrimping and scraping to make ends meet, of a childhood in which clothes were mostly home-made or "hand-me-downs" and of having various "labels" attached to us because of the expectations of other people, "the manse" gave me the kind of background which I now see is priceless. My father's ministerial training was in the Cowcaddens of Glasgow during the "hungry thirties" and I have lived in the very different manses of Uyeasound, Shetland (where I was born), Old Kilpatrick (during the first part of the Second World War), Tain, Alford, Kippen, the chaplaincy of the then new University of Stirling and now in association with the great church of St Michael's, Linlithgow.

It was in the manse that I learned early about the rich diversity of the human condition and the wide variety of people's needs, developing a strong social consciousness in the process. People will argue, quite rightly, that these things can be learned anywhere but I do believe that we were given a special experience through our manse life and I know other "children of the manse" who feel the same. The current Chancellor of the Exchequer, Gordon Brown (whose father was my grandfather's last Assistant in St Mary's Govan) once described how being brought up in a manse in Kirkcaldy shaped his future in politics. "Parishioners would come to my father for help. They were people suffering bereavement or poverty - at that time the textile and coal industries were falling away."

Lord Steel of Aikwood quotes his father, the Very Revd Dr David Steel, in his autobigraphy *Against Goliath, p.13* as saying something similar: "A manse child has a considerable advantage over others in that he (and she) meets all kinds of people from all strata of society in the manse. He might be meeting the Lord Lieutenant one minute and a miner the next and he's taught to treat all people automatically the same way. Manse society is a very democratic society."

In my childhood home we learned early that other people always came first: from the evacuees from near-by Inver, far-away Czechoslovakia and different parts of England, who shared it from 1942 to 1946, to the local parishioners who had first claims. Always there were also countless visitors, both those "passing through" and those who stayed for longer spells, some of them to be nursed to their graves by my remarkable mother in an age when nursing homes and hospitals were simply not available in the quantity of to-day. During the war years the house seemed to be bursting at the seams for at times there seemed to be families in every room. It was enriching to be touched by the lives of all sorts of people -"gentle and semple", as my father described them. Three little cameos from his book *Looking Back - A set of Recollections,* published privately for the family in 1984, may serve to illustrate what I mean.

In 1948 one of our guests was the Moderator of the General Assembly, the Very Revd Dr Alexander Macdonald (his son, Donald, was to be my father's successor in Kippen in 1975) who stayed with us during the eight days of his visit to the Presbytery of Tain. My oldest brother, then nine, had been listening intently to a conversation, in kindly terms, between the Moderator and my father about the Free Church of Scotland. In a moment of silence, John piped up: "Please, Dr Macdonald, if we went to the Free Church would we get in for nothing?" "No, sonny," the Moderator replied, laughing. "We'd pay more!" and he went on to explain how the Free Church depended on the givings of the people alone, while the Church of Scotland had various other sources from which to draw revenue." Our first lesson in church history and politics had been given!

A visitor of a different sort was Lord Gibson, Chairman of the Scottish Land Court and a notable Baptist layman. On circuit in the Scottish Highlands, he attended the morning service in Tain on a Sunday when my father, being unwell, was not preaching. However, my ever hospitable mother, with no realisation of who he was and hearing that he was alone in one of the local hotels, invited him to supper in the evening. When she reached home, she discovered that her tins were emptier than expected and, Sabbath or no, she had therefore to bake something which she dredged up from what she had in her cupboard - mainly flour, breakfast cereal, coconut, condensed milk and butter. "In due course," writes my father, the worthy Lord polished off eleven of these" - my brothers were counting - "a great tribute indeed to their baker, but a disappointment to the children who enjoyed them too and were hoping for more after all had left the table." Ever afterwards these cakes were known as "Gibson Cakes" and, more importantly, we had learned that noble Lords are human beings with simple tastes.

My father served as Town Councillor in Tain for three years. The most controversial issue at every Council meeting in those post-war years was housing and the day after the meeting our telephone and door-bells rang with calls asking "Who got these houses?" Then would follow "an argument beginning `I was more entitled to one than so and so' to which [my father] tried to respond with long-suffering patience, courtesy and explanation of the system of allocation." He was the only one of the fifteen councillors who was so questioned and it was the issue of housing which made him withdraw from the Council at the next election. He writes: "I suppose it was a kind of compliment to the minister, from whom they knew they would receive civility and patience." Episodes like this made me eager to do something for people, although more via the church and Guiding rather than politics. However, it may have been part of my middle brother's motivation in standing twice for Parliament in the 1970s and having particular involvements in Scottish housing in the 80s. Like Gordon Brown our political consciences had been aroused!

In my own generation concern for people expressed through involvement in politics rather than the Church, as it might have been in a previous age, has brought several "sons of the Scottish manse" (and, for all I know, daughters, although I have not yet found any!) to the political arena. Notable among these, in addition to the two mentioned above, are Lord Mackay of Drumadoon (son of the Revd Donald Mackay late of Greenbank Parish Church in Edinburgh), Douglas Alexander (a son of the manse of Bishopton) and Lord Fraser of Carmyllie whose father was a distinguished missionary in what is now Zambia.

As in our own family, where two of us are committed Christians and two are not yet persuaded, some of these men are motivated by Christian conviction and others are not. I suggest that their childhood setting was a significant influence on their later work, offering them, as it did our family, a knowledge of the Scriptures, teaching in the Christian faith, examples of public service, opportunities to meet with a wide cross-section of the population, a healthy inquisitiveness, deeply interesting conversation, the value of reading, a rich cultural heritage, awareness of needs and of the disadvantaged and a desire to challenge and question beliefs and attitudes, the better, it was hoped, to be of service.

I suggest also, however, that valuable as the contribution of these men is, perhaps even more valuable in the lives of ordinary people is the contribution and influence of countless ministers' wives who, with their husbands, served communities the length and breadth of Scotland. Sometimes described as "unpaid Assistants", the work they did is incalculable and will never be fully known.

There was a down-side, too, however, to life in the manse. People's expectations were sometimes unfair, in that they regarded the offspring of ministers to be either paragons of heavenly virtue or wimpish or both. I recall vividly the day when a righteous woman in our parish rang the door bell to enquire if my parents were aware that one of my brothers was smoking on the school bus! "Yes!" the astonished woman was told. In our family some of us, understandably, rebelled against the expected *status quo* and expressed our rebellion in various ways. For my mother, as a daughter of the manse, and two of my brothers, sport, for example, became the great "god" for whom excellence must be achieved and strength developed. Scripture shows, however, that rebellion can be part of growth, as can learning to forgive - a word often heard in our manse training - and training in standards.

In her chapter on *Protestantism and Gender* in *Sermons and Battle Hymns*,[14] Kay Carmichael describes how the standards (of household and family management) were "normally set by the Protestant women. For reasons I as a child did not understand, their houses were better furnished, tidier, their brasses shone more brightly, even their washing seemed to hang out on the line in more organised ways. In their persons they were better dressed, the aprons they wore to do their housework never seemed to get dirty, their hair was always neat and tidy, their husband's dinner always ready on the table when he came home from work. Most important, they never, ever, seemed to get into debt."

These reflections echo part of my manse up-bringing - except that about houses being "better furnished"! Standards were inculcated in us which remain to this day, although they may not always be achieved in the stress and rush of modern living. The Biblical injunction "To whom much (perhaps not in a material sense) is given, of him much shall be required" underpinned these standards. For example, it was my job, in later childhood, to see that the brasses, especially those at the front door, "shone brightly" and we were all trained not to get into debt, my father being the sort who paid all bills almost the day they arrived, no matter how hard that might be for him on a minimum stipend. Standards of integrity, justice and fairness were also "dinned into" us, as was the need to work hard and act responsibly, and these remain to this day even when misfortune strikes.

Kay Carmichael states that she "didn't realise that she was watching the Protestant ethic.... alive and well and functioning". Perhaps I was, too, although I certainly did not appreciate that at the time. But our imperceptible training was far from dull and my recollections are of growing up in a home where there was much fun and laughter as we learned with Kipling to take "delight in simple things", to argue constructively and to debate a range of issues. Mealtimes were elongated by much lively discussion, particularly as we grew up and we had to learn to listen with respect to people from all walks of life as well!

We did not have family worship in our manse, partly because of my mother's unhappy experience of having her sporting activities curtailed by lengthy morning prayers and partly because it was difficult to find a time when we would be all together for long enough to do something worthwhile. But grace was always said at meals, we were early taught prayers we could use on our own and the Bible stories came alive in my father's telling of them to us round the fire with great dramatic effect for he was a brilliant raconteur. We therefore grew up very much in the *atmosphere* of the faith and something of that atmosphere must have been evident in our home for visitors frequently commented on it.

So what does all this amount to? I have been at the hard edge of the working church, living it in manses and working for the Church of Scotland Guild - and have been immeasurably enriched in the process. But the influences which have touched my life have filtered down through society in the lives and work of countless Scots, both in manses and among the laity of the Church. The contribution which women have made from first to last in imparting our Christian values is, to a great extent, responsible for the Christian tradition which has shaped Scotland. Despite the sense we sometimes have that our world is falling apart and standards of social and moral conduct are declining in the increasing secularism of the modern world, nevertheless that fundamental Scottish tradition enables me to look forward with some confidence to a future in the new Scotland. In his sermon: *Today's Christian Duty* published in *A Time To Serve*,[15] Dr John Brown, Gordon's father, says: "Let us never underestimate the influence of lives that have been renewed and transformed by the Gospel. It is Christian living that is the strongest evidence for Christianity and the most powerful influence on its behalf."

Parliaments may come, administrations may go, but the Kingdom of God is eternal.

[1]   When greater perils men environ
       Then women show a front of iron;
       And, gentle in their manner, they
       Do bold things in a quiet way.
          (Thomas Dunn English in *Betty Zane*)

[2]   Graham Walker and Tom Gallagher, *Sermons and Battle Hymns: Protestant Popular Culture in Modern Scotland* (1990) - essay by Christopher Harvie on *The Covenanting Tradition*.

[3]   The Revd D.P. Thomson, *Women of the Scottish Church* (1975)

[4]   Elizabeth G.K. Hewat, *Vision and Achievement 1796 - 1956* (1960)

[5]   Mrs H.E. Scott, *A Saint in Kenya - the life of Marion Scott Stevenson* (1932)

[6]   Mary Sherrard (ed.), *Women of Faith* - sections on Helen Wilson and Elsie Inglis by Ruth Forbes (1993)

[7]   Angela Cran and James Robertson (ed.), *Dictionary of Scottish Quotations* (1996)

[8]   *New Dictionary of National Biography* (publication pending)

[9]   Tom Begg, *The Excellent Women* (1994)

[10]   Mary Levison, *Wrestling With The Church* (1992)

[11]   Mamie Magnusson, *Out of Silence* (1987)

[12]   Jane Gray, *20:20 Vision* (1997)

[13]   David Steel, *Against Goliath* (1989)

[14]   Graham Walker and Tom Gallagher, *op. cit.* - essay by Kay Carmichael on *Protestantism and Gender*

[15]   John E. Brown, *A Time to Serve - a collection of Sunday Sermons* (1994) No. 16 "Today's Christian Duty"

9   THE BURNING ROSEBUSH

Africa, ecumenism and country parishes

Catherine Hepburn

It was at a pastoral care and counselling course I attended in the early years of my ministry that I first encountered the rosebush meditation. Guiding us into a state of relaxation the leader invited each participant to imagine his or herself as a rosebush. "A rosebush?! No way!" But such is the grace of God's sense of humour, as I closed my reluctant eyes I found that I was indeed a rosebush with a clear sense of where and how I was growing. "Where" was the front garden of the first home I remember, the Manse at Mulanje, in the land of my birth then known on the pink map of Empire in Central East Africa as Nyasaland, and now in independence is called Malawi. "How" was with roots deep, easy and at home in the warm red soil, with branches blossoming well and freely in the gracious sunshine under a spacious blue heaven; and the whole bush ablaze with roses.

It was a lovely gift of a meditation that has ever after alerted me to the understanding that my deepest sense of God is rooted in my earliest experience of life and faith and church in Africa.

As a person (and as a parson) I am a daughter of the missionfield of the church and in particular of the Church of Scotland. This fundamental fact of my life has been a source of both joy and pain. It is highlighted every time I am asked where I come from or where I belong.

The answer is complicated: I belong and I don't belong. I am Scottish but Africa is the continent of my birth and baptism. I'm a member and minister of the Church of Scotland but my first experiences of worship and church life were within the welcoming shade of her daughter church, the Church of Central Africa Presbyterian. I ask the questioners how far back they want me to go and in many a children's address and sermon I have traced my lifeline back through the Gospel mustard seed tree to its Jesus root.

> Again Jesus said, "What shall we say the kingdom of God
> is like, or what parable shall we use to describe it? It is like
> a mustard seed, which is the smallest seed you plant in the
> ground. Yet when planted, it grows and becomes the largest
> of all garden plants, with such big branches that the birds
> of the air can perch in its shade." Mark 4:30-32 (NIV)

At the centre there is Jesus, the single seed that falls to the ground
and dies to rise again, and around him Peter and Mary of Magdala
and the rest of the first disciples, the first flowering of the new
community of women and men living the new relationship of God's
love. The Gospel tree, blazing with the light of faith, springs up; the
church grows. St Paul (1st century A.D.) travelled widely, preached
powerfully and brought many into the light of Christ that once
blinded him, as he grafted on the Gentiles to the Gospel tree growing
across the Roman Empire. A Hungarian Roman soldier in France,
Martin (4th century) met Christ in a beggar and found his place in
the light and in the story of the church as a loving and enegetic
evangelist and Bishop of Tours. Story has it that Ninian (4th / 5th
century ?) on his way home to Britain after being consecrated a bishop
in Rome was befriended by Martin in Tours before carrying his
blazing branch to Whithorn, in the South West of Scotland. The
light shone out in that luminous place, Candida Casa, and the younger
British Patrick (c.389-461), abducted from his home in South West
Scotland, discovered the darkness of slavery in Ireland could not
quench it. Returning to Ireland as a free man, bishop and missionary,
Patrick started out on the dangerous task of banishing the snakes of
superstitious ignorance and the darkness of unbelief. Under the
branch of the tree he set burning throughout all Ireland was nurtured
Columba (C.521-597), that "beloved lamp, pure, clear".

In 563 Columba set out on his resurrection pilgrimage and
mission to Scotland, founding a monastic community on Iona that
became the heart of Celtic Christianity and a centre of mission to
Scotland, England and beyond. The call to mission pulsed through
the sap of the Scottish church and down through the centuries bearers
of the light and cultivators of the tree went out into all the world. In
1859 as David Livingstone (1813-1873) explored his way to Lake
Nyasa in Central East Africa he had a vision of a Scottish mission in
that place. The Revd Dr Alexander Hetherwick (1860-1939) in his
book "The Romance of Blantyre" tells the story of how that vision
was realised by the Church of Scotland and the Free Church when
they, in Livingstone's memory, respectively founded the Blantyre

Mission and the Livingstonia Mission in what is now Malawi. From 1885 until 1928 Dr Hetherwick worked in Blantyre Mission. Retiring to Aberdeen, he was Moderator of that Presbytery when it ordained the Revd Stuart Louden whose preaching in Dailly Parish Church, Ayrshire inspired a young teacher to offer herself for the Church of Scotland's work of mission in Africa and later dedicated her as a missionary to teach in Blantyre Mission.

The golden chain of apostolic succession runs through the Reformed tradition; the Church of Scotland provides its share of the living links of the fishing net with which God catches and saves the world; and as the great George MacLeod, founder of the Iona Community, is often quoted as saying: "If you think it's a coincidence, you deserve a dull life!" The tree grows, the light burns and the romance of Blantyre thrived as the Church of Scotland sent out on the same ship to the same place the Ayrshire teacher and a newly ordained minister from Perth. My parents were married in the church of St Michael and all Angels set at the heart of Blantyre Mission. In due course I too arrived on the missionfield and so began my journey in life and faith, rooted in the Church of Scotland to which my parents belonged and yet through the mission of the church, to which I owe my life, aware that this particular tradition is part of an ongoing, growing movement and multi-coloured community of people rooted in Jesus Christ and reaching through the centuries and around the world. Around the apse of St Michael's in Blantyre are the words of Jesus: "My house shall be called of all nations the house of prayer". (Mark 11:17 KJV)

My personal vision of the rosebush, ablaze with blossom, puts me in touch with the gift of my missionary childhood: open-doored and full churches with people free to come in late or go out as the service overruns by an hour or so, breastfed babies and lively children everywhere and welcome - especially when my father with his African colleague baptised 80 babies at the one service, the rhythm of the music and dance, the colours of difference - black white and brown - in the one congregation, the everyday reality of the bigger, extended family, the importance of the personal and the political as discipleship places you firmly in the world and its pain and struggle, a community in which who you are is accepted and what you do matters. Of course there were thorns: times of pain, anxiety and grief; but even my first funeral at the age of six was an experience of deep sorrow set in the perspective of Easter joy as the whole congregation moved to the graveside singing resurrection hymns.

Welcome, warmth, acceptance, shelter and freedom, a space to
live and grow, a life bigger than death: my childhood experience of
the Church of Scotland in Africa gave me first-hand knowledge of
the fulfilment of Jesus' parable and promise: "What shall we say the
kingdom of God is like ....when planted, it grows ... the birds of the
air can perch in its shade." My academic knowledge of Hebrew is
very limited but when I read in *A Theological Word Book of the Bible*,
edited by Alan Richardson, that the Hebrew word for *save* and
salvation in the Old Testament "... is expressed by a word which has
the root meaning to be wide or spacious, to develop without
hindrance and thus, ultimately, to have victory in battle...", I
understand.

The rosebush is my personal entry into the living meaning of
the kingdom parable of the mustard seed. The Gospel tree grows; it
offers salvation shelter to the nations, and its branches flame with
the light of faith. Growth means change. My childhood in Nyasaland
took place at a time of great change for that country - change in the
church as Scottish missionaries laboured to become less that African
collegues might become more and this daughter church grow into
interdependent adulthood; change in the country as it struggled to
move from dependent British Protectorate to independence; drastic
and painful change for our family when the time came to move to
Scotland - a return home for my parents, a going into exile in a foreign
land for myself.

If I view some of the past through rose-tinted spectacles, then
my memories of coming to live in Scotland are seen through a very
dark glass. Instead of vast expanses of sunlight, there was the learning
of the word "dreich". Instead of the excitement of tropical storms,
there was drizzle. Churches kept their doors closed, lively children
were frowned upon and not a baby was to be seen being fed anywhere.
It didn't feel right that congregations were mostly made up of people
who all looked the same with their white skin-colour, and above all
there was that great and solemn affirmation of faith: "We've aye
done it this way!"

Suddenly horizons were no longer wide but narrow. The pulsing
sap of the tree had gone and dead wood seemed to be the new perching
place. Please make allowances for the harsh judgements of a confused
child. There was welcome given, though I found the decent Scottish
reticence and due Presbyterian order with which it was given strange
and unfamiliar. In later years I have pondered the difference climate
makes to culture and faith and the complex relationship between

culture, faith and church. But even as a child I knew the creed "we've aye done it this way" to be not, as it appeared, an expression of faithful tradition but rather a life-restricting and unfaithful lie. My first experiences of the Church of Scotland in Scotland I remember as difficult and restrictive. Settling into my father's first charge in Scotland, it seemed as if his dog-collar enclosed not only his neck but his children too and we were thereby marked as a different order of humanity from others; and being a daughter of the missionfield as well as the manse was only an added cause of suspicion to those of my peer group who had never travelled across Scotland. The missionfield was often not seen as a cutting edge of the chuch's life and work but as second best; as an elderly relative announced with sadly shaking head when my father was ordained for Blantyre Mission: "A first-class degree and he couldn't get a kirk in Scotland!"

There was a tension between the view that regarded the parish as the world, and that which understood the world as the parish. When I overheard my parents say that it was time the African missionaries came to Scotland, I agreed with them. Today I balance the pain of exile with the global horizons the church has given me. However precious any one branch of the tree is, the whole tree matters; and thanks to the Church of Scotland's partnership in mission around the world, missionaries from Africa and elsewhere are coming to Scotland today to nourish our roots and enrich our growth.

If Africa was for me a significant and positive experience of the life and work of the Church of Scotland, so too is ecumenism. As a six year old who didn't know the word "ecumenical", far less its meaning, I yet ventured a toe in the turbulent waters of intercommunion when I made a tray of chocolate fudge to give the Anglican Archdeacon who visited us in Zomba Manse. With immense graciousness and gravity Archdeacon Lacey accepted my sticky offering and insisted on sharing it. I felt accepted; different but equal, free to be who I was aged six as he was himself aged sixty and both of us united in the sharing. As a teenager I often came in the back door of our manse after school to find the local Roman Catholic and Episcopal priests sitting around the kitchen table with my parents planning the next joint Bible study group or Retreat day or who would open whose Sale of Work: different but equal and our differences a gift to each other. I took it for granted that "our church: the Kirk" has its valuable place and giftedness: it is a room in the house of many mansions, it is a branch on the tree, a limb on the body, but the God we worship whom "heav'n cannot hold ... nor earth sustain" (Hymn 178 - *In the bleak midwinter*, by Christina Rossetti) requires at least the whole house, the whole tree, the whole body of Christ; the light is not limited or confined, the Spirit blows where she wills.

Two ecumenical experiences in particular have had a profound effect on my "knowledge and love of God and of his Son Jesus Christ our Lord": Diss and St Beuno's. Taking a year out of my theological studies at New College in Edinburgh, I became a candidate for the ministry of the Church of Scotland and then spent four months working as parish assistant in the Church of England parish of St Mary's, Diss, in Norfolk, learning to chant the psalms, cherish Evensong, tolerate Matins, and appreciate weekly communion.

Diss as a market town is the church centre for many other denominations. In the course of my four months I shared in worship with them all. I clapped my hands with the Assemblies of God and celebrated the sacrament of communion with the Baptists. I was strengthened by the singing of Wesleyan hymns with the Methodists, remembered the great communion of saints with my Roman Catholic sisters and brothers, and thrilled to the tambourines and trumpets of the Salvation Army. I sank gladly into the deep and supportive silence of the Quakers, and felt at home with the United Reformed Church. In each different church and congregation I heard the Word of the Lord and was touched by the grace of God.

The welcome in worship and the warmth of personal contacts in a community large enough to be varied, small enough for people to know each other beyond the circles of separate congregations, ruled out any easy dismissive criticism of any one denomination including my own. I was glad to remain a member of the Church of Scotland but made aware by the other denominations I was privileged to encounter that Christ is a living presence and not a possession, that the church is a body "... and if the whole body were an eye, where would the sense of hearing be? ... the eye cannot say to the hand, "I don't need you!" (1 Corinthians 12:17a, 21a).

There are different traditions of worship and theology, different histories of faith and doctrine and so often these differences painfully divide us and I would not wish to minimise the suffering caused by separation. In Diss I discovered that my own tradition resembled the others, no more and no less, in this truth: in so far as any tradition shares "the living faith of dead people" it is an open door to faith, a living branch of the tree. In so far as each clings to "the dead faith of living people" - "we've aye done it this way" - it is dead wood and a stumbling block. Encountering these other denominations of the church I learned that what - or rather who - we have in common is more fundamental than our differences and these very differences can help us each discern the dead wood from the living tree in our particular branch. Too often difference is used to divide us when in God's good providence it points to the truth that is so much bigger than who we are: "... For we know in part and we prophesy in part, but when perfection comes, the imperfect disappears..." (I Corinthians 13: 9-10). It is a challenge in today's world to cherish the roots and story of who we are, to value our specific place and history while being open to others and to a changing future; to accept that our giftedness does not invalidate the different giftedness of the other.

The Church and the churches have so much potential for showing "the world" how to live in community where one does not have to be a loser for the other to win, nor one member to be demonised as wrong and weak for another to be right and strong, nor unity be understood as uniformity. As a wise father of the church once said: "It's time we got out of our separated flowerpots and bloomed together in God's herbaceous border."

Some years later, at a retreat at St Beuno's Spiritual Centre in North Wales I walked through the pied beauty of Gerald Manley Hopkins' poetry:

Glory be to God for dappled things...
All things counter, original, spare, strange...
He fathers-forth whose beauty is past change;
Praise him.

I was spending 30 days in silent prayer following the Spiritual Exercises of St Ignatius - a form of spirituality no longer confined to the Jesuit order of the Roman Catholic Church but one of its gifts to the wider church and those beyond the church who are seeking to know God in their lives. Never have I worked so hard, cried so bitterly and laughed so much in the space of a single month. This was an intense and intimate journey in the knowledge and love of God mediated in part through forms of worship that confronted me daily with the doctrinal and theological differences between the Roman Catholic and Protestant churches.

As a nine year old, ignorant of the significance of the question from my new classmates: "Are you Catholic or Protestant?" I was astonished (and hurt) to be beaten up in the Edinburgh school playgound when I replied: "I'm a Protestant Catholic." There was mutual incomprehension. As daily mass followed daily mass at St Beuno's I comprehended more fully my baptism into the "one, holy, catholic and apostolic church". I envied some elements of worship and devotion such as an everyday awareness of the communion of saints, while my Protestant roots were strengthened and affirmed as I recognised those elements I could not accept. It was hard work and a lesson I was glad to learn again (and again) that difference does not need to mean division and that the real presence of Christ in communion and community is deeper and wider than the doctrines we do not share. To quote a badge once seen and never forgotten: the heart of God is greater than the mind of any church council. I cherish the discipline and freedom the Church of Scotland gives me in its faith and doctrine to belong to a particular branch of the church and through that belonging to be part of the whole people of God.

Nec Tamen Consumebatur

My most immediate and continuous experience of the life and work of the Church of Scotland is as a Minister of Word and Sacrament in a rural area where I have served for the past seventeen years - first one parish on its own: Gargunnock, and then that parish linked with a second: Kincardine-in-Menteith. What is there to say about a long term ministry in a small, rural congregation? There are the solid joys and lasting treasures: the privilege of being woven into the life and several generations of a family through the blessing of the significant times especially funerals, baptisms, and weddings; a congregation and community small enough to know each other where church and community are clearly still part and parcel of each other.

There are the stresses shared with so many other trades and professions today: on the one hand the short term contract and living with no job security - for the first twelve years of my ministry Gargunnock was a terminable appointment; on the other the expansion of job descriptions to cover the work once done by several people - Gargunnock is now linked with Kincardine-in-Menteith: two churches, two congregations, two parishes. There is an ongoing tension between "keeping the familiar show on the road", while trying to discern the shape of the church's life and work that is faithful obedience to God in this place and community for today's world and tomorrow rather than yesterday.

The other day I conducted the funeral of yet another elderly village worthy, a good, decent, hard-working soul; the kind of man of whom the writer of Ecclesiasticus says: "...they do not hold high rank in the assembly... but they give solidity to the created world... they hold the world in their hands; their worship is in their work..."

"We won't see his like again," was one comment made after the service and it sometimes seems that over the many years that I have been minister of these small rural parishes it has been my duty to celebrate the funeral rites of a dying way of life in the community and the church. The people who lived all their lives in this place, maturing in a community that knew and accepted them "warts and all" are fewer now. Lack of affordable housing for young village people, development, and an influx of people whose centre of work and leisure gravity is elsewhere in town and city have changed the texture of village and country life. This is still a community in which neighbours care, but "I used to know everybody" is a frequent cry. Where once farmers and their workers formed small communities on each of the surrounding farms, now there are fewer and fewer farmers on the land. Seventeen years ago all but one of the Gargunnock church elders was a farmer, now only one of the fourteen elders is a farmer and he is retired.

When I first came to Gargunnock, a brand new minister, I could see traces of what the church had been: the "good old days" of full pews with the church firmly at the centre of village and community life, the glory days that people often use as a yard stick for describing what they would like to see happening now. Now the congregations get smaller, and two parishes share one minister. The community centre has taken over from the church hall and there are so many other choices that people can and do make for their time and talents. As the only church in the community, the importance of the parish church lingers on as people still need and want, in the midst of busy and complicated lives, to celebrate the rites of passage. The church may no longer be overtly the centre of community but church members are to be found participating in every village event and organisation. Many people still look on the village church as their church though that belonging does not entail attendance. In the years of my ministry here I have seen the church change from being the centre of a single circle of community life, to being the centre of a small and decreasing circle of committed members, important for a larger circle, there if needed for many, and completely irrelevant for others.

If no longer the centre, how can we be the heart of the community awaking people to the pulse of God's love in their lives and choices? How can we offer the welcome and shelter of God's salvation space in Jesus Christ? How can the limitations and weaknesses of a small congregation become its gift and opportunities for new life? What needs to change so that we can meet the need for God that doesn't change? The Church of Scotland has many resources to face the dying that leads to resurrection. Its logo and motto are more than an identifying brand but a powerful story of change that leads to life: the bush burns but is not destroyed; "What name shall I tell them?" asks tongue-tied Moses... And God said to Moses, "I AM WHO I AM - I WILL BE WHAT I WILL BE. This is what you are to say to the Israelites: `I AM has sent me to you.'" (Exodus 3).

Our history is one of changing shape as secession and disruption and reunion have lived out the motto of the Reformed church family: Ecclesias reformata semper reformanda - the reformed church always reforming and always requiring to be reformed. We have partnership around the world with churches that are grew from the seeds of mission and now have so much to share with us. There is our partnership in the Action of Churches Together in Scotland (A.C.T.S.) exploring what we can do better together than apart with our sisters and brothers in Christ of other denominations. There is the central commitment to and headship of Jesus Christ that anchors the Church of Scotland and a breadth of theological position around it that gives freedom and variety of movement to this limb of the body, this branch of the living tree.

In the Iona Community, founded by George MacLeod in the living tradition of St Columba, to which I have belonged all the years of my ministry, I have found a space where my rosebush of African mission, the Church of Scotland's burning bush and Jesus' mustard-seed tree of God's kingdom grow together. The prayer for the Iona Community in its daily office is one I pray also for my parishes and the whole church:

> O God, our Father, who gave to your servant Columba the gifts of courage, faith and cheerfulness, and sent people forth from Iona to carry the word of your evangel to every creature, grant, we pray, a like spirit to your church, even at this present time. Further in all things the purpose of our community, that hidden things may be revealed to us, and new ways found to touch the hearts of all. May we preserve with each other sincere charity and peace, and, if it be your holy will, grant that a place of your abiding be continued still to be a sanctuary and a light. Through Jesus Christ our Lord. Amen.

10 THEOLOGICAL AND NATURAL SCIENCE

Thomas F. Torrance

In "reflections on the conceptual interface" of theology and science, Professor Torrance describes the reforming roles of John Philoponos, theologican and scientist in the early Church, and James Clerk Maxwell - a supremely important scientist who was also a great man of faith and devoted Kirk elder. Their work helps explain how "access to God and access to science belong together".

Access to God and access to science considered together, access to scientific understanding of the creation, and access to theological understanding of God, go back to the great theologians and scientists of Alexandria in the first six centuries of the Christian era.

Shortly before the first century scientists arose there who were dissatisfied with trying to understand the world in *a priori* abstract theoretical forms in Platonic, Aristotelian, or Stoic ways. They set about developing a new kind of open inquiry in which they asked positive questions or framed "thought experiments" designed to disclose the nature of the realities into which they inquired. These natural scicnists, called *physikoi*, were sharply criticised by sceptical thinkers of the New Academy like Sextus Empiricus who called them the *dogmatikoi* - not because they were dogmatic in the later sense of that word, but because they were concerned to ask questions that might yield true answers under the positive or dogmatic constraint of nature.[1]

They regarded science as proceeding strictly in accordance with nature, *kata physin*, in order to disclose the actual nature of any reality in question. This was called *dogmatike episteme* or dogmatic science in which scientific thinking was pursued faithfully under the constraint of what the nature of something really is, and allowed the conceptual assent of of our minds to that reality, as it becomes progressively disclosed to us, to determine how we are to think truly of it and express our understanding of it. In this context the terms nature and reality were equivalent. This rigorous scientific method of inquiry was held to apply in every field of scientific knowledge, when an appropriate modality of the reason was developed under the constraint of the specific nature of the object and information it yielded.

In Alexandria that was how scientific theological inquiry concerned with the nature and activity of God was regarded and developed by the great theologians of the ancient Church.[2] They too, especially Cyril of Alexandria, spoke of Christian theology as "dogmatic science", in which they allowed the nature of God, as he has revealed himself to mankind through the reality of his incarnate Word, to govern how they were to think out and give rigorous expression to its truth in faithful conformity to it - that is, strictly in accordance with the nature of God. In the course of that development of dogmatic science it was understandable that theologians and scientists (*theologoi, physikoi*) should influence each other.

That is my concern here, with the way in which access to God through his self-revelation affected access to natural science, and thus in which access of theological science to creation affected access of natural science to God.

It was such a movement of thought that took place when the Fathers of the Church hammered out their basic forms of thought and speech, not only in the literary and philosophical culture of the day but in the midst of the most advanced scientific achievements of the ancient world.

It was in Alexandria particularly that theological and scientific traditions flowed together and theology and science interacted with each other, conceptually, epistemologically and linguistically. Owing to the fact that immense attention was devoted to the doctrines of the incarnation and creation, and of the incarnation within the created order of space and time, a radical transformation in the foundations of knowledge and in cosmological outlook took place. Theology and science began to be pursued together within the same unitary world of space and time so that careful attention had to be given to the whole created order, as it came from God and as it is sustained in his Word or Logos.

It is, above all, I believe to John Philoponos of Alexandria in the sixth century,[3] theologian and physicist, that we must turn if we are to grasp best something of how knowledge of God and knowledge of the cosmos interacted with each other in a very fruitful and utterly astonishing way, one in which, as we now know, the ultimate foundation for all modern empirico-science was laid. It is on that ground, I believe, that we may understand how access to God and access to science belong together and how we may with appropriate reserve speak of science in our day as opening and serving access to God.

Already Christian theologians like Athanasius, Basil, and Cyril had begun to think out the Christian understanding of God and the world in ways which John Philoponos realised had revolutionary implications for classical philosophy and science. Three basic points may be noted:

1   The biblical doctrine of the one God, the creator of all things visible and invisible, called in question Greek polytheism and pluralism, polymorphism, hylomorphism (finding the cause of the universe in matter), and dualism, and demanded a unitary view of the created universe which required a scientific way of knowing that answered to its rational order.

2   The biblical view of the goodness of the creation, reinforced by the doctrine of the incarnation of the eternal Logos or Son of God within the creation, destroyed the idea that sensible and empirical events are not accessible to rational thought, and established instead the reality of the empirical world in the recognition that temporal and sensible realities have a common rationality of a contingent kind, open to scientific investigation and understanding.

3   And the fact that God himself in creating the universe out of nothing has conferred upon it one comprehensive rational order, dependent on his own, had the effect of destroying the Aristotelian and Ptolemaic separation between the sensible and the intelligible worlds, and so between terrestrial and celestial mechanics, and at the same time gave rise to dynamic and relational concepts of space and time as bearers of rational order in the created universe. That was the Christian view of God and the created universe which John Philoponos inherited and set out to develop and defend against Neoplatonic and Aristotelian attacks, and on that basis to deepen and develop scientific and theological understanding of the created order.

Reflection on two major ingredients in this theological inheritance opened up for Philoponos a revolutionary conception of natural science, which then fed back into his incarnational theology giving it a more realistic and dynamic emphasis, not least in respect of the understanding of space and time. These were: (a) the demand of the Judaeo-Christian doctrine of creation *ex nihilo* for a radical rethinking of the classical Greek conceptions of the universe; and (b) the bearing of the distinction between uncreated and created light upon the classical sciences of optics, physics, and dynamics. Both of these had the effect of generating a scientific outlook upon the created order that was congenial and conducive to doctrinal formulation of the Christian faith.

First, the Christian doctrine of creation understood from the perspective of the incarnation of God the Word in space and time.

Alexandria was the great centre where classical science and cosmology had reached their height, but where a stultifying amalgam of Aristotelian and Neoplatonic ideas had come to prevail under the teaching of Proclus. It was there that John Philoponos opened his attack on the pagan ideas of the eternity of the world in his work *De aeternitate mundi contra Proclum*, and followed it up by *De aeternitate mundo contra Aristotelem*, developed in a series of critical commentaries on the the works of Aristotle.[4] In them he set out a philosophico-scientific account of the Christian doctrine of creation out of nothing, and of the unitary universe, with a rejection of epistemological and cosmological dualism which he claimed obstructed scientfic investigation of empirical and cosmological realities.

He demolished Aristotle's notion of the "aither" or the so-called fifth element[5] and with it the myth of eternal cycles and unending time,[6] and throughout advanced a powerful account of the open-structured nature of the universe as freely created by God and endowed with a contingent rational order of its own. Of particular importance for Philoponos was the idea that God created both matter and form out of nothing, and created it in a non-temporal way, while creating time itself along with the world.[7]

Added to these critical scientific and epistemological arguments against Neoplatonists and Aristoteleans, John Philoponos offered a more positive account of the Christian doctrine of creation in the *De opificio mundi*.[8] In it he had in mind Saint Basil's *Homilies on the Hexaemeron*[9] but throughout he was concerned to give scientific expression to the biblical doctrine of creation. Here it becomes clear that it was his distinctively Christian understanding of creation that had opened up for Philoponos the possibility of a genuinely scientific account of the world of space and time, freeing it from the philosophical myths of the Greeks. Here also we see that it was his theological understanding of the contingent rational order of the universe of space and time free from necessity that provided him with access to the actual nature of the universe, and helped him to put forward a genuine scientific understanding of the empirical laws of its order.

Second, the theological distinction between created and uncreated light.

The understanding of God as Light, not just in a symbolic sense, was a primary element in the teaching of Athananius about God as Creator and Logos: God **is** Light.[10] Due largely to the teaching of Saint John, light had early become a primary element in Christian thought in worship and theology alike, particularly as identified with Christ.[11] Like Saint Basil in his Homilies, John Philoponos gave attention to the biblical account in Genesis of creation through the majestic fist of God, including the creation of light: "Let there be light, and there was light." And he distinguished this created light from the uncreated light of the divine Logos.[12] That was a distinction similar to that between creative Spirit and created spirit which became became all-important for Philoponos,[13] for it exercised a major role not only in his theology but in his science, and not only in optics but in dynamics. It had the effect of reinforcing his rejection of the radical dualism in Hellenic philosophy and science between visible and invisible, tangible and intangible realities, and thus between terrestrial and celestial mechanics. All this called in particular for fresh thinking about the physics of light, which he undertook in controversial examination of the teaching of Aristotle, especially as expressed in the *De anima*,[14] which opened the door for something like a dynamic field theory (called *hexis*) of light.[15]

In contrast to Aristotle's static notion of light, Philoponos put forward a conception of light as a real activity. Thus he spoke of light as an immaterial or incorporeal dynamic force, invisible in a medium like air, which moves directionally and continuously at a timeless or unlimited velocity.[16] As Philoponos wrote in his work against Proclus, the movement or speed of light is so fast that it can be said to be "timeless".[17]

The concept of light as incorporeal kinetic activity, which Philoponos called *phostike dynamis*,[18] had far-reaching applications for optics, physics, and dynamics; it involved a new kinetic theory in sharp antithesis to that of Aristotle. What Philoponos did, taking his cue from the kinetic propagation of light, was in fact to propound a new theory of impetus on the analogy between the impetus imparted to a projectile in being hurled and the incorporeal kinetic force or momentum in the movement of light imparted to it by its Creator. Philoponos' light theory and impetus theory together amounted to a radical rejection of Aristotelian physics and mechanics and registered an immense advance in scientific understanding of the universe, approaching that of modern times. This combination of light theory and impetus theory was congenial, as Philoponos realised, to the Christian doctrine of creation out of nothing, for God himself is is the creative source of all matter and form, and all light and energy in the universe.[19] Thus for Philoponos light theory and impetus theory together scientifically reinforced and contributed to the unitary view of heaven and earth, matter and form, space and time, freely created by God Almighty out of nothing, for it was through the eternal Word or Logos incarnate in Jesus Christ, the Light of the world, that he has freely endowed them with their active force (*kinetike dynamis*) and continues to maintain and hold them together in their rational order.

The combination of Philoponos' dynamic and relational theories of light and motion reinforced the open-structured notions of space and time already developed by theologians, and gave rise to a conception of the universe as governed by an internal cohesion (*hexis*) affecting and unifying all activity within it.[20] Thus light theory and impetus theory constituted together a kind of dynamic field theory,[21] anticipating that of James Clerk Maxwell in the nineteenth century. The immediate effect of this was to liberate science from the closed world of Aristotle, nowhere more apparent than in his quantitative notion of space and the immobile limit within which a body is contained,[22] and to replace it with a unified open-structured kind of rational order. The change in the conception of space applies, *mutatis mutandis*, also to Philoponos' relational conception of time in the reciprocal bearing of time and motion upon one another.[23]

All this had the effect of profoundly altering the fundamental conception of the nature of things, and consequently the understanding of scientific inquiry as pursued strictly "in accordance with the nature of things", that is, in accordance with their dynamic nature or natural force. This change towards a radically dynamic and relational conception of the inherent nature and order of the universe carried with it a basic change in the precise meaning and handling of scientific terms. That was nowhere more apparent than in the dynamic conception and meaning of "nature" itself, and of "reality", e.g. in their frequently synonymous relation to one another.

We must not overlook the fact that already in the course of Alexandrian theology, particularly through Athanasius and Cyril, there had come about a steady development in the use of theological terms. Thus in their actual use the Greek terms for nature, being, hypostasis and face (*phusis, ousia, hypostasis, prosopon*) had already been stretched, changed, and developed, so that attention must be given to their actual use in particular contexts rather than to their classical Greek definitions. It was in line with that on-going conceptual, epistemological, and linguistic activity that the changes in the scientific use of terms under Philoponos took place, but the results of his scientific revolution had a feed-back upon Christian theology, giving it a more realistic and dynamic slant, especially in the Alexandrian tradition which I fear the West has not properly appreciated.

That change is nowhere more important than in the use of the expression *mia physis* or one nature to speak of the *mia aletheia* or one truth of the incarnate son of God. It was because that was not recognised by the Aristotelian Establishment in Byzantium that Philoponos was condemned and then anathematised as a monophysite heretic, which had the disastrous effect of condemning and rejecting his revolution in natural science, resulting in its loss for many, many centuries. In fact it was not until the revolutionary change that started with the work of James Clerk Maxwell in the combination of light theory and impetus theory that our modern empirico-theoretical science actually arose.

James Clerk Maxwell was a very devout Christian believer, brought up by a Presbyterian father, who founded Corsock Parish Church in Kirkcudbrightshire, and an Episcopalian mother. He went to school at Edinburgh Academy, studied physics and philosphy at Edinburgh University and then went on to Trinity College, Cambridge. After lecturing at Marischal College, Aberdeen, and King's College, London, he was called back to Trinity College, Cambridge, where he built up the famous Cavendish Laboratory. Like his father, Clerk Maxwell was a devoted churchman and became an elder in Parton Kirk. Even when he lived in England he used to make a point of riding back to Parton during the Communion seasons in order to prepare the parishioners committed to his charge for Holy Communion. It was undoubtedly his Christian commitment and deep evangelical faith which prompted and guided him in working out the conceptual interface between his science and Christian belief. And in bringing together light theory and impetus theory, to which he gave expression in his famous differential equations, he revolutionised natural science, laid the foundation on which empirico-theoretical science has rested ever since, and supplied it with the platform for further advance.

My concern here is not to pursue that but to discuss the fruitful way in which through John Philoponos, theologian and physicist, and James Clerk Maxwell, Christian theology and natural science can bear fruitfully on one another. Clerk Maxwell and John Philoponos did not intrude their theology upon their science, or their science on their theology. However their theological grasp of divine truth opened their eyes to a more realistic understanding of the contingent nature of the world and its distinctive rational order, and exercised a regulative role in their choice and formation of scientific concepts and theories and their explanatory development.

John Philoponos was rather more a theologian than Clerk Maxwell - the dynamic character of his physical science as its developed under the impact of his Christian faith had a remarkable feed-back effect on his theology. He never thought of arguing from the world to the Creator, for that would have presupposed a logically necessary relation between them. No, he regarded the world as created freely by God and endowed with a contingent form of rationality different from God's transcendent Rationality but which, as such, points openly beyond itself to the Creator. That is to say, his Christian theology opened up for him access to science, and his science thus understood opened up for him access to God.

John Philoponos anticipated the kind of empirico-theoretical science in which we engage today on the foundation laid down by James Clerk Maxwell in his epoch-making work, *A Dynamical Theory of the Electromagnetic Field*.[24] It was his concept of the continuous dynamic field that Einstein hailed as the greatest change in the rational structure of science.[25]

What lay behind that change, however, which Einstein did not realise, was Clerk Maxwell's adaptation to physics of his relational way of thinking, which in Scotland went back through Sir William Hamilton and Robert Boyd of Trochrig, and to the kind of onto-

relations expressed in the Christian doctrine of the Holy Trinity in which the relations between the three divine Persons belong to what they really are.[26] Clerk Maxwell's way of thinking out in a non-necessary, non-mechanistic, and non-logical way the dynamic relations of light particles with one another in the magnetic field revealed the kind of access which Christian theology can have to natural science, and thereby also revealed the kind of access on *epistemological grounds* that natural science can have for Christian theology. It is, I believe, in this epistemological perspective, in which we engage in the conceptual interface of theological and natural science, that we may rightly ask questions about the way in which natural science, pursued in this dynamic relational way hand in hand with theology, can open for us today a mode of access to God.

In the rest of this article I want to discuss the way in which we may consider the kind of access in which natural science in relation to theological science may be said to serve access to God. Theologians and scientists live and work within the same empirical world of space and time, which both have to take seriously, when there is inevitably an overlap in their inquiries, and in the modalities of the reason which they develop under pressure from the different realities with which they have to do. How then in our modern era may we think of the access of natural science to God?

Of massive significance, of course, is the concept of *contingence*, contingent reality and contingent order,[27] upon which all our modern science, particularly since Clerk Maxwell and Einstein, is based.[28] As we have already noted it was the biblical concept of creation *ex nihilo* radicalised by Christian theology that made empirical science rationally possible and indeed gave rise to its early beginnings. By contingence is meant that the whole universe of matter and form was freely created by God and endowed with a rationality of its own utterly distinct from the transcendent reality of God, but dependent or contingent on it. It is a serious error to think of contingence as chance or to equate the contingent with the accidental, but that is what is often being put forward today by scientists, especially in the field of biology. Appeal to chance is a way not to think, but contingence refers to a positive form of rational order which is not self-explicable but points beyond itself to a transcendent ground of order as the ultimate reason for what it is. In the nature of the case contingence is not something that natural science could ever have come up with and cannot explain - and yet all our natural science and the laws of nature which it seeks to formulate have to do with the intrinsically contingent nature of the universe and its contingent form of rationality.

This means that natural science cannot explain itself, and that there is no way of arguing from the contingent nature or rationality of the world explored by science to God, for that would presuppose that the world is not contingent but necessary. It cannot be said, therefore that natural science, or the world of nature which it explores and seeks to comprehend, actually gives us access to God. However because the world is contingent in its rational order, by its very nature it points openly beyond itself, and cries out (so to speak) mutely for the Creator. Far from closing access to God, natural science can be an open door to a way of knowing God beyond itself. By the very nature of its contingent rational order, natural science reaches out in its formulation of the laws of nature beyond the boundary of being with non-being, in a tacit semantic reference to some form of "law beyond law", to an ultimate *why* or "transcendent reason" for the laws which it formulates. In virtue of its contingent nature the world is not finally understandable without God.

That was the issue raised by Albert Einstein in his remarkable lecture in Zürich in 1929 on the present state of field theory, when he claimed that science has now reached the point where we cannot remain satisfied with knowing how nature is and how its laws operate, for we want to know why nature is and what it is and not otherwise (*warum die Natur so und nicht anders ist*). He went on to say that to aim at a "logical uniformity" somehow related to God would be a "Promethean" undertaking, but here nevertheless science has to do with the "religious basis of its scientific struggle" (*die religiöse Basis des wissenschaftlichen Bemühens*).[29] That is to say, there is no way by which science by itself can penetrate into the ultimate core of nature's secrets - there can be no ultimate justification for the laws of nature except on a transcendent basis. Expressed otherwise, the concept of order which science assumes and with which it operates is not open to scientific demonstration, for order has to be assumed in any proof or disproof. Belief in order is a *sine qua non* for science, as indeed for all rational thought. Einstein's discussion of unified field theory certainly indicated that he had abandoned a positivistic notion of science, but he declined to press on with the question "why" with a view to clarifying understanding of the ultimate ground of rational order on which the laws of nature rest and from which they derive their unity. Instead he went on trying to find a solution to a unified field-theory through mathematical calculations and failed. The mathematical texture of the universe which fascinated Einstein is a very important one to which I shall return shortly.

Meanwhile let me ask: what are we to make of the role of a so-called "natural theology"? To answer that question scientifically today two points need to be considered. First, we have to take seriously the notion of "dogmatic science" developed by scientists and theologians alike in the early Christian era. Second, we have to examine the epistemological implications of general relativity theory in our own times.

In rigorous science we pursue inquiry in any field in such a way that we allow the nature of the field or the nature of the object to govern how we know it, think about it, formulate knowledge of it, and how we verify that knowledge. That applies equally to natural science and to theological science, in each of which we develop a modality of the reason appropriate to the specific nature of the object. The modality of the reason appropriate to the nature of an inanimate reality is different from what we develop in knowing an animal, and different again from knowing a human person. Here we switch from an impersonal to a personal modality of our reason, but with a person we are not in a position to exercise control over him or her as the object of knowing - a human being is personally other than we are and more profoundly objective, for example, than a rock or a cow, for a person would object to our attempts to control him or her. However, when we turn to inquire of God and seek to know him in accordance with his Nature, there is and must be a radical change in our knowing of him in accordance with his Divine Nature as the Lord God the Creator of our being: we cannot objectify him in the same way.

Thus before God as the object of our knowledge there takes place an "epistemological inversion" of our knowing relation. In knowing God in accordance with his ultimate divine nature we can only know him through his self-revelation and grace, and thus only in the mode of worship, prayer, and adoration in which we respond personally, humbly, and obediently to his divine initiative in making himself known to us as our Creator and Lord. How God can be known must be determined by the way in which he is actually known - that is, through his self-revelation. Here the modality of the human reason undergoes a radical adaptation in accordance with the compelling claims of God's transcendent nature. That is precisely what scientific theology or dogmatic science involves: knowing God strictly in accordance with his nature and in accordance with his truth or reality. And that, in the strictest sense, is natural theology, theology in accordance with the nature of God.

To the second point. Today this way of knowing has been considerably reinforced through the epistemological revolution initiated with general relativity theory in its rejection of dualism, and its finding that empirical and intelligible relations inhere in one another at all levels in nature and in our knowledge of it. This has not a little relevance for traditional natural theology. I refer here to Einstein's own account of this in his 1921 lecture on "Geometry and Experience".[30] With relativity theory he rejected the Newtonian dualism between absolute mathematical space and time and bodies in motion, between geometry and experience, i.e. between theoretical and empirical factors in scientific knowledge. He argued that instead of idealising geometry by detaching it from experience and making it an independent conceptual system which was then used as an external framework within which physical knowledge is to be gained and organised, geometry must be brought into the midst of physics where it changes and becomes a form of natural science indissolubly bound up with physics.

Instead of being swallowed up by physics and disappearing, however, geometry becomes the epistemological structure in the heart of physics, although it is imcomplete without physics. It is in a similar way, I believe, that natural theology is to be rejected as a *praeambula fidei* or an independent conceptual system antecedent to actual knowledge of God, which is then used as an epistemological framework within which to interpret and formulate real or actual empirical knowledge of God, thereby subjecting it to distorting forms of thought. To set aside an "independent" natural theology in that way is demanded by rigorous scientific method, according to which we must allow all our presuppositions and every preconceived framework to be called in question by what is actually disclosed in the process of inquiry. However instead of rejecting natural theology altogether, what we need to do is to transpose it into the material content of theology where, in a changed form, it serves the epistemological structure of our knowledge of God. As such, however, it cannot be used as an external parameter or independent logical structure detached from the actual subject-matter of our knowledge of God. This would be in line with a faithful interpretation of Saint Anselm's *Fides Quaerens Intellectum*[31] and, I believe, with a proper understanding of natural science as it arose under the impact of the Christian doctrine of the contingent rational order of the universe.[32]

Now let us turn to mathematics as the language of the created universe and consider whether a realist co-ordination of mathematics with the rational structures of nature may open up access to God. Mathematics certainly has a remarkable effectiveness helping to disclose and describe the inherent patterns of order in the created universe. In it we elaborate symbolic systems as refined instruments enabling us to extend the range of our understanding of those patterns beyond what we are capable of without them. The significance of mathematical symbolisms, however, is to be found not in the mathematical equations themselves but in their bearing beyond themselves. Mathematics is effective because it belongs to the actual contingent world, and reflects and expresses the patterned intelligibilities embodied in it, even though they cannot be captured in abstract mathematical form. In this event mathematical propositions and equations share with the universe its contingent character and reinforce the way in which as contingent its order points beyond itself altogether.

Let it be stressed that mathematics rigorously used does not lead to a closed necessitarian or self-explanatory system of the world (which lends itself to aprioristic thinking), but to an open contingent universe. Whenever mathematics is intimately correlated with the structures of the empirical universe it operates with open-textured or incomplete symbols, for in rigorous operation it is found to have reference outside its own system which limits the validity of formalisation.

What I wish to stress here in the necesary openness of precise mathematical propositions, which Pascal showed long before when he pointed out that in defining anything in one set of terms we must tacitly assume other terms that remain undefined. Even in the strictest mathematical operations we rely upon informal thought-structures. It is impossible to operate with a set of formally complete mathematical propositions or equations - true and effective mathematical formalisations are incomplete in themslves but are open to completion beyond themselves.

That truth was established in cognate ways by Georg Cantor and Kurt Gödel. Thus, as Gödel demonstrated, in any arithmetical system of sufficient richness there are, and must be, certain propositions that are not capable of proof or disproof within the given system. That is to say, while formal mathematical systems are inconsistent and incomplete in themselves, they are open to completion and are true and consistent only by reference beyond themselves.

Here we have also to take into account the facts established by Alan Turing, the Cambridge mathematician, who demonstrated through an idealised computing machine that there are mathematical functions and intelligible relations in nature that are inherently non-computable, which reinforces the open reference of the contingent nature of the universe and its rational order beyond itself altogether. Thus, as John Barrow has argued, "If the universe is mathematical in some deep sense, then the mysterious undecidabilities demonstrated by Gödel and Turing are part of the fabric of the universe rather than merely products of our minds. They show that even a mathematical universe is more than axioms, more than computation, more than logic - more than mathematicians can know."[33]

I believe that rigorous scientific and mathematical accounts of the universe in space and time have the effect of reinforcing the conception of the universe as an open system of contingent rational order that points beyond itself to a transcendent ground of rationality and order in the Creator. This does not mean that science by itself or on its own independent ground gives us access to God, but that it serves the access to God which he has given us through his Word and Light incarnate in Jesus Christ. It has a very important role in opening up the scientific understanding of the space-time world to God in ways congenial to the Christian faith. Thus the rigorous scientific understanding of the world in accordance with its actual nature and reality, harnessed together with the access to God given in Christian theology, has today a very significant epistemic role in opening the minds of people to faith and trust in God as our Lord and Saviour.

[1]   Sextus Empiricus, *Adversus Dogmatikos*, I, viii-xxix

[2]   See my account of this scientific method in "The Hermeneutics of Clement of Alexandria", *Divine Meaning*, 1994, pp.130-178

[3]   See *The Physical World of Late Antiquity* by Samuel Sambursky, 1962, and *Philoponos and the Rejection of Aristotelian science*, edit. Richard Sorabji, 1987, and John McKenna *The Life-Setting of the Arbiter of John Philoponos*, 1997

[4]   Preserved by Simplicius in *Commentaria in Aristotelem graeca*, vols. 13-17 ed. H. Diels, Berlin 1882-1909. See also *Philoponos against Aristotle on the Eternity of the World*, tr. C. Wildberg, 1987

[5]   Cf. Aristotle, *De Caelo*, 1; and Philoponos, *Contra Proclum* (edit. H. Rabe, 1899) XIII 485-491

[6]   Cf. Aristotle, *Physica* 8.1; Philoponos, *In physica*, Fragment 108 & *Contra Proclum*, I.6-8, XI.12

[7]   Philoponos, *In Physica* 189, & Fragment 73; In *De Caelo*, 136-138; In *Physica*, Fragment 108-126 & 132. Cf. Wildberg op. cit. pp.122ff, 128ff

[8]   Edit. G. Reichardt, Leipzig, 1897

[9]   See my account of this in *The Christian Frame of Mind*, 1989 pp.1-6

[10] See for example *De decretis*, 27, & *Ad Serapionem*, 1.19

[11] See for example the great hymn *phos hilaron* attributed to Gregory the Theologian of Nazianzus

[12] Basil, *Hexaemeron*, VI.2. This was a distinction also found in the West as with St Augustine, *Contra Faustum Manichaeum*, 20.7

[13] *De Opificio Mundi* edit W. Reichardt 1897, Or. II & III, and cf. p.10, 74f & 76ff. See also McKenna op. cit. pp.93ff.

[14] See Sambursky op. cit. pp.110ff.; Walter Böhm, *Johannes Philoponos*, 1978, pp.139ff, 182ff. & 188ff; and Richard Sorabji, *Philoponos and the Rejection of Aristotelan Science*, 1987, pp.26ff.

[15] See Philoponos *In de anima* 438b & 430a. Cf. Böhm op. cit. pp.176ff, 188ff, 195 & 308

[16] See Böhm op. cit. pp.185, 187f., 315f., & 445; also Samnbursky op. cit. p.115

[17] *De aeternitate mundo contra Proclum*, 1.8.22

[18] *Ibid.* 1.8.22

[19] Philoponos, *In de anima*, 330, 21, & 428 b.9

[20] For the use of the word in this way see Philoponos *In de anima* 418b & 430a, and cf. Böhm op. cit., pp.195, 308

[21] Cf. John McKenna op. cit. pp.96ff.

[22] I have discussed this in *Space, Time, and Incarnation*, 1969 & 1997, pp.1-21, and in *Divine Meaning*, 1995, pp.343-373

[23] See Sambursky op. cit. p.96f.

148

[24] Refer to my edition of this work (1982, reprinted 1987) and to my account of his thoughts in *Transformation and Convergence in the Frame of Knowledge*, 1984, ch. 6 pp. 215-242; in *Senso del divino e scienza moderna*, tr. G. Del Re, 1992, pp.317-352; and in *Das Verhältnis zwischen christlichem Glauben und moderner Naturwissenschaft. Die geistesgeschichtliche Bedeutung von James Clerk Maxwell*, 1982.

[25] Albert Einstein, Leopold Infeld, *The Evolution of Physics*, 1938 "Field Relativity", pp.125ff.; also Einstein, *The World as I See It*, pp.156-161; and Einstein's appreciation of Clerk Maxwell pp.29-32 in my edition of *A Dynamical Theory of the Electromagnetic Field*

[26] For that he was evidently indebted to Robert Boyd, *Praelectiones in Ephesios*, 1661, cc. 487 et seq.

[27] I have discussed this at length in *Divine and Contingent Order*, 1981 & 1998

[28] Refer to my contribution to *John Paul II on Science and Religion. Reflections on the New View from Rome*, 1990, pp.105ff.

[29] *Über den gegeenwärtignen Stand der Feld-Theorie*, Festschrift Prof. A. Stodola, Orell Füssli Verlag 1929, p.126f. Also cf. Lanczos's discussion of this in "Rationalism in the Physical World", *Boston Studies in the Philosophy of Science*, Vol. III 1954-56, New York, p.185

[30] *Geometrie und Erfahrung*, Preussische Akademie der Wissenschaften, Sitzungsberichte 1921, pt.1, pp. 123-130

[31] Consult Karl Barth, *Fides quaerens intellectum. Anselms Beweis der Existenz Gottes*, 1931 & 1935; Alexander Broadie, *The Shadow of Scotus*, 1995, p.9ff.

[32] Refer to my discussion "The Transformation of Natural Theology", ch. 4 of *The Ground and Grammar of Theology*, 1980 & 1998, pp.75-109

[33] John Barrow, "The Mathematical Universe", *Natural Science*, May 1989, pp.311

11   THE LIVELINESS O' MITHER TONGUES

Reflections on biblical language, common speech, and the Lorimer New Testament

George Bruce

> It would be no gain whatever for English culture, for the Welsh, Scots, and Irish to become indistinguishable from Englishmen - what would happen, of course, is that we should all become featureless "Britons", at a lower level of culture than that of any of the separate regions. On the contrary, it is great advantage for English culture to be constantly influenced from Scotland, Ireland, and Wales.[1]
> (*Notes towards the Definition of Culture*, T.S. Eliot)

The title is macaronic. Even the greatest masterpieces of translation implicitly acknowledge the homologizing of words of diverse origins, before they become one thing. So it was with the plays of William Shakespeare, and the King James translation of the Bible, by the date of which speech and the written word had been sharpened and enriched. Before the King James translation were Tyndale's Bible and the Geneva Bible. From both much was accepted in the King James version of 1611.

The greatness of the King James or Authorised Version is undeniable. It has entered the minds and possessed the hearts of people world-wide. It would be helped on its way in Scotland by the advocacy of the *First Book of Discipline* (1560) that there should be "a school in every parish". In his essay,"The Commun Buke of the Kirke",[2] David F. Wright comments: "The Scottish Reformation rediscovered the Bible not for liturgical recitation, but for common apprehension of its mind and message." Over the years, from the seventeenth century, the practice of evening family worship with readings from the King James version at its

centre, and the preaching of the Word, modified Scottish speech
in its rhythm and language.

Wordsworth, in his poem *Resolution and independence*,
recognised this effect when he described the speech of the old leech-
gatherer as

....a stately speech; Such as grave Livers do in Scotland use,
Religious men, who give to God and man their dues.

Some 150 years later, as Joseph Macleod, the BBC wartime announcer,
strode forward to shake the hand of the fisherman, James Buchan,
then an old man, he was greeted with the words: "I admire your
speech Mr Macleod", to which Macleod replied: "I admire your
speech, Mr Buchan."

Generations had gone to the making of that speech. It was not
anglicized by James Buchan's regular reading of the Bible, for the
enunciation of the consonants and vowels, the pitches of the voice,
the delivery, though fortified and given grace by the translation,
remained singularly Scottish in effect.

In considering the King James translation the presence of
vernacular expressions in epithets and proverbs, the currency of the
"folk" arising from domestic and work practices, must be taken into
account. In the uses of language this was an adventurous age - new
geographic discoveries meant new words - but their absorption into
a language where there was no disjunction between the root and the
flower was not difficult. From the Jacobean stage in a play by
Shakespeare came the epithet: "There's a divinity that shapes our
ends, rough-hew them how we will."

A matter of 350 years later a hedger in Warwickshire was
overheard to say to his companion: "You rough-hew the ends
and I'll shape them". Nevertheless social stratification developed
and continued in England, less so in Scotland, until the concept
of there being a single correct way of speaking English - standard
English it was called - was nationally accepted, even to the extent
of candidates for posts being rejected because they did not have
the "right" accents.

As a schoolboy in the early 1920's it was brought home to me
that Scots was an inferior means of communication. It was "threeped
down my throat" that "we only speak standard English here" by a
teacher unaware that she was incapable of speaking "standard"
English, and who when in a "teen" would tell us we were gowks and
"eediots", thereby demonstrating the invigorating effects of the Scots

tongue. So we were safe from the affectation of English, spoken by those who sought to climb the social ladder. Of all the writers in the nineteenth century whose style in English showed the deadening and falsifying effect, Sir Walter Scott in his high-falutin vein led the way - the wrong way. Virginia Woolf in her essay on *The Antiquary*[3] contrasts the ineffectiveness of Scott's English with the effectiveness of his Scots. She dismisses Scott's description of ladies and gentlemen:

> They are equally futile; equally impotent; from their poor dried breasts; they squeak; they flutter; and a strong smell of camphor exudes from their poor dried breasts, then with a dismal croaking and cawing they emit the astonishing language of their love-making.... Never was a change more emphatic... He showed us the languor of the fine gentlemen who bored him by the immense vivacity of the common people whom he loved. Images, anecdotes, illustrations drawn from the sea, sky, and earth, race and bubble from their lips. They shoot every thought as it flies, and bring it tumbling to the ground in metaphor. Sometimes it is a phrase - "at the back of a dyke in a wreath o' snaw, or in the wame o' a wave"; sometimes in a proverb - "he'll no can haud down his head to sneeze for fear o' seein' his shoon"; always the dialogue is sharpened and pointed by the use of the Scottish dialect which is at once so homely and so pungent, so colloquial and so passionate, so shrewd and so melancholy into the bargain.

The essay ends: "And he is perhaps the last novelist to practise the great, the Shakespearean art of making people reveal themselves in speech."[4]

Virginia Woolf does not exclude from Scott's greatness passages in English of moment and great percipience and wide perspective, but those which pierce the heart or give a fundamentally comic view are in Scots - that is to say those which the community provided, who spoke (or rather sang) through the ballads. Yet it was this medium which the Kailyarders vulgarised or deadened in their novels and verses. This, however, did not mean that Scots was dead, though its imminent demise was forecast by Lord Cockburn in the 1840's. Even so the question had to be asked - what remained of the tongue by the 1920's and therafter? Education was against its use in the classroom, though it was generally permitted in the playground. The new means of communication, broadcasting - of necessity to reach the greatest number of listeners, especially as spoken through newsreaders - presented an English readily understood, and as an ideal mode of speech. In these circumstances the least that might be expected was an etiolation of Scots speech. Certainly the number of Scots words in common use in Scots speech has diminished, but now in a very different climate of opinion there are other factors to be taken into account.

First there is the idea of communication itself. For facts alone English is adequate, though of course numbers, devoid of being anything other than what they say, may be more useful than words. Again, one must query what is meant by English. In Wichita Falls, Texas, I found myself in conversation with a CPA (Chartered Public Accountant). It was a country voice, and with images from the country. I asked him, with such a speech as he possessed, if he was happy to live in the city. He replied: "I was a cotton-picker in the sun. Now I'm in the shade I'm stayin' here." The nutrition of the imagination that he had gained, brought up a poor white boy on a cotton plantation, had informed his speech. It implied a traditional community behind him to have such a fulfilling expression. How fortunate I was to have had a teacher who imagined she was speaking "standard" English, yet with a routh of Scots words in her head on tap for the appropriate occasion.

It seems to me the invigoration of spoken English is dependent on the existence of communities between which there is a free flow of words, idioms, epithets, without a presumption of superiority. So far from "standard" English being a guarantor of the continuing life of the language, its exclusiveness - had it been successfully imposed - would have resulted in anaemia. Social change, scientific discovery, the mobility of peoples, ended the restriction but not before its imperialism threatend the life of the so-called inferior speech of Scots. Gaelic and Scots were bound for the ghetto.

Gaelic had the advantage over Scots of being a language in itself, not sharing (as Scots does) a common area of speech with English, but it too has suffered, and more strongly than Scots, from the attacks of official policy. Its danger was to retreat into itself and fail to develop its great traditions of poetry and song. It took the genius of Sorley Maclean in the 1940's to free the bonds of Gaelic poetry from its past, yet not to cut it off from its inheritance.

The sentimentality of the Kailyard school boded ill for the future of Scottish literature. Those elements which showed the liveliness of Scottish minds, contradictions and debate, were denied expression. By the 1930's novelists such as Blake, Gibbon, and Gunn, by their invoking significant continuities from our past, bringing into play in their novels the circulation of ideas, reflected more truly the spirit of the nation.

Yet until comparatively recently, despite MacDiarmid's achievement in radical poetry, the impression was general that a radical politics had not found expression in print. Two books by William Donaldson corrected this impression, *Popular Literature in Victorian Scotland* (1986) and *The Language of the People, Scots Prose from the Victorian Revival* (1989). They revealed that so far from Scots avoiding political and social issues, articles, humorous and serious, were meat and drink to *The People's Journal* and *The Aberdeen Weekly Free Press*. William Donaldson begins his article on "The Press and the Vernacular":

> One of the most striking things about the popular press in Victorian Scotland was its readiness to use the language of the people - vernacular Scots. This took place on an extensive scale and in some respects was pioneering, indeed revolutionary, in its implications. A whole new vernacular prose came into being with a range and diversity unknown for centuries.[5]

There was, of course, a wide readership avid for the comment, especially on social change. But this was in the last century, and the readership of the tabloids today would be at a loss in the presence of such writing. Yet when I hearken to the speech about me, throughout the North-East of Scotland, it is not English that I hear; and in view of the favourable climate towards the encouragement of vernacular speech and the character and quality of the written word in Gaelic, Scots, and Scots English, a reappraisal is desirable of where we stand with regard to continuity and possible innovation. Here a few indices can only be touched on. An evidence of the true fulfilment of a language is when one becomes aware that a verbal contribution has been made from all levels of society to the written word. The power house is from those who provide elementary needs, and today this includes technology.

These are as germane to the final art work as are the contributions of those who define and refine statements. Lose one level and the physical properties of the word are lost: lose another and the sharpening of the tool is blunted. Fortunately this matter may be illustrated by focusing on the genius of Hugh MacDiarmid and on the scholarly genius of W.L. Lorimer in his translation of the New Testament.

Before dealing with Lorimer, with regard to the title of this essay, *The Liveliness o' Mither Tongues*, I find it useful to place a translation into English by George Reavey of the first verse of a Russian poem by Boris Pasternak, "Star Swarm", alongside William Soutar's translation of Reavey's English into Scots.[6] First the English translation:

> Stars swarmed. Promontories splashed the sea.
> Salt blinded. Tears were drying up.
> Bedrooms plunged in darkness. Thoughts swarmed.
> The Sphinx listened in the Sahara.

Then the Scots:[7]

> Up and atour the Grampian snaw
> Gaed stern, and owre the sauty links;
> And owre the rocks that runch'd the sea;
> Wa's murl'd in mirk;
> And thochts breeng'd oot o' chinks
> Whaur tears forgat to fa'
> Alane in its Sahara smirl'd the Sphinx.

The aspiration of the English translator is evident, but the language strains after an effect. Admitted, Soutar is the finer poet, but the rough surge of sound belongs to the instrument which the Scots community provided. The effect inheres in the language. It is available to the translator. More unexpectedly, Soutar can venture into areas sentimentalised by the Kailyard and produce a poetry of great delicacy and tenderness. Here is the first verse of *A Volkslied* translated from the German by Odell Shepard:[8]

> I stood in the Maytime meadows
> By roses circled round,
> Where many a fragile blossom
> Was bright upon the ground;
> And as though the roses called them
> And their wild hearts understood,
> The little birds were singing
> In the shadows of the wood.

Fresh and agreeable as is the singing of this verse, a personal note is added in the Soutar version:[9]

> I stude upong a green holt,
> Abune a windy muir,
> Whan the sma' white rose was fa'in
> Doun through the simmer air.

The falling of the petals of the rose mirrors the transience of life. When he wrote the poem - as all good translations must become - he had been bed-fast for three years (1933) and he had looked on changing nature from his bed through a great glass window designed by his father. His poems were much influenced by the ballad tradition, and throughout that tradition there was a purifying of feeling. This poem, and others, link with such ballad lines as,[10]

> O think ye na my heart was sair
> When I laid the moul on his yellow hair
> O think ye na my heart was wae
> When I turned about awa tae gae.

The language of his finer poems was the language he inherited from his people - not that they spoke Scots all the time; but when it is used generations speak through us. When I go North I speak it, not in reminiscence but because it is active in me and my place still resonates with its sound. If we lose this tongue we lose part of our being, and we arc diminished by the loss. It is hard to take account of the fact that during the centenary year of Soutar's birth (1998) no selection of his poems was available in this country, other than those in anthologies. However a bilingual edition of *Seeds in the Wind* - bairn-rhymes written by Soutar - was published in 1998 in Austria in their orginal tongue and in Viennese, with illustrations by Colin Gibson, reproductions of the edition published in 1948.[11] The translations are by Heidelinde Prüger:

It is a little odd, if not humiliating, that Soutar's poems for children can find a market in Austria, presumably principally in schools, and not one here. Is it not high time that concerted efforts should be made to keep such books of high quality and character in print? Should they not belong to the Scottish National Curriculum for schools?

The question may be asked - why Viennese? In some sense the relationship of Viennese to German parallels Scots to English. One is the official language, the other the language of the community.

Also published last year in Frankfurt (in English) was *The Righteousness of Life* by Heidelinde Prüger, its title taken from a Soutar diary. Its publisher states that "taking Soutar's philosophy of the Righteousness of Life as a starting point.... she establishes fully for the first time the width of this Scottish writer's philosophic range."[12]

The matter pertains to the concern of this essay - the keeping alive of a distinctive consciousness of the Scottish nation. Thus the homely is an aspect, as is the intellectual. Without the achievement of Hugh MacDiarmid and of Lorimer in his New Testament translation, Scots was on the way to regression; Scottish poetry, despite many poems of quality, to becoming preoccupied with old models and excluding matters of contemporary debate.

Of MacDiarmid, David Daiches wrote that "Dunbar, Burns, and MacDiarmid are the great Scottish trio. Let pedants wrangle over which of these deserves the precedence; there can be little doubt that MacDiarmid is the greatest miracle."[13]

Well might Professor Daiches be suprised, for the music of the early lyrics - named as "cosmic lyrics" by Kenneth Buthlay - was so strange it might seem the right accompaniment for the astronomical discoveries of our time. In *Prelude to Moon Music* MacDiarmid wrote:

> But wheest! - Whatna music is this,
> While the win's haud their breath?[14]

And in *Moonstruck* (peerieweerie - diminished to a thread of sound; whuds - dashes):

> An' the roarin o' oceans noo
> Is peerieweerie to me:
> Thunner's a tinklin' bell: an Time
> Whuds like a flee....[15]

and in *The Innumerable Christ*:

> An' when the earth's as cauld's the mune
> An' a' its folk are lang syne deid,
> On coontless stars the Babe maun cry
> An' the Crucified maun bleed.[16]

Though there was not a neologism in this poetry, so strange was the apprehension of what indeed was, and is, strange - even to the poet himself - that he published the first of the lyrics anonymously. If anything the mysterious universe of today is more mysterious than it was in the early 1920's when MacDiarmid wrote the poems. He was accused of inventing an artificial Scots language, which was nonsense. He did consult Jamieson's Scots dictionary, as did William Soutar, but he was rooted in Border speech, to the extent that when listening to him speaking English it was difficult to believe that he was not speaking Scots.

On one occasion when giving a talk in Dumfries I was explaining some of the Scots words in the early lyrics, which I thought were not in common use, and for which I presumed MacDiarmid had resorted to the dictionary, when I noticed an elderly member of the audience standing and attempting to draw attention to himself. He explained he had just retired from being a shepherd, his district having been on the hills above Langholm. He then said: "If MacDiarmid did not know these words he must have been deaf. I have known them all my life."

This was one aspect of MacDiarmid's genius. Another is *A Drunk Man Looks at the Thistle*. David Daiches wrote of the poem: "It is not only MacDiarmid's finest sustained performance but also the greatest long poem (or poem-sequence) in Scottish literature and one of the greatest in any literature. It is hardly less than miraculous than in an age when Scottish culture is so confused and adulterated a poem, with this kind of originality, this kind of integrity, and this kind of technical brilliance has been written."[17]

In the poem he puts under scrutiny the hypocrisies, personal, social, and political of the day. There is indignation, even wrath, humour, laughter at human absurdities as witnessed in Scotland. The poem was published in 1926, so we have the expression of one form of genius in the first quarter of the twentieth century, and another in the last quarter, the translation of the New Testament into Scots by W.L. Lorimer.

When Tom Fleming was approached by the director of the Edinburgh International Festival to compose and present a programme of Burns's works, there being no special reason for this, he suggested instead a programme made from MacDiarmid's *A Drunk Man Looks at the Thistle*. It was 1976, the 50th anniversary of publication of the poem. The suggestion was not received with acclaim, for it was believed it would make a loss. Mr Fleming was adamant. It was the first event of the Festival to be sold out. Since then other performances by Tom Fleming of *The Drunk Man* have fared similarly.

When in 1982 Tom Fleming read the whole of St Luke's Gospel in the Lorimer translation to a large congregation in St Andrew's and St George's Church in Edinburgh the attention was complete. The congregation was deeply moved, sometimes to laughter.

On his father's death Robin Lorimer undertook the editing of the translation. In his Introduction he tells how his father's interest in the translation was aroused:

> ....It was while reading the neutral press in 1916 to 1919 that he had first become keenly interested in the problems encountered by linguistic minorities in reviving or developing their language. Before the beginning of the Second World War further study had convinced him that, if Scots were ever to be resuscitated and rehabilitated, two great works must first be produced: a good modern Scots Dicionary and a good modern Scots translation of the New Testament.[18]

Both requirements were under way by 1946 - the dictionary, edited by David Murison, was to be completed in 1976: Lorimer was chairman of its executive council until his death in 1967. He had finished his work on the translation before his death, though the book required an editor.

Finally the question must be answered: What new contribution to understanding the New Testament is made by translating it into Scots? First there is the requirement of telling a tale. In this case the translator depends on the character of the language. The habit of the tale-telling community will provide him or her with a convention which will draw the people together. The portents in this century with the dominance of mass communication, expressed finally in television, pointed strongly to the ending of this means of communal expression, yet the reverse is the case. The story-teller has once again found a place in Scotland. Even the status of Scottish literature, in Gaelic, Scots, and English, has risen, and studies in the subject have burgeoned throughout Europe and the American continent; so the story-tellers have found their way even into educational establishments. He or she will look at the listeners and begin "Ae day ..." So Alex Borrowman began his translation of Chapter 3 of *The Buik o Ruth*:

> Ae day, Ruth's guidmither Naomi said tae her, "Ma dochter,
> Ah suld be blyth gin ye had a guid doonsettin."

This harks back to a Scottish oral tradition of tales passed down through generations, mainly of travelling folk. We feel intimate with the teller of the tale, sensing an intake of breath after the first two words, "Ae day", as the tale gets going. Set alongside this is the King James version rendering:

> Then Naomi her mother in law said unto her, My daughter,
> shall I not seek rest for thee, that it may be well with thee?

The elegance and eloquence of the great King James Version is here less applicable to the expression of Naomi's concern for Ruth than Borrowman's Scots: "Mother in law" has the neutrality of a legal term and nothing more, but "guidmither" conveys that relationship and human warmth. This tradition becomes available to Lorimer.

In the same year as the Borrowman (1979) the Four Gospels and the Revelation were translated into English by Richard Lattimore. In a review in *The New York Review of Books* (July 19, 1979) Frank Kermode described Lattimore as "a translator of very great experience". But whilst the review is generally appreciative, one problem is referred to several times: "....Lattimore may be just a little too smooth.... To me the original sounds astonishingly rugged and its uncouthness powerfully affects my sense of what Mark's Gospel is.... I seem to want more clangour, more roughness."

For the translator into Scots the problem does not exist. Lorimer, indeed, felt the need to justify his creation of a carpenter Jesus who could be rough-spoken, but if the language is anaemic, what vitality will the biblical characters possess? The fault, then, is not in the individual translator but in the condition of the language, just as, to take the reverse case, the achievement of Shakespeare was based on the common speech of the Elizabethan community. There is no cut-off of the supply of sap, so the flourish of the tree benefits, and of course the "lower" social orders were themselves enriched by the benefaction of Shakespeare's plays. This two-way traffic was to end in England as the class-system developed. The stratification resulted in the belief in the superiority of a class speech and the exclusion of a vocabulary and pronunciation not in accord with the rules.

Passage after passage in Lorimer has the imprint of the teller of a tale, one who belonged to the people, and who so identified Jesus. David Ogston, in his *Appreciation of Lorimer*, writes: "If it is not too fanciful a way of putting it, the Word in English became flesh of our flesh in Scots."[19] In the Gospels, in Lorimer's translation, Jesus and the disciples become physical presences. In the King James translation of the retort to Peter's denial of Jesus (Matthew 26:73) is reported: "Surely thou also art one of them; for thy speech betrayeth thee." Lorimer translates the passage (p.55):

> A wee efter, the stauners-by gaed up til him an said, "Ay,
> but ye war sae wi him, tae: your Galilee twang outs ye."

Lorimer does not hesitate to use old and modern Scots but also to use effective words from the shared vocabulary of English, such as "twang", which strikes the ear with force, its resonance reinforced by the abrupt "outs ye". The intensity of the drama is heightened by Peter being depicted in a small space, "sittin furth i the close". The incisive sound penetrates the claustrophobic atmosphere. This is great story-telling. But more was required; more in the realisation of the deeply human that is a potential of our kind. The arrival home of the Prodigal Son is told by Luke in the King James version thus (15:20):

> But when he was yet a great way off, his father saw him, and had compassion and ran, and fell on his neck, and kissed him.

This is beautiful and tender and dignified. Lorimer translated the passage (p.136):

> When he wis ey a lang gate aff, his faither saw him, an a stound o pitie gaed til the hairt o him, and he ran an flang his airms about his craig and kissed him.

"And had compassion" prompts the words dignity and beauty, but there is also a detachment in their refined rhetoric from the object pitied, whereas "a stound o pitie" pierces, and we are intimate with grief. Here Lorimer draws on the oral ballad tradition and also on Robert Henryson. In *The Testament of Cresseid*, smitten with leprosy, Cressida suddenly recognises her former lover, Troilus, as he passed by on horseback.

> Stiffer than steill, there stert ane bitter stound
> Throughout hir hart, and fell doun to the ground.

Henryson in the late fifteenth century, Lorimer in the twentieth, use almost the same phrase; the physical effect of the language survives the centuries. The other side of this coin is in the provision of a language of condemnation. In the impassioned attack on the Pharisees (Matthew 23:13) the Greek presents a good wailing word in *ouia* and the King James version comes near to it in: "But woe unto you scribes and Pharisees, hypocrites! for ye shut up the kingdom of heaven against men." This is strong direct writing. The New English Bible translators, however, recognising that "woe" no longer carries conviction, render the apostrophe thus: "Alas for you lawyers and Phariseees, hypocrites!" The Good News Bible, recognising presumably that "Alas" was simply feeble and was not current speech begins the sentence, "How terrible...". There is apparently no way in English of keeping close to the Greek and communicating the condemnation of the falsity of the Pharisees and doctors of law. Lorimer's translation departs from the Greek text and realises the intention (p.45):

> "Black s' be your faa, Doctors o the Law and Pharisees, hypocrites at ye ar! Ye steik the yett o the Kingdom o Heiven in men's faces; ye gangna in yoursels, and them at seeks in ye hender tae win ben."

The passage begins in imprecation and the power this generates carries into "Ye steik the yett..." Put the gentle "close the door" of English alongside and one knows better the hit of the Scots consonants. This is high drama, and the intensity mounts in the opening phrase "Black s' be your faa" is repeated no less than six times in the verses that follow. The rhetoric in the Authorised Version has a similar affect, but only the Lorimer can stand beside it. The capacity of the Scots tongue here is what might be expected, for imprecation in Scots has travelled without adulteration from the flyting found in William Dunbar's poetry to the stair-heid rammies of today.

Travel throughout Scotland, though pay special attention to Glasgow, and you will find confirmation that the art of the expression of indignation and vilification carries on, especially on the lips of women: admittedly not in the tongue of Lorimer nor in classic Scots, but in an "English" so distinctly Scots in tone, temper, and presentation that it is bonded to the user's community in time present and time past. The country places of Scotland have had their due of admiration, largely because they spoke in Scots with a lacing of English words, but not the townships, and particularly the city of Glasgow. Outstanding in its habilitation has been the work of Tom Leonard as practitioner of verse and as advocate. The novels of James Kelman, abrasive to some at first with their staple of Glasgow vernacular shot through with the life of this extraordinary city, gave new life to the Scottish novel. This was recognised outwith Scotland by the award of the Booker Prize.

More signficant, perhaps, than any literary achievement is the creation of rare phrases and never-say-die quips in circumstances where the human spirit might well be depressed. It finds expression in its own popular art forms, and especially in pantomime.

Pantomime used to be looked down upon: it was not straight theatre. However in January 1958 as producer of the BBC Radio Programme "Arts Review" I appointed John Grierson, the film producer, to review "Mother Goose" at the Alhambra Theatre in Glasgow. For additional comment Professor David Daiches went with him. They returned to the studio vastly entertained and enamoured of the proceedings. The inspiration of the humour was in the performances of Duncan Macrae and Stanley Baxter as plumbers making their way through the sewers of Glasgow, invisible to the audience until they popped up above ground in unexpected places, as in Kelvinside, where they immediately assumed the appropriate style of voice and manners with ironic social comment. Again in the Gorbals of Glasgow - a less salubrious place than now - they became local inhabitants, survivors of bad times, who spoke their minds ripe with Glasgow comment on current affairs. The sketches reached their climax as they emerged in Peking (as it was then called) with gestures of Eastern dance and observations on the human race.

This was Theatre of the Absurd, which words generally refer to a genre of theatre, and which is the title of Martin Esslin's book, which deals mainly with the plays of "Beckett, Adomov, Ionesco, and Genet". Between the low-brow Glasgow pantomime and the puzzling high-brow *Waiting for Godot* by Samuel Beckett there appeared to be an insuperable distance, yet for John Grieve and Walter Carr, inheritors of the style of Glasgow pantomime, it was but a short step. They were born to the parts of the two tramps.

I had seen *Waiting for Godot* in the Royal Lyceum, Edinburgh, in 1956, played by English actors - well done; but this was a different matter in 1985. Then in 1956 about half the audience in the stalls, and they were not many, walked out at the interval. Now in the same theatre, in 1985, the principal actors straight from Glasgow, as members of the Scottish Theatre Company directed for the occasion by Peter Dews, held us to laugh and weep with them and the company from the first word to the last. Why should this be?

First with their Scots accents they gave the play a place. We were in that place. Lost souls they might be, and as the play proceeded we began to recognise that we were not far from that condition. As John Grieve indeterminately wandered to the edge of the stage, to explain to us how horrible it was to be tied to his companion; and his companion, Walter Carr, stood centre-stage simply amazed, the sensation grew that here was lost humanity, vaguely seeking solutions, increasingly giving the impression that the problems and attempted solutions were ours.

In his introduction to his book, *The Theatre of the Absurd*, Martin Esslin quotes Ionesco on Kafka, defending his understanding of the term as follows: "Absurd is that which is devoid of purpose.... Cut off from his religious, metaphysical, and transcendental roots, man is lost; all his actions become senseless, absurd, useless." Yet in the very act of giving flesh to the thesis, Beckett's tramps, in their survival as persons bound by an un-named force to each other, imply a different valuation of life.

In 1984 the Scotish Theatre Company, under its director Tom Fleming, put on stage in Poland Sir David Lindsay's *Ane Satyre of the Thrie Estaitis*, where in contest with companies from Berlin, Warsaw, and Moscow, it won an award. The play speaks out in a more direct way than *Waiting for Godot* against evils in society. It found the Three Estates - the Scottish Parliament - guilty of corruption. The new Scottish Parliament begins its life in the same theatre, the hall of the General Assembly of the Church of Scotland, in which *The Thrie Estaitis* was first presented in this century by Tyrone Guthrie. As an aid to keeping us human we need such theatre and poetry and music. The hope is that this will be recognised.

1   *Notes towards the Definition of Culture*, ch.3. p.50
2   *The Bible in Scottish Life and Literature*, edited by David F. Wright, p.173
3   *Collected Essays by Virginia Woolf*, vol.1, p.140
4   *Ibid.* p.143
5   *The Scoatch Depairtment*, p.35, Popular Literature in Victorian Scotland
6   *Poems in Scots and English* by William Soutar, selected by W.R. Aitken
7   *Ibid.* - Theme and Variation, p.111
8   *Ibid.* p.99
9   *Ibid.* p.114
10 *Ibid.* p.104
11 William Soutar: *Distln im Wind: Seeds in the Wind. Aus dem Scottischen ins Wienerische übertragen von Heidelinde Prüger*
12 *The Righteousness of Life* (1998)

[13] *Hugh MacDiarmid, a Festschrift.* Edited by K.D. Duval and Sydney Goodsir Smith. "The Early Poems", by David Daiches, p.47

[14] *The Complete Poems of Hugh MacDiarmid*, vol 1, p.23

[15] *Ibid.* p.24

[16] *Ibid.* p.32

[17] *Hugh MacDiarmid, a Festschift*, p.46

[18] The New Testament in Scots by W.L. Lorimer. Introduction by the Editor, R.L.C. Lorimer, p.xiv

[19] *The Bible in Scottish Life and Literature. An Appreciation*, p.55

[20] *The Theatre of the Absurd* by Martin Esslin, p.17

12   CROSSING PARLIAMENT SQUARE

Thoughts, musical and theological, on singing and shouting

Ian Mackenzie

You might not expect an essay on the Scottish politico-historical hinterland to begin with opera; but did the unlikely plots of Scottish history ever start, fizzle out, or splutter back into life where expected? I'm starting with singing because it is both an activity and a metaphor.

Singing is not the same as shouting. You could divide the Scottish experience into shouting and singing. Since most of the singing is for rather than against, what this categorisation would be about is the conflict between the for-ness elements in Scottishness, particularly religious Scottishness, and the against elements. In my experience whether singing or shouting wins in Scotland is a close-run thing.

I am not a historian. All those facts! Well, no, it's otherwise, isn't it? The problem is the paucity of facts. What remains is an arbitrary collage of documents, artefacts, and verbal traditions which the historian interprets in order to uncover alleged facts. Lacking these skills, I'm on safest ground if I relate what I know from experience; though I'm presumably as free as anyone else to place an interpretation on it.

Having harvested a father, two grandfathers, four uncles, and a father-in-law who were preachers, not to mention a brother-in-law who still is, I was from an early age prey to pulpit intelligence. Despatches from the sermonic front line reached me continually without any evidence of a "need to know" classification. Indeed, for all I know, it was as I was being delivered into this world that I first heard the dictum, "When in doubt, shout"; though as I do not recall my mother ever subsequently raising her voice, I think it was improbable that she did even at that point of historical importance.

My father did raise his voice in the pulpit. He had to. The Fraserburgh High Kirk of my boyhood was not only high, perched

on a steep hill over the harbour, but long; and if modern amplification
had existed my father would have thought the use of it in worship as
unnecessary as Maria Callas singing Norma through a megaphone.
After I preached in an Aberdeen church before the vacancy committee
of the Muckle Kirk of Peterhead, a Peterhead elder asked me if I
could shout, as the Muckle Kirk was very muckle and had no
microphone.

At my first session meeting in Peterhead, a more diffident elder
conveyed the request of an old lady in his district that I might shout
more quietly as I was frightening her. Between the devil and the
deep blue sea of those two elders I learnt the useful lesson that being
considerably audible is not the same as shouting. Raising one's voice
is a matter of audibility or the rhetorical projection of passion. (One
can sing loudly, yet musically.) Shouting is qualitatively different; it
grates and, like the monotonous beat of heavy metal, doesn't take
long to bore.

If I were to lay end to end all the Scottiish preachers I've heard
loudly boring for God, I'd be a happy man; all these bellowers quiet
at last. But for many of their victims, the only sure way to be rid of
the turbulent vocalisers was themselves to pass away into the quietness
of post-incineration or a space under the ground - though, even then,
could one be sure of one's decomposing parts not being subject to a
final bombardment of ecclesiastical overspeak? I once went to a
Glasgow crematorium to support a BBC technician whose mother
had died. Also present were another colleague and two distant
relatives. The minister screamed his way through the service as if
addressing in a gale the entire population of Scotland spread across
Rannoch Moor. Emotion recollected in tranquillity it was not.
Emotion recollected it was not. Emotion it was not.

So what was it? The accidental result of incompetence? The by-
product of a physical dysfunction? Or the primal exploitation of
power? Yes, power. Which brings us to the new Scottish Parliament.

Will the inhabitants of the upturned boats be shouting (which
upside down in a political gale you could understand) or might they
find it within themselves to sing? For me that is a substantive question;
and it might be so for many Scots, even though they might not put
it like that.

It is ultimately a matter of education, of being civilised. Pavarotti
said singing tenor was "an educated yell". Germaine Greer, glossing
it, described Maria Callas as a educated scream. Will our first home
legislature since the horse-drawn carriage carry not only educated

minds but educated larynxes and ears - in other words the grace to weave harmony and discord, accord and counterpoint, in the music of ideas? Is that really such a bizarre question?

One might insert here a passing note. It's obvious that singing is not confined to any one style. There are as many styles as there are composers and singers. It is possible, therefore, to categorise both Donald Dewar and Alex Salmond as singers, except when they're addressing each other. To be sure, Mr Dewar is not a *lyrical* singer. The noises his mouth makes are not legato, let alone cantabile. The "Ums" which function as bar lines, rests, sforzandos, phrasing-marks, and contrapuntal stretti are more neoclassical Stravinsky than romantic Puccini. But sound, qua sound, is only a physical instrument. It's what you use it for that counts! Whatever the style of a composer, what your ear registers is a connection to the *brain*. And the Dewar brain is capable of song. As is the Salmond brain.

The mechanics of good politics, just as much as of good engineering, are designed to produce singing, not clattering. I know when my car has been well serviced: it sings. We all know when the political machine is not working: it grunts, rattles, clunks, crashes, judders, and as often as not conks out till it can cool off and be restarted. I once saw a singer who shall be absolutely nameless do six rapidly deteriorating record takes of an aria before being sent away to cool off with a whisky. It was unconventional vocal therapy, but it worked. She sailed back and took her top E by storm.

Not, as I've made plain, being a historian, I don't have the expertise to catalogue the arias of the political and ecclesiastical rogues' gallery of the last 300 years and match them to current performers. But there's no need for long lists. We all instinctively recognise our current characters. Dewar, Salmond, Wallace, Rifkind, Lally (I put him in because, like Ben Nevis, he's there). Hopefully the Holyrood Palace of Varieties will be bursting with characters, the more the merrier and the merrier the better. But... Ah, yes, in Scottish affairs there's always a but. And that "but" is at the heart of the shouting or singing choice. Because you can't sing with a "but". A "but" leads to *cantus interruptus*. It's the "buts" that throughout history have sent Scots off to recoup with a dram. The "but" is where our nerve fails, our brain defaults, our heart quivers, our soul punctures. Singing is about breath control. All at the service of emotional freedom. Singing is the soul and body at full stretch. Shouting is a nasty wee activity, throat clenched, diaphragm clenched, brain clenched, fist clenched. Alas and alack, Scotish religion has had its fill of that, and if much of our politics has been infected, should we be surprised? Who learned the rhetoric from whom? God's on my side, so you're damned. Pulpit or Parliament, where's the difference?

That the bad news, The good news is that there's another way of sweet reason. The way of singing logic. The lyricism of rationality. The tune of persuasion, The fugue of close argument. That has always been the best of the Scottish way.

Reflecting on this almost persuades me that I misjudged Donald Dewar over the site of the new Parliament. When Calton Hill was rejected I was - for me - quite angry. My mind, though not my mouth, went into shouting mode. How *could* this educated man do something so plainly wrong, historically, symbolically, theatrically? The chance not of a lifetime but of many lifetimes, of centuries, carelessly trash-canned: new Scottish democracy, citzenship set on a hill; Athens of the North; behold, the mountain of the people. Something so inspirational would transcend lesser squabbles.

But now I think rather than emote; and perhaps thinking is something Mr Dewar does. Is the new Parliament to be a theatre for demagogues or a laboratory for thought? I forget which actor, when asked what he did, said he went out in the evenings and shouted a bit. We'd have enjoyed, I suppose, the spectacle of the members of the Scottish Parliament climbing the hill to a great debating theatre in the sky in order to hurl to the four winds volleys of incandescent imprecations. Wonderful telly, or a day out in the visitors' gallery on a wet day. But there's a danger in political rhetoric. It may be pardonable entertainment in a pulpit, where no vote follows and where no life is directly affected by a consequent decision; but on the floor of a decision-making body it can muddy the waters. Perhaps rather than our new political repertory company (or will it still be the old one?) pretending Calton Hill is Bayreuth and proclaiming "We are the Meistersinger now!", it may be better to play *Peter Grimes* down among the upturned boats. Not that Britten lacks emotion, but there is a waspish grittiness and sense of human limitation underpinning his tragedy which may relate more directly to the Scottish experience.

Unfortunately the new Parliament will convene neither on Calton Hill nor at Holyrood. Nobody is to blame for this, one supposes, but meeting in the Kirk's Assembly Hall is a symbolic muddle. If I withdraw my charge against Donald Dewar for spurning a Sydney Opera House in the sky, I'm still girning a bit about his volte-face over an opening session in Glasgow. All the reasons which now reconcile me to Holyrood argued for the defining opening year of the Parliament being clearly labelled a non-romantic, down-to-earth laboratory for thought and decision in a city which once engineered the Empire. Well, it can't be changed now; but at least one can hope that the first year on the Mound does not slip into a theatrical *folie de grandeur*.

It has been said that meeting in the Assembly Hall will provide a link of continuity between the old and the new - this based on the mantra which has appeared in some corner of a public print every year I can remember, to the effect that the Kirk's General Assembly was the nearest thing we had to a Scottish Parliament. But that's the problem. If the General Assembly was the nearest thing, then only a slight adjustment is required to have the real thing.

But the General Assembly was never in function remotely like a Parliament. It just had some of its theatrical trappings, including the ceremonial links with the *Palace* of Holyrood. Aye, and there's the rub. Instead of the first Parliament in Scotland for three centuries looking like a new democratic instrument for the twenty-first century, its trappings will look similar to those of a religious assembly which has, in one form or another, been meeting throughout these centuries, applauded, cushioned, and choreographed by the Establishment. The television coverage of processions passing up and down the Royal Mile or up and down the Mound between the Palace of Holyroodhouse and the Assembly Hall will be eerily familiar; and there's the symbolic muddle, for this Parliament should not appear familiar. It should - it must - be radically different.

I don't disparage traditional theatre in religion or in politics. Worship is theatre. Preaching is theatre. It is the drama in Old or New Testament stories that has reignited theology (or, sadly, cemented bigotry) down the ages. It is the raw theatre of religious confrontations, from Paul facing Peter with his racism down to the Drumcree stand-off and the three murdered boys contending for the soul of Ulster in July 1998, that has time and again refocused stale minds on primal issues. And what about the primitive theatre of the Covenanters marching up the High Street singing the 124th Psalm while the gutters flowed with blood? Not a pretty image, but one reminding us that the Kingship of Christ was not the title of a sermon or lecture series but in its time a life and death struggle for the title deeds of raw power in Scotland, a theologically crystallised struggle for freedom.

How much of that is myth and how much is factuality is not exactly the point, any more than King Lear fighting in the storm to keep his kingship and his sanity, only to lose his daughter, is factual history - or, come to that, whether Jesus revealing a sovereignty over the cosmos by getting the wind and waves to calm down was a factual precursor to rising from the dead. What is always the issue is how things are perceived, for that is what motivates individuals and kingdoms. What is definitely true about the old 124th Psalm tune is that it would provide as stirring a national anthem as any, of such nobility that Holst borrowed it shamelessly for a church anthem. On the other hand, whether the words of that Psalm in the Scottish Metrical Psalter would find sufficient resonance in devolution as against independence is a moot point: "Even as a bird out of the fowler's snare escapes away, so is our soul set free." One of the truly great musical sounds Scotland has produced from its austere culture is its psalm-singing.

Others will have insights to share about the developing Church-State relationship in a devolved Scotland, though such insights may be undermined by the symbolic obfuscation of the Parliament launching itself in a famous building associated with one particular Presbyterian tradition, albeit the currently Established one.

When I was a theological student living in the New College residence a posse of Soviet students visited Edinburgh University. Some were billeted in our residence. Simultaneously the Scottish Tories were holding their annual conference in the Assembly Hall next door.

The young Soviet apparatchiks nodded understandingly. Yes, it was the same with them: the State tolerated the Church so long as it toed the line. A couple of theological students decided the clearest way to disprove this was to climb on the roof and remove the Conservative banner which had been hung across the Assembly Hall entrance at the head of the well-worn steps. Our Russians were wide-eyed. Would there be executions?

All things pass. The Soviet Union has passed into history. So may the union of Scotland and England. So may the hegemony of the Kirk. What will remain?

Us. Five million souls who need a context and a song to sing. The question I'm highlighting is whether our devolved public speech will degenerate into shoutings and bickerings or sing with intelligence and vision.

The answer is, of course, that one doesn't know. It could go either way. In my small lifetime (as against three centuries) I've seen triviality and malice among politicians and churchmen; and I've seen greatness.

The small-mindedness I've seen and heard would demean me to write and anyone to read, so let me at this crossroads of Scottish State and spirituality celebrate the greatness. There lies our hope. Here are some exemplars like torches, too specific to illuminate a whole historical landscape, yet burning with such intensity as to encourage the belief that we can step forward into the shadows of a politically unsure future.

My Free Kirk grandfather had an obsession all through the Second World War. He kept saying it: education, education, education. The only way to rebuild a shattered Europe after the war would be for all European peoples to be educated into a consensual understanding. Now this was no doddery liberal sentimentalist. For a part of his life he was principal clerk of the Free Church Assembly and successfully fought through the House of Lords the 1911 legislation which won for the Free Church its historical position as the repository of the Reformed tradition. (It was a broader Church then than now.) In the midst of the more apocalyptic battle with the forces of Fascist evil, when all civilised values seemed wrecked, he saw with a steady intelligence that only educated intelligence could restore harmony. Quite a lineage of such believers in education: John Knox, my grandfather, R.A. Butler, David Blunkett; and, I hope we can believe, a Dewar, a Salmond, a Wallace, and some at least of those who will emerge at Holyrood.

My next three examples are famous, at least among those who were there, as I was privileged to be; in the Assembly Hall where the new Parliament is to be born.

When I was a very small boy, for reasons I can't fathom my father took me to the visitors' gallery of the Assembly Hall. John Baillie was presenting his special report on God's Will for our time. That was probably not the title, and I can't remember a word that was said. What I do recall is the overwhelming intensity. My father was exceptionally serious. The hundreds amd hundreds of men in dark clothing were grave. What they were listening to was a not very tall man with a noble face and a Highland lilt talking in what even as a wee person I understood to be a very special kind of music. When twenty years later I heard John Baillie preach and pray and lecture I understood what kind of music it was: it was reason. The musical voice was not the music. The clarity was the music. The logic was the music. The lucidity was the music. The width of the argument was the music. The transparency of the spirit was the music. The humility was the music.

My father and John Baillie came from Gairloch. They were in the same class at Inverness Academy. The music I had heard in public from the one, I was lucky enough to experience privately from the other. I knew the coinage was sound. I'd like to hear the music of that reason in our Parliament.

When George MacLeod famously locked horns with Professor James Pitt-Watson over "The Bomb" the earth moved. George's Götterdämmerung conflagration on Church and Nation Day had become an annual ritual. The contemptible element in the ritual was that after George's Wagnerian music had taken us soaring through the clouds and crashing to doom there would be a moment of traumatised silence, followed by applause for a great performance. Then as night follows day there would be the statutory plod of mediocrity to the microphone to say that of course we were moved by Dr MacLeod's eloquence, but now could we get back to the real world? One May, however, the case against George was put by Pitt-Watson with an intellectual and emotional voltage to match. "Dr MacLeod impales me on the horn of the dilemma which is Hiroshima", shouted Pitt-Watson, wagging his finger. "I impale him on the horn of the dilemma which is Belsen." Ah, but it was not shouting. Or it was educated shouting. It was liturgy groaning in travail; it was opera at full stretch; it was a debate fusing reason and emotion in a molten moment. I wish the new Parliament could give birth to at least an occasional such tournament of blistering reality.

In 1956, at the height of the Suez crisis, the then twice-yearly Commission of the Assembly was holding its day-long meeting. The convener of the Church and Nation Committee was Dr Nevile Davidson of Glasgow Cathedral. His was a safe pair of hands. I once met him in a Glasgow store, and his deft manipulation of the lift buttons was a joy to behold. On this day of crisis, he pressed all the right buttons, gravely informing the Assembly that it was our duty to pray for the Government. One wouldn't expect dissent from such an unremarkable remark. The minister of Glasgow Cathedral had kicked the ball unerringly into an undefended net as wide as the Great Glen. But there was, after all, a defender. Down on the benches something stirred. It was Dr George Gunn, minister of Broughton Place Church; scholar, theologically educated preacher of sermons of magnitude, and so highly regarded as a Church statesman that he was tipped to be the next, or next to the next, Moderator. He marched to the microphone.

"Moderator!", he shouted in his flat Caithness sing-song. If it was not yet clear that he was unchuffed, it would have been a careless observer who would have put a bet on his being chuffed. The Assembly shuddered in delicious anticipation. How safe were these hands? Not at all. He raised one hand. It held a newspaper. It was the (then *Manchester*) *Guardian*. There, in the twinkling of an eye, sank his Moderatorship. *The Scotsman*, The *Glasgow Herald*, possibly the *Telegraph* or *Times* - these were sound organs. What on earth was Gunn doing brandishing a left-wing broadsheet? He told us.

The Government's *raison d'être* for Britain and France sending armed forces to Egypt was to separate the opposing combatants, Israel and Egypt. But the paper Dr Gunn was still waving above his head had a front-page photograph of French and Israeli pilots chatting on the ground. It was apparent proof of collusion. (It was in fact just that: a set-up.)

George Gunn gave an educated yell. "We can't pray for the Government until we know what they are doing." He was shouted down. The Assembly in baying mode is not a pleasant noise. The Moderator that day was Dr Robin Scott of Pont Street. His son Tom went to lunch with him in the New Club immediately afterwards, and Tom told me that afternoon how senior panjandrums had chuckled over their sherries: "That's finished George Gunn for Moderator."

That self-immolation of a proud, lonely Christian man with a brain remains with me as one of the most anguished arias I've heard in public. Despite the flat unattractive voice it was music because it was independent, brave, selfless - and true. It would be nice if the new Parliament threw up more independent spirits like him and fewer self-serving careerists than those who chuckled over their sherries at the political unwisdom of a friend.

The examples I've quoted were either grand operatic moments or significant statements in the symphony of truth. But truth is mined in chamber music also; perhaps more often. I have in my notebooks accounts of many such occasions, mainly during the sixteen years in which I was responsible for the BBC's coverage of the General Assembly on radio and television. As in a Mozart divertimento, Brahms trio, or late Beethoven string quartet, the depth of the utterance was equal to that in any symphony or opera, but the performing figures were not stars. What made these moments elemental was that quiet people sang their song of pain, protest, or prophecy in the face of indifference, incomprehension, contempt, or baying hostility of General Assembly Christians, transmogrified into a mob. Will quiet, modest, truthful men and women be heard in our Parliament?

What passes? What remains?

When I was two years old, my parents took me for a year to Prague, where my father on behalf of the Church of Scotland ministered to a wide English-speaking diaspora. It was there I first learned to speak English; from the exiled daughter of the city architect of St Petersburg. Back in Fraserburgh, over the next few years till 1939, that draughty north-eastern manse with nothing between it and the Arctic played host to a procession of pilgrims from Central Europe, all warning us of the holocaust to come. My grandfather, the one who believed in education, would sit with my father over the wireless to hear the latest news of Hitler's unresisted annexations, and then they'd shake their heads. They saw the war coming, step by step. I had little sense then of being a Scots boy, still less British. That manse had always felt like a part of the wider world because of overseas relatives and a stream of visiting missionaries; but increasingly it felt like a part of Europe, and as Czechoslovakia fell, I felt Hitler's hot breath on my own neck.

Decades later the Salmond doctrine of Scotland in Europe is as new to me as Arthur's Seat; and when Blair and Brown finally dip their toes into monetary union, it will feel like a consummation infinitely postponed.

In the early 1960's, when I worked for the Student Christian Movement, my wife and I attended a European student conference in Prague and were able to look up people my parents had known, and their families. The older generation was miserable. Neither the Dubcek Spring nor its grisly aftermath had happened. The golden Europe that had burnished my parents' lives had gone forever, buried as Prague was that February under uncivilised slush. But the new generation was keeping the faith. We went to an unadvertised evening Communion service. It was packed with young Czech Christians, including soldiers in uniform who hurried in at the last minute and left quickly at the end. Farther north, a year later, I led a students' conference in Lund, and preached in Lund Cathedral about the Cuban crisis, whose angel of death had just passed us by. There was no sense there in Sweden of a detached or neutral society. The students and their tutors were yoked to a European and world view of a future whose structures had to be forged anew under God. I experienced an equal solidarity on a visit to Taizé; then after the Berlin Wall came down I was able to return to Prague to make a film, in golden autumn days, of a people led by a poet emerging into light, the same wonderful people, but fragile, brittle, unsure of their landmark values in the world of a new kind of bright brutality: survival in the market.

As I do not just see it, but have known it, Scottish Christianity owes more to Europe than to England. That isn't a querulous, argumentative, or political statement, merely a factual one. I could have written a quite different affectionate piece about what I personally owe to England and English Christianity. I could have written yet another different piece about my roots in Celtic Christianity, through Highland parents and instinctive pantheism. But the strand of faith that seems immediately relevant to the new Parliament is that broad European river of educated theological intelligence that has over centuries carried forward our religious perspective and bolstered our courage; though the Kirk's connections with the New World and the Third World have never allowed it to rest in a provincial Europeanism.

I finish with two last pictures; one of perspective the other of courage.

As a student, when I grew weary of the dogmatism of the Churches and the demagoguery of the General Assembly, I'd cross Parliament Square and sit for a quiet hour or two in the Court of Appeal. It was pure delight, like slipping into a cool bath on a hot sticky day. Lawyers and judges talked quietly, logically, clearly. Everyone appeared actually to listen to the other. There was no sense of an agenda dictated by ideology. Above all, it was reasonable. The jokes, though not frequent, were worth waiting for, based as they were in a perceived flaw in logic or nuance of language. As criminality was not involved, not much raw emotion intruded. It was civil law. It was civilised. Judgmentalism was absent. What was sought was judiciousness: a sense of perspective. I usually left craving all that quiet reasonableness for my turbo-charged Church.

A few yards across the square was St Giles' where I was for several years assistant organist, and later assistant minister. As if those experiences didn't give me a sufficient perspective on what was going on there, I married the daughter of the then minister, Harry Whitley.

At St Giles' I learned a more fundamental lesson: that reason, however civilised, is not enough. Perspective, however nicely poised, is not enough. Emotion, however deep, is not enough. The story of how Harry Whitley, called from the slums of Glasgow to the highest pulpit in the land, survived the most savage onslaught from several Edinburgh Establishments, including the Law and the Church, both of which I had in so many ways admired, is too complex and multi-layered to insert here. Had I not observed them at first hand I would not have believed the things I saw done and heard said. But I did see and I did hear; and so I did finally face reality. *Civilisation is not enough*. Because we are not, at bottom, reasonable. We're not even always sensible. We're animals with appetites, bent by our brains into a a steep curvature of potential for good amd for evil; most commonly for both. And that's what great music is about: the struggle out of chaos towards redemption. It was such a redemptive process that I observed Harry Whitley bringing to a singing conclusion.

We musn't expect too much from our new Parliament. One lesson from history is that we are indeed sinners. From that proposition the Reformed faith has never deviated. Whether seen in macrocosm in Europe's holocausts, or in microcosm in Scotland's sleaze, the human species is flawed. The elevation of the Parliament building, whether Calton, Holyrood, or Mound is, as Lady Bracknell would say, immaterial. It's the elevation of soul that counts in the end. All we can do, as Matthew Arnold did say, is to go on, on to the bound of the waste, on to the city of God. And on that historic march to pray that one day, however distant, the shouts of *Dies Irae* will be drowned out by the singing of *Pax in Terris*.

Amen, so let it be.

BIBLIOGRAPHICAL POSTSCRIPT

On books vital and books neglected

R.D. Kernohan

I thought of rounding off this book with an impressive bibliography, a device used by authors who know how to mix the books they have actually read with reputedly important books which they have heard of from afar. That didn't seem such a good idea once the contributions came in for the book, with contributors playing by their own rules in citing the sources that mattered to them. It may have been my own fault for not even trying to law down the law in advance, but even if I had tried I don't think any bibliographical law could have been imposed on such different contributions and contributors.

But good bibliographies make good reading. Both as reader and reviewer I have encountered some which made better reading than the works to which they were appended. They certainly make better reading than summings-up by the editors of symposia who have already pitched their ideas into their introductions.

Then the idea occurred to me to let a very subjective sort of bibliography, or bibliographical commentary, take the place of a summing-up. That is why I have selected a handful of books, either because they are exceptionally useful and enlightening, or because they express ideas and experiences that reveal marvellous things in Scotland's past and its potential. I would never suggest that anyone's basic reading about the Reformed style of the universal or catholick Christian faith should consist only or even mainly of Scottish books. But part of our contemporary neglect of our historic faith and achievements involves a neglect of some of our greatest literature.

First, a concession to objectivity, and three reference books. I have always found the British edition of *The New International Dictionary of the Christian Church* edited by J.D. Douglas (Exeter and Grand Rapids, 1974) the best source-book for setting Scottish religion in an international and ecumenical context. The book to keep beside it, a treasury of Scottish religious history and experience, is *The Dictionary of Scottish Church History and Theology* (Edinburgh 1993) initiated by Rutherford House. Many of the concerns I feel about modern Scotland's ignorance of its spiritual and religious history can be be addressed by anyone ready to delve into this remarkable and scholarly "dictionary", which is really an encyclopaedia with major essays as well as brief notes.

The third reference book is the *Handbook to the Revised Church Hymnary* (Oxford 1928), which is some ways has a wider range than its current and now obsolescent successor. Millar Patrick's brief introduction is a mini-classic, though anyone deeply interested in Reformed worship must also seek out his fuller work on the Psalms. Incidentally those who think that Presbyterians are dull dogs might look up another of his great works: *The Scottish Students' Song-Book*.

And so to subjectivity, and to John Knox's *History of the Reformation in Scotland* (various editions, Edinburgh 1949 etc), which is also an autobiography of a sort, although as its admirer Thomas Carlyle said, a "hasty loose production". It shows the great Reformer as a man of his time, context, and controversies. But it also shows his faith and power, and not least his power with words. How much other prose of its era, apart from Cranmer's Prayer Book and the English Bible, stands the rest of time or is even readable today? Knox mingles an astonishly restrained style in places, not least in the famous passage about the galley-slaves' off-shore view of St Andrews, with great fluency and power in others, notably the fascinating dialogues with his devious but determined Queen. And it remains important that we should take the view of Carlyle - and of Knox - that through the imperfections of fallible humanity there shine "the unspeakable mercies of God to this poor realm of Scotland".

For the following century I slip in a mention of John Buchan's *Montrose*, (London 1928). But both the book and the character of its hero, the Covenanter who changed sides, seem to me to raise questions rather than teach the clear lessons that Buchan wanted. I have found a surer place for Buchan later, but his biography of "the Presbyterian Cavalier" is a masterpiece of Scots literature.

Things are far easier after skipping another century to John Galt's *Annals of the Parish* (many editions from 1821). This deceptively simple Ayrshire chronicle, put in the form of an aged minister's account of his life and times in the long reign of George III, is probably too unpretentious to be accounted a great novel but it is a work of considerable art, human sympathy, and insight that conveys better social and religious history than more ponderous books.

Next a dip into what might reasonably be described as the literature of Presbyterian civil war. In fact I began to dip into *The Annals of the Disruption* (Edinburgh 1884) when I found it on the bookshelf of a West Highland holiday house during a wet spell. I could't put it down even when the sun came out.

Although put together long after the event and rather untidy as a book, it marvellously conveys the moods of the great conflict - the high principles, the sacrifice, the bitterness, even the pettiness, for example in its scorn of those waverers who stayed with the Establishment. No book tells so much Scottish history with such passion and directness.

One other item from the age of the Disruption and its most eminent lay publicist: Hugh Miller's "First Impressions of England and its People". Miller, stonemason turned geologist as well as journalist, edited "The Witness", a newspaper of the evangelicals who were to become the Free Kirk. The book appeared in 1846, ten years before Miller's tragic death, but has at least one modern edition (Hawick 1983).

This is a travel book, but one with a difference - or rather two differences. The first is that a good deal of it is about religion; the second that it is a Scots view of England which takes it as a matter of course that the two nations are different in many things, including religious ones, but part of the same political and cultural community. It is a gem of a book. In a completely non-nationalist, pre-nationalist way it assumes and affirms Scottish identity but treats the English as equals as well as friends and partners!

But even the most selective bibliography of the Reformed tradition in Scotland must look farther afield. The most obvious item is David Livingstone's *Missionary Travels and Researches in South Africa* (various editions from London publication in 1857). Livingstone, although both a national and international hero, stands slightly apart from the main Scots missionary tradition: his Reformed background was "Independent", which we would now call Congregationalist, and he went to Africa with the London Missionary Society. He also proved a very independent spirit indeed and became a "loner". Yet no-one better exemplifies the power that was created in Scotland when the Reformed tradition fused with the Evangelical revival.

Something else out of Africa. Henry Drummond is usually remembered for his testimony in *The Greatest Thing in the World* but there is a fascination in his *Tropical Africa* (London 1888), which is about Malawi and adjacent regions. Drummond was one of the most successful Victorians in integrating the advance of scientific knowledge with an evangelical view of the chief ends of humanity. His book is also a corrective to two fashionable views of our time: that we should be ashamed of the British Empire and that imperialism and colonialism can all be lumped together with jingoism.

Robert Louis Stevenson was in many things a rebel against parental and patriarchal Presbyterianism but *Travels with a Donkey in the Cévennes* (many editions since 1878) shows how deeply and positively even a wayward Victorian genius was shaped by his Calvinist heritage. The book is a travel classic. But the passage where Stevenson reacts to an ill-judged and rather disparaging attempt to talk him out of his residual Presbyterianism should strike a chord even today.

I have a special soft spot for books by travellers in the Holy Land, including a forgotten treasure by Norman MacLeod of the Barony - *Eastward* originally serialised his magazine *Good Words* in 1863. To read it is to understand why he was as influential in his day as, in the next century, his grandson George. It also helps explain why such men as MacLeod could rescue the Establishment after the Disruption. But the Presbyterian classic of the Holy Land is the *Narrative of a Mission of Enquiry to the Jews* by Robert Murray McCheyne and Andrew Bonar (Edinburgh 1842, with later editions). This is a remarkable Protestant discovery of Palestine and a bid, admittedly on very Christian terms, for Christian reconciliation with the Jews. In a pre-Zionist way it saw Palestine as the Land of Israel and envisaged the Jewish people, as a nation and national Church, finding the Messiah in Christ. But it also displays both the mind and soul of the Evangelical revival.

I put Bonar and McCheyne on a par, in their way, with the greatest Scots work of scholarship about Palestine and the Land of Israel, the immensely successful and influential *Historical Geography of the Holy Land* (London 1894) by the U.F. Professor George Adam Smith, later Principal of St Andrews University. But Smith was also a partner with John Buchan in another literary enterprise that, better than anything else, defines where the Reformed tradition stood at the time of the reunion of the Auld Kirk and the United Free Church. Their book, *The Kirk in Scotland 1560-1929* is now hard to come by, though Buchan's part, a brilliant historical and theological essay, has since been republished (Dunbar 1985) in a rather unsatisfactory modern edition. Its publisher included a postscript narrative of later history but not the introduction which is really needed. Incidentally the very welcome modern revival of Buchan's reputation as a novelist should not be allowed to obscure his quality as a serious writer and lay theologian. It is a sad sign of the times that he is often only seen as author of what he called "shockers", splendid though these are.

Maybe it is time to offer a last few and less subjective selections. Despite the quality and power of Ian Henderson's writing, I still think that the best post-war general book about the Church of Scotland is the one which J.M. Reid, a Glasgow editor and superb journalist, wrote at the time of the fourth centenary of the Reformation: *Kirk and Nation* (London 1960). For history in more depth covering the time from the 1688 Revolution to the beginning of the twentieth century there is the very fine trilogy in the names of Andrew Drummond and of James Bulloch, who took over and developed the work on Drummond's death. The titles are *The Scottish Church 1688-1843; The Church in Victorian Scotland 1843-74; The Church in Late Victorian Scotland 1874-1900* (Edinburgh 1973-78).

For those anxious to understand how the Reformed tradition responded to the social, economic, and scientific impact of the nineteenth century there are also Professor Alec Cheyne's Chalmers Lectures, *The Transforming of the Kirk,* (Edinburgh 1983), which make an immensely valuable short book. A new book of studies in Scottish Church history by Professor Cheyne was also due to appear shortly before this book.

It is also worth adding, for serious researchers, that the various journals of the Reformed Church in Scotland - notably *Life and Work* and the various *Records* associated with the Free and U.F. Church as well as the Auld Kirk - provide a superb record of the mixture of essential things, ephemeral things, and trivial pursuits in the life and thought of the Church.

I also fit in a book which is not about religion, but which recognises its importance - Duncan Macmillan's magnificent *Scottish Art 1460-1990*. It is a fair and broad-minded as well as a masterly book in its field. Anyone who thinks that the Calvinist and Reformed tradition blighted Scottish art should read it to discover the quality of Scotish achievement, not just in the ages of Enlightenment but of Evangelical revival and Victorian religion.

Of course not all Scottish artists even then were Presbyterians; but of the many who were an unexpected number (and not just David Wilkie and Octavius Hill) were very positive Christians. That may be even more widely realised as some undervalued forms of Scottish and Victorian art come back into fashion and get the gallery space they deserve. But it suggests that the problem for Reformed Christianity to grapple with is not some stifling legacy of Calvinism, ill-defined and misunderstood, but the gulf which developed in the twentieth century between religion and the dominant tendencies both in intellectual and artistic life.

And what to end with (almost but not quite)? I thought about George MacLeod with his great influence in the twentieth century but his impact was through power of personality and the spoken word - he was the greatest orator I have heard - and much less through the written word. Instead I think it ought to be Mary Levison's *Wrestling with the Church* (London 1992). Compared to some other Protestant parts of the Church the Kirk was slow to recognise the logic, spiritual as well as temporal, of ordaining women on the same terms and conditions as men. On the other hand the travails of the Church of England, before it came to the same decision, show that the decision could not be easy for any Church with conservative procedures and a strong sense of historic succession.

That there was so much less pain in the Church of Scotland obviously says much about the way the determined campaigner and petitioner Mary Lusk (as she then was) was seen even by those parts of the Church which were nervous, uncertain, or hostile. But it also suggests something about the way in which the procedures of the Kirk, still so conservative in an age when fashions favour the radicals in ephemeral politics and experimental theology, can handle continuing reformation and the right kind of reform when it really matters.

I also add a book which is not easy reading, and not always read by those who venture opinions about it: the Westminster Confession of Faith, preferably in an edition adding the Larger and Shorter Catechisms. It contains some great prose and much powerful argument set out with logic and lucidity. Some of the difficulties it presents derive from a tendency to generalise over-much from particular biblical passages. Others, more profound, are difficulties inherent in understanding and interpreting Scripture itself, for example in Paul's concept of pre-destination (see Romans 8). But those in the modern Kirk who think of the Confession only in relation to its unflattering description of the Vatican should re-read the rest of it.

But the last word must go to the most influential book in Scottish history, which Americans call after a Scotsman, James VI and I, but which Britain knows as the Authorised Version. It was not the Bible of the Scottish Reformation any more than of the English one, though it inherits much from Tyndale and the Geneva Bible. It seems to have taken several decades to be fully accepted in Scotland at a time when Presbyterianism had good reason to suspect royal initiatives in religious matters. Once accepted, however, it shaped much of the language, written and spoken, as as well as the faith and worship of the Scottish people.

For centuries it co-existed with Scots (and indeed still does) but also nourished the best English speech of Scotland as well as of England, Ireland, and North America.

Its merit and historical importance might seem to make a mention needless. But today many Christian congregations no longer make active use of it, preferring modern translations that range from excellent to inadequate. Bible societies promote the new versions in trying to reach beyond the Churches. The ecumenical mood also encourages revisions which all Churches can approve without seeming to turn their backs on distinctive traditions. The schools, in so far as they use and teach the Bible in religious education, also seem to use newer versions.

Taken together these factors justify a call to Church and nation to cherish the Authorised Version. Christians raised or quickened in faith through newer versions will find unexpected stimulation in it as well as deeper understanding of the way the Church was shaped. But everyone who cares for English language and the cultures of English-speaking peoples needs some familiarity with the style and range of the Bible in the Authorised Version.

This is not something additional to our Scottishness but part of it. Our share in the things we hold in common with others is as vital a part of our identity and as enriching a part of our traditions as those things distinctive to us.

BIOGRAPHICAL NOTES ON CONTRIBUTORS

RUSSELL BARR: minister of Cramond Kirk, Edinburgh, with previous parishes in the East End of Glasgow (Garthamlock) and Greenock town centre. Emphatically from Kilmarnock (b.1953) but an Edinburgh graduate in arts and divinity, later taking an M.Th. at New College and now completing a doctorate from Princeton University, USA. "More importantly, he captained the Church of Scotland golf team to a famous victory over their Anglican opponents in 1997." Major roles in Church and Nation Committee and Edinburgh Churches' project for homeless.

GEORGE BRUCE: leading Scottish poet and literary authority. B. 1909 in Fraserburgh. "Consequently it's not surprising to discover the impact of the elements in his seven collections of poetry." Aberdeen graduate who taught for nine years before becoming an outstanding BBC producer (1947-70) with leading role in Scottish arts broadcasting. Visiting professor or fellow at American and other colleges and first fellow in creative writing at Glasgow University. Prose writings range from the arts and essays on contemporary poets to a review of Lorimer's Scots New Testament for *The Times Literary Supplement*. His latest collection of poems (1986-98) in English and Scots, *Pursuit*, has just been published.

CATHERINE HEPBURN: Minister of the linked parishes of Gargunnock and Kincardine-in-Menteith in Stirlingshire since 1994. Also had a long spell as interim moderator of a continuing vacancy in another country parish, Kilmadock. Previously had twelve-year "terminable appointment" at Gargunnock! Edinburgh graduate. Spent her first nine years (b.1955) in Malawi, previously Nyasaland, where her parents were missionaries who returned respectively to parish ministry and presidency of the Woman's Guild.

ROBERT D. KERNOHAN: Elder, journalist, and ex-editor, Glaswegian settled in Edinburgh; b. 1931, ed. Glasgow University and Balliol College, Oxford. Sometime Conservative candidate and party director, former London Editor *The Glasgow Herald*; author of various books. Editor of the Kirk journal *Life and Work* 1972-90. Served on Monopolies and Mergers Commission and Broadcasting Standards Commission, also as H.M. Lay Inspector of Constabulary for Scotland.

STEWART LAMONT: Minister, writer, and broadcaster. B. 1947, Broughty Ferry. Science and divinity graduate of St Andrews, where he was president of the Union. Ordained as BBC religious producer, later freelance broadcaster and minister. Minister of Kinning Park, Glasgow, since 1991. Religious Affairs Correspondent *The Herald*. His books include a life of John Knox (*The Swordbearer*).

IAN MACKENZIE: Minister and broadcaster; Head of BBC Religious Programmes Scotland 1973-89. B. Fraserburgh 1931. Ed. Fettes College and Edinburgh University; was both assistant organist and assistant minister at St Giles' Cathedral, but not at same time. Worked for Student Christian Movement and independent television companies (ABC, LWT) before returning to Scotland as minister of Peterhead Old Parish Church. Was chairman of IBA Scottish religious panel. Delivered Baird Lectures on Church Music, 1990.

DONALD MACLEOD: Professor of Systematic Theology at Free Church College in Edinburgh since 1978. B. 1940, Ness, Lewis; ed. Nicolson Institute, Glasgow University, Free Church College. Editor of the *Monthly Record* 1977-90. Previously Free Church minister in Kilmallie and Partick. No stranger to controversy, within and beyond his own denomination, but noted for power and clarity of his writing and reflections from theologically conservative but strongly evangelical viewpoint. Recreations include "dreaming about cricket".

JOHNSTON R. McKAY: Minister and broadcaster; senior producer BBC religious programmes since 1987. Previously minister of Paisley Abbey and Bellahouston Steven Parish Church after spell as assistant minister at St Giles' Cathedral. b. 1942; graduate of Glasgow University and Cambridge. Chairman BBC Scottish Religious Advisory Committee 1981-86. Noted for style, polish, and determination in his broadcasting. Lives in Largs.

LORNA M. PATERSON: General Secretary Church of Scotland Guild (formerly Woman's Guild) 1985-98. B. 1938 in Unst, Shetland, ed. at Tain and Inverurie. Aberdeen graduate. Worked as teacher in Aberdeen and Stirling and in university administration (Strathclyde and Stirling). Former Guide district commissioner. Elder at St Michael's Linlithgow; married to minister there.

DONALD SMITH: Director of the Netherbow Arts Centre (which operates under the aegis of the Church of Scotland) and Curator of the neighbouring John Knox House on Edinburgh's Royal Mile. b. 1956. Brought up in Stirling, Edinburgh graduate (M.A., Ph.D). Before coming to the Netherbow was a researcher at the Edinburgh University School of Scottish Studies. Director of the Scottish International Storytelling Festival.

WILLIAM STORRAR: Minister, scholar, and university teacher; b. 1953. Senior Lecturer in Practical Theology at Glasgow University Department of Theology and Religious Studies. Previously lecturer at Aberdeen University after parish ministry at St John's Carluke; ordained 1984. Triple graduate of Edinburgh University (Arts, Divinity, Ph.D).Working on a book about the concept of "the republic of consent" in political theory and theology.

THOMAS F. TORRANCE: B. in China of missionary parents, 1913. Leading Scottish theologian of international eminence, honoured in wide range of countries and demominations, and authority on the relation of religion and science. Moderator of General Assembly 1976-77. Awarded Templeton Prize for Progress in Religion 1978. Professor of Christian Dogmatics at Edinburgh 1952-79 after holding Church History chair there. Previously parish minister in Alyth and Aberdeen. Author of many books on varied themes including Calvin, Barth, the early Church Fathers, and the relation of theological and natural science.

DAVID F. WRIGHT: About to move into personal professorial chair in Patristic and Reformed Christianity at Edinburgh University after being Senior Lecturer in Ecclesiastical History there. Dean of Divinity Faculty 1988-92. B. 1937, Hayes, Kent. Ed. Christ's College, Cambridge; Lincoln College, Oxford. Chairman Tyndale Fellowship for Biblical and Theological Research. Chief general editor of Scottish Dictionary of Church History and Theology; author or editor of many other theological and historical works. Church of Scotland elder and member of Edinburgh Presbytery. Chairman Handsel Press Board.